Just The Facts 101
Textbook Key Facts

Connecticut Investment & Business Guide

by Cram101
Textbook NOT Included

Table of Contents

Title Page

Copyright

Foundations of Business

Management

Business law

Finance

Human resource management

Information systems

Marketing

Manufacturing

Commerce

Business ethics

Accounting

Index: Answers

Just The Facts101

Exam Prep for

Connecticut Investment & Business Guide

Just The Facts101 Exam Prep is your link from
the textbook and lecture to your exams.

**Just The Facts101 Exam Preps are unauthorized and comprehensive reviews
of your textbooks.**

All material provided by CTI Publications (c) 2019

Textbook publishers and textbook authors do not participate in or contribute to these reviews.

Just The Facts101 Exam Prep

Copyright © 2019 by CTI Publications. All rights reserved.

eAIN 444426

Foundations of Business

A business, also known as an enterprise, agency or a firm, is an entity involved in the provision of goods and/or services to consumers. Businesses are prevalent in capitalist economies, where most of them are privately owned and provide goods and services to customers in exchange for other goods, services, or money.

:: Economic globalization ::

_____ is an agreement in which one company hires another company to be responsible for a planned or existing activity that is or could be done internally, and sometimes involves transferring employees and assets from one firm to another.

Exam Probability: **High**

1. *Answer choices:*

(see index for correct answer)

- a. Outsourcing
- b. global financial

Guidance: level 1

:: Insolvency ::

_____ is a legal process through which people or other entities who cannot repay debts to creditors may seek relief from some or all of their debts. In most jurisdictions, _____ is imposed by a court order, often initiated by the debtor.

Exam Probability: **Medium**

2. *Answer choices:*

(see index for correct answer)

- a. Financial distress
- b. Bankruptcy
- c. Insolvency law of Russia
- d. Official Committee of Equity Security Holders

Guidance: level 1

:: ::

_____ is a means of protection from financial loss. It is a form of risk management, primarily used to hedge against the risk of a contingent or uncertain loss

Exam Probability: **High**

3. *Answer choices:*
(see index for correct answer)

- a. personal values
- b. co-culture
- c. corporate values
- d. Insurance

Guidance: level 1

:: Employment ::

_____ is a relationship between two parties, usually based on a contract where work is paid for, where one party, which may be a corporation, for profit, not-for-profit organization, co-operative or other entity is the employer and the other is the employee. Employees work in return for payment, which may be in the form of an hourly wage, by piecework or an annual salary, depending on the type of work an employee does or which sector she or he is working in. Employees in some fields or sectors may receive gratuities, bonus payment or stock options. In some types of _____ , employees may receive benefits in addition to payment. Benefits can include health insurance, housing, disability insurance or use of a gym. _____ is typically governed by _____ laws, regulations or legal contracts.

Exam Probability: **Low**

4. *Answer choices:*

(see index for correct answer)

- a. Employment
- b. Employment reference letter
- c. Cyberloafing
- d. Temporary duty assignment

Guidance: level 1

:: Marketing ::

A _____ is a group of customers within a business's serviceable available market at which a business aims its marketing efforts and resources. A _____ is a subset of the total market for a product or service. The _____ typically consists of consumers who exhibit similar characteristics and are considered most likely to buy a business's market offerings or are likely to be the most profitable segments for the business to service.

Exam Probability: **Low**

5. *Answer choices:*

(see index for correct answer)

- a. Target market
- b. Fixed value-added resource
- c. Market intelligence
- d. Product bundling

Guidance: level 1

:: Project management ::

In political science, an _____ is a means by which a petition signed by a certain minimum number of registered voters can force a government to choose to either enact a law or hold a public vote in parliament in what is called indirect _____, or under direct _____, the proposition is immediately put to a plebiscite or referendum, in what is called a Popular initiated Referendum or citizen-initiated referendum).

Exam Probability: **Low**

6. *Answer choices:*

(see index for correct answer)

- a. PM Declaration of Interdependence
- b. Project anatomy
- c. Initiative
- d. Project management office

Guidance: level 1

:: Social security ::

_____ is "any government system that provides monetary assistance to people with an inadequate or no income." In the United States, this is usually called welfare or a social safety net, especially when talking about Canada and European countries.

Exam Probability: **High**

7. *Answer choices:*

(see index for correct answer)

- a. SNILS
- b. Social security
- c. Baby bonus

- d. Mahatma Gandhi Pravasi Suraksha Yojana

Guidance: level 1

:: Statistical terminology ::

_____ is the magnitude or dimensions of a thing. _____ can be measured as length, width, height, diameter, perimeter, area, volume, or mass.

Exam Probability: **High**

8. *Answer choices:*

(see index for correct answer)

- a. Treatment group
- b. Permutation test
- c. Testimator
- d. Scale parameter

Guidance: level 1

:: Market research ::

A _____ is a small, but demographically diverse group of people and whose reactions are studied especially in market research or political analysis in guided or open discussions about a new product or something else to determine the reactions that can be expected from a larger population. It is a form of qualitative research consisting of interviews in which a group of people are asked about their perceptions, opinions, beliefs, and attitudes towards a product, service, concept, advertisement, idea, or packaging. Questions are asked in an interactive group setting where participants are free to talk with other group members. During this process, the researcher either takes notes or records the vital points he or she is getting from the group. Researchers should select members of the _____ carefully for effective and authoritative responses.

Exam Probability: **Medium**

9. *Answer choices:*

(see index for correct answer)

- a. Central location test
- b. Focus group
- c. Respondent error
- d. Brand elections

Guidance: level 1

:: Private equity ::

_____ is a type of private equity, a form of financing that is provided by firms or funds to small, early-stage, emerging firms that are deemed to have high growth potential, or which have demonstrated high growth. _____ firms or funds invest in these early-stage companies in exchange for equity, or an ownership stake, in the companies they invest in. _____ists take on the risk of financing risky start-ups in the hopes that some of the firms they support will become successful. Because startups face high uncertainty, VC investments do have high rates of failure. The start-ups are usually based on an innovative technology or business model and they are usually from the high technology industries, such as information technology, clean technology or biotechnology.

Exam Probability: **High**

10. *Answer choices:*

(see index for correct answer)

- a. Growth capital
- b. Private equity in the 1990s
- c. Venture capital
- d. Management fee

Guidance: level 1

:: Decision theory ::

Within economics the concept of _____ is used to model worth or value, but its usage has evolved significantly over time. The term was introduced initially as a measure of pleasure or satisfaction within the theory of utilitarianism by moral philosophers such as Jeremy Bentham and John Stuart Mill. But the term has been adapted and reapplied within neoclassical economics, which dominates modern economic theory, as a _____ function that represents a consumer's preference ordering over a choice set. As such, it is devoid of its original interpretation as a measurement of the pleasure or satisfaction obtained by the consumer from that choice.

Exam Probability: **High**

11. *Answer choices:*

(see index for correct answer)

- a. Decision fatigue
- b. Omission bias
- c. Dominance-based rough set approach
- d. Utility

Guidance: level 1

:: Public relations ::

_____ is the public visibility or awareness for any product, service or company. It may also refer to the movement of information from its source to the general public, often but not always via the media. The subjects of _____ include people, goods and services, organizations, and works of art or entertainment.

Exam Probability: **High**

12. *Answer choices:*

(see index for correct answer)

- a. Sparkpr
- b. International Association of Business Communicators
- c. Public relations of The Church of Jesus Christ of Latter-day Saints
- d. Kompromat

Guidance: level 1

:: International trade ::

_____ or globalisation is the process of interaction and integration among people, companies, and governments worldwide. As a complex and multifaceted phenomenon, _____ is considered by some as a form of capitalist expansion which entails the integration of local and national economies into a global, unregulated market economy. _____ has grown due to advances in transportation and communication technology. With the increased global interactions comes the growth of international trade, ideas, and culture. _____ is primarily an economic process of interaction and integration that's associated with social and cultural aspects. However, conflicts and diplomacy are also large parts of the history of _____, and modern _____ .

Exam Probability: **Medium**

13. *Answer choices:*

(see index for correct answer)

- a. Foreign Agricultural Service
- b. Globalization
- c. Authorized economic operator
- d. Gains from trade

Guidance: level 1

:: Globalization-related theories ::

_____ is the process in which a nation is being improved in the sector of the economic, political, and social well-being of its people. The term has been used frequently by economists, politicians, and others in the 20th and 21st centuries. The concept, however, has been in existence in the West for centuries. "Modernization, "westernization", and especially "industrialization" are other terms often used while discussing _____ . _____ has a direct relationship with the environment and environmental issues. _____ is very often confused with industrial development, even in some academic sources.

Exam Probability: **Medium**

14. *Answer choices:*
(see index for correct answer)

- a. post-industrial
- b. Capitalism
- c. Economic Development

Guidance: level 1

:: Information systems ::

_____ are formal, sociotechnical, organizational systems designed to collect, process, store, and distribute information. In a sociotechnical perspective, _____ are composed by four components: task, people, structure, and technology.

Exam Probability: **Low**

15. *Answer choices:*

(see index for correct answer)

- a. Vehicle Information and Communication System
- b. Question Manager
- c. Information systems
- d. Notify NYC

Guidance: level 1

:: Currency ::

A _____ , in the most specific sense is money in any form when in use or circulation as a medium of exchange, especially circulating banknotes and coins. A more general definition is that a _____ is a system of money in common use, especially for people in a nation. Under this definition, US dollars , pounds sterling , Australian dollars , European euros , Russian rubles and Indian Rupees are examples of currencies. These various currencies are recognized as stores of value and are traded between nations in foreign exchange markets, which determine the relative values of the different currencies. Currencies in this sense are defined by governments, and each type has limited boundaries of acceptance.

Exam Probability: **High**

16. *Answer choices:*

(see index for correct answer)

- a. Debasement
- b. York rating
- c. Currency money
- d. Currency

Guidance: level 1

:: Bribery ::

_____ is the act of giving or receiving something of value in exchange for some kind of influence or action in return, that the recipient would otherwise not offer. _____ is defined by Black's Law Dictionary as the offering, giving, receiving, or soliciting of any item of value to influence the actions of an official or other person in charge of a public or legal duty. Essentially, _____ is offering to do something for someone for the expressed purpose of receiving something in exchange. Gifts of money or other items of value which are otherwise available to everyone on an equivalent basis, and not for dishonest purposes, is not _____ . Offering a discount or a refund to all purchasers is a legal rebate and is not _____ . For example, it is legal for an employee of a Public Utilities Commission involved in electric rate regulation to accept a rebate on electric service that reduces their cost for electricity, when the rebate is available to other residential electric customers. Giving the rebate to influence them to look favorably on the electric utility's rate increase applications, however, would be considered _____ .

Exam Probability: **Medium**

17. *Answer choices:*
(see index for correct answer)

- a. English football bribery scandal
- b. Bribery
- c. Global Corruption Barometer
- d. Cockerham bribery case

Guidance: level 1

:: Monopoly (economics) ::

A _____ is a form of intellectual property that gives its owner the legal right to exclude others from making, using, selling, and importing an invention for a limited period of years, in exchange for publishing an enabling public disclosure of the invention. In most countries _____ rights fall under civil law and the _____ holder needs to sue someone infringing the _____ in order to enforce his or her rights. In some industries _____ s are an essential form of competitive advantage; in others they are irrelevant.

Exam Probability: **High**

18. *Answer choices:*

(see index for correct answer)

- a. Ownership unbundling
- b. Practice of law
- c. Patent
- d. Natural monopoly

Guidance: level 1

:: Marketing ::

A _____ is something that is necessary for an organism to live a healthy life. _____ s are distinguished from wants in that, in the case of a _____, a deficiency causes a clear adverse outcome: a dysfunction or death. In other words, a _____ is something required for a safe, stable and healthy life while a want is a desire, wish or aspiration. When _____ s or wants are backed by purchasing power, they have the potential to become economic demands.

Exam Probability: **Medium**

19. *Answer choices:*

(see index for correct answer)

- a. Azerbaijan Marketing Society
- b. Need
- c. Brandjacking
- d. Product

Guidance: level 1

:: ::

_____ is the means to see, hear, or become aware of something or someone through our fundamental senses. The term _____ derives from the Latin word perceptio, and is the organization, identification, and interpretation of sensory information in order to represent and understand the presented information, or the environment.

Exam Probability: **High**

20. *Answer choices:*

(see index for correct answer)

- a. Character
- b. functional perspective
- c. similarity-attraction theory
- d. co-culture

Guidance: level 1

:: International trade ::

An _____ is a good brought into a jurisdiction, especially across a national border, from an external source. The party bringing in the good is called an _____ er. An _____ in the receiving country is an export from the sending country. _____ ation and exportation are the defining financial transactions of international trade.

Exam Probability: **Low**

21. *Answer choices:*

(see index for correct answer)

- a. Import
- b. Neomercantilism

- c. Agreement on Agriculture
- d. Foreign trade multiplier

Guidance: level 1

:: Foreign direct investment ::

A _____ is an investment in the form of a controlling ownership in a business in one country by an entity based in another country. It is thus distinguished from a foreign portfolio investment by a notion of direct control.

Exam Probability: **High**

22. *Answer choices:*

(see index for correct answer)

- a. EB-5 visa
- b. International Centre for Settlement of Investment Disputes
- c. Foreign direct investment
- d. Oligopolistic reaction

Guidance: level 1

:: Accounting software ::

_____ is any item or verifiable record that is generally accepted as payment for goods and services and repayment of debts, such as taxes, in a particular country or socio-economic context. The main functions of _____ are distinguished as: a medium of exchange, a unit of account, a store of value and sometimes, a standard of deferred payment. Any item or verifiable record that fulfils these functions can be considered as _____ .

Exam Probability: **High**

23. *Answer choices:*

(see index for correct answer)

- a. You Need a Budget
- b. Money
- c. Digital Insight
- d. Gem Accounts

Guidance: level 1

:: Product management ::

A _____ , trade mark, or trade-mark is a recognizable sign, design, or expression which identifies products or services of a particular source from those of others, although _____ s used to identify services are usually called service marks. The _____ owner can be an individual, business organization, or any legal entity. A _____ may be located on a package, a label, a voucher, or on the product itself. For the sake of corporate identity, _____ s are often displayed on company buildings. It is legally recognized as a type of intellectual property.

Exam Probability: **Medium**

24. *Answer choices:*

(see index for correct answer)

- a. Promise Index
- b. Trademark
- c. business name
- d. Product family engineering

Guidance: level 1

:: Corporate crime ::

_____ LLP, based in Chicago, was an American holding company. Formerly one of the "Big Five" accounting firms, the firm had provided auditing, tax, and consulting services to large corporations. By 2001, it had become one of the world's largest multinational companies.

Exam Probability: **High**

25. *Answer choices:*

(see index for correct answer)

- a. Medco Health Solutions
- b. Walter Forbes
- c. Corporate manslaughter

- d. Arthur Andersen

Guidance: level 1

:: Strategic alliances ::

A _____ is an agreement between two or more parties to pursue a set of agreed upon objectives needed while remaining independent organizations. A _____ will usually fall short of a legal partnership entity, agency, or corporate affiliate relationship. Typically, two companies form a _____ when each possesses one or more business assets or have expertise that will help the other by enhancing their businesses. _____ s can develop in outsourcing relationships where the parties desire to achieve long-term win-win benefits and innovation based on mutually desired outcomes.

Exam Probability: **Medium**

26. *Answer choices:*

(see index for correct answer)

- a. Strategic alliance
- b. Management contract
- c. Defensive termination
- d. Bridge Alliance

Guidance: level 1

:: Investment ::

In finance, the benefit from an _____ is called a return. The return may consist of a gain realised from the sale of property or an _____, unrealised capital appreciation, or _____ income such as dividends, interest, rental income etc., or a combination of capital gain and income. The return may also include currency gains or losses due to changes in foreign currency exchange rates.

Exam Probability: **High**

27. *Answer choices:*

(see index for correct answer)

- a. Buy-write
- b. Investment
- c. Foreign portfolio investment
- d. Acertus Market Sentiment Indicator

Guidance: level 1

:: Generally Accepted Accounting Principles ::

Expenditure is an outflow of money to another person or group to pay for an item or service, or for a category of costs. For a tenant, rent is an _____. For students or parents, tuition is an _____. Buying food, clothing, furniture or an automobile is often referred to as an _____. An _____ is a cost that is "paid" or "remitted", usually in exchange for something of value. Something that seems to cost a great deal is "expensive". Something that seems to cost little is "inexpensive". "_____s of the table" are _____s of dining, refreshments, a feast, etc.

Exam Probability: **Medium**

28. *Answer choices:*

(see index for correct answer)

- a. Revenue
- b. Expense
- c. Write-off
- d. Operating income

Guidance: level 1

An _____ is the production of goods or related services within an economy. The major source of revenue of a group or company is the indicator of its relevant _____ . When a large group has multiple sources of revenue generation, it is considered to be working in different industries. Manufacturing _____ became a key sector of production and labour in European and North American countries during the Industrial Revolution, upsetting previous mercantile and feudal economies. This came through many successive rapid advances in technology, such as the production of steel and coal.

Exam Probability: **Medium**

29. *Answer choices:*

(see index for correct answer)

- a. Industry
- b. similarity-attraction theory
- c. personal values
- d. hierarchical perspective

Guidance: level 1

:: Service industries ::

_____ are the economic services provided by the finance industry, which encompasses a broad range of businesses that manage money, including credit unions, banks, credit-card companies, insurance companies, accountancy companies, consumer-finance companies, stock brokerages, investment funds, individual managers and some government-sponsored enterprises. _____ companies are present in all economically developed geographic locations and tend to cluster in local, national, regional and international financial centers such as London, New York City, and Tokyo.

Exam Probability: **Medium**

30. *Answer choices:*

(see index for correct answer)

- a. Graham Company
- b. Allotment
- c. Financial services in China
- d. Financial services

Guidance: level 1

:: Summary statistics ::

_____ is the number of occurrences of a repeating event per unit of time. It is also referred to as temporal _____, which emphasizes the contrast to spatial _____ and angular _____. The period is the duration of time of one cycle in a repeating event, so the period is the reciprocal of the _____. For example: if a newborn baby's heart beats at a _____ of 120 times a minute, its period—the time interval between beats—is half a second. _____ is an important parameter used in science and engineering to specify the rate of oscillatory and vibratory phenomena, such as mechanical vibrations, audio signals, radio waves, and light.

Exam Probability: **High**

31. *Answer choices:*

(see index for correct answer)

- a. Summary statistics
- b. Frequency
- c. Quartile
- d. Lorenz asymmetry coefficient

Guidance: level 1

:: Materials ::

A _____, also known as a feedstock, unprocessed material, or primary commodity, is a basic material that is used to produce goods, finished products, energy, or intermediate materials which are feedstock for future finished products. As feedstock, the term connotes these materials are bottleneck assets and are highly important with regard to producing other products. An example of this is crude oil, which is a _____ and a feedstock used in the production of industrial chemicals, fuels, plastics, and pharmaceutical goods; lumber is a _____ used to produce a variety of products including all types of furniture. The term "_____" denotes materials in minimally processed or unprocessed in states; e.g., raw latex, crude oil, cotton, coal, raw biomass, iron ore, air, logs, or water i.e. "...any product of agriculture, forestry, fishing and any other mineral that is in its natural form or which has undergone the transformation required to prepare it for internationally marketing in substantial volumes."

Exam Probability: **High**

32. *Answer choices:*

(see index for correct answer)

- a. Three-dimensional quartz phenolic
- b. Raw material
- c. Semimetal
- d. Muka

Guidance: level 1

:: Problem solving ::

In other words, _____ is a situation where a group of people meet to generate new ideas and solutions around a specific domain of interest by removing inhibitions. People are able to think more freely and they suggest as many spontaneous new ideas as possible. All the ideas are noted down and those ideas are not criticized and after _____ session the ideas are evaluated. The term was popularized by Alex Faickney Osborn in the 1953 book Applied Imagination.

Exam Probability: **Low**

33. *Answer choices:*

(see index for correct answer)

- a. Brainstorming
- b. Spider mapping
- c. Social heuristics
- d. Tar-Baby

Guidance: level 1

:: Decision theory ::

A _____ is a deliberate system of principles to guide decisions and achieve rational outcomes. A _____ is a statement of intent, and is implemented as a procedure or protocol. Policies are generally adopted by a governance body within an organization. Policies can assist in both subjective and objective decision making. Policies to assist in subjective decision making usually assist senior management with decisions that must be based on the relative merits of a number of factors, and as a result are often hard to test objectively, e.g. work-life balance _____ . In contrast policies to assist in objective decision making are usually operational in nature and can be objectively tested, e.g. password _____ .

Exam Probability: **Medium**

34. *Answer choices:*

(see index for correct answer)

- a. Choice architecture
- b. Weighted sum model
- c. Scoring rule
- d. Strategic assumptions

Guidance: level 1

:: Legal terms ::

An _____ is an action which is inaccurate or incorrect. In some usages, an _____ is synonymous with a mistake. In statistics, "_____" refers to the difference between the value which has been computed and the correct value. An _____ could result in failure or in a deviation from the intended performance or behaviour.

Exam Probability: **Low**

35. *Answer choices:*

(see index for correct answer)

- a. Curator bonis
- b. Detention
- c. Contravention
- d. Error

Guidance: level 1

:: Management occupations ::

_____ ship is the process of designing, launching and running a new business, which is often initially a small business. The people who create these businesses are called _____ s.

Exam Probability: **High**

36. *Answer choices:*

(see index for correct answer)

- a. Entrepreneur
- b. Councillor
- c. City manager
- d. Corporate trainer

Guidance: level 1

:: Credit cards ::

The _____ Company, also known as Amex, is an American multinational financial services corporation headquartered in Three World Financial Center in New York City. The company was founded in 1850 and is one of the 30 components of the Dow Jones Industrial Average. The company is best known for its charge card, credit card, and traveler's cheque businesses.

Exam Probability: **High**

37. *Answer choices:*

(see index for correct answer)

- a. SecurityMetrics
- b. Ingenico
- c. American Express
- d. Payments as a service

Guidance: level 1

:: Management accounting ::

_____ s are costs that change as the quantity of the good or service that a business produces changes. _____ s are the sum of marginal costs over all units produced. They can also be considered normal costs. Fixed costs and _____ s make up the two components of total cost. Direct costs are costs that can easily be associated with a particular cost object. However, not all _____ s are direct costs. For example, variable manufacturing overhead costs are _____ s that are indirect costs, not direct costs. _____ s are sometimes called unit-level costs as they vary with the number of units produced.

Exam Probability: **Medium**

38. *Answer choices:*

(see index for correct answer)

- a. Profit center
- b. Variable cost
- c. Standard cost
- d. Cash and cash equivalents

Guidance: level 1

:: Planning ::

_____ is a high level plan to achieve one or more goals under conditions of uncertainty. In the sense of the "art of the general," which included several subsets of skills including tactics, siegecraft, logistics etc., the term came into use in the 6th century C.E. in East Roman terminology, and was translated into Western vernacular languages only in the 18th century. From then until the 20th century, the word "_____" came to denote "a comprehensive way to try to pursue political ends, including the threat or actual use of force, in a dialectic of wills" in a military conflict, in which both adversaries interact.

Exam Probability: **Low**

39. *Answer choices:*

(see index for correct answer)

- a. Reproductive life plan
- b. Strategy
- c. Disruption
- d. Group information management

Guidance: level 1

:: Electronic feedback ::

_____ occurs when outputs of a system are routed back as inputs as part of a chain of cause-and-effect that forms a circuit or loop. The system can then be said to feed back into itself. The notion of cause-and-effect has to be handled carefully when applied to _____ systems.

Exam Probability: **Low**

40. *Answer choices:*

(see index for correct answer)

- a. Feedback
- b. feedback loop

Guidance: level 1

:: Globalization-related theories ::

_____ is an economic system based on the private ownership of the means of production and their operation for profit. Characteristics central to _____ include private property, capital accumulation, wage labor, voluntary exchange, a price system, and competitive markets. In a capitalist market economy, decision-making and investment are determined by every owner of wealth, property or production ability in financial and capital markets, whereas prices and the distribution of goods and services are mainly determined by competition in goods and services markets.

Exam Probability: **Medium**

41. *Answer choices:*

(see index for correct answer)

- a. post-industrial
- b. postmodernism

- c. Capitalism

Guidance: level 1

:: Production and manufacturing ::

_____ is a set of techniques and tools for process improvement. Though as a shortened form it may be found written as 6S, it should not be confused with the methodology known as 6S.

Exam Probability: **Medium**

42. *Answer choices:*

(see index for correct answer)

- a. Positive recall
- b. Cellular manufacturing
- c. Advanced Manufacturing Software
- d. Follow-the-sun

Guidance: level 1

:: ::

_____ refers to a business or organization attempting to acquire goods or services to accomplish its goals. Although there are several organizations that attempt to set standards in the _____ process, processes can vary greatly between organizations. Typically the word " _____ " is not used interchangeably with the word "procurement", since procurement typically includes expediting, supplier quality, and transportation and logistics in addition to _____ .

Exam Probability: **Medium**

43. *Answer choices:*

(see index for correct answer)

- a. co-culture
- b. surface-level diversity
- c. Purchasing
- d. corporate values

Guidance: level 1

:: Real estate ::

_____ s serve several societal needs – primarily as shelter from weather, security, living space, privacy, to store belongings, and to comfortably live and work. A _____ as a shelter represents a physical division of the human habitat and the outside .

Exam Probability: **Medium**

44. Answer choices:

(see index for correct answer)

- a. Building
- b. 99-year lease
- c. Deeds registration
- d. American Measurement Standard

Guidance: level 1

:: Macroeconomics ::

A foreign _____ is an investment in the form of a controlling ownership in a business in one country by an entity based in another country. It is thus distinguished from a foreign portfolio investment by a notion of direct control.

Exam Probability: **Low**

45. Answer choices:

(see index for correct answer)

- a. Net material product
- b. Direct investment
- c. Depression
- d. Demand shock

Guidance: level 1

:: Health promotion ::

_____ , as defined by the World _____ Organization, is "a state of complete physical, mental and social well-being and not merely the absence of disease or infirmity." This definition has been subject to controversy, as it may have limited value for implementation. _____ may be defined as the ability to adapt and manage physical, mental and social challenges throughout life.

Exam Probability: **Medium**

46. *Answer choices:*

(see index for correct answer)

- a. PRECEDE-PROCEED
- b. Health
- c. Breastfeeding promotion
- d. Lifestyle management programme

Guidance: level 1

:: Marketing ::

_____ is the percentage of a market accounted for by a specific entity. In a survey of nearly 200 senior marketing managers, 67% responded that they found the revenue- "dollar _____" metric very useful, while 61% found "unit _____" very useful.

Exam Probability: **Low**

47. *Answer choices:*

(see index for correct answer)

- a. Market share
- b. Next-best-action marketing
- c. Effie Award
- d. Emailing

Guidance: level 1

:: Logistics ::

_____ is generally the detailed organization and implementation of a complex operation. In a general business sense, _____ is the management of the flow of things between the point of origin and the point of consumption in order to meet requirements of customers or corporations. The resources managed in _____ may include tangible goods such as materials, equipment, and supplies, as well as food and other consumable items. The _____ of physical items usually involves the integration of information flow, materials handling, production, packaging, inventory, transportation, warehousing, and often security.

Exam Probability: **Low**

48. *Answer choices:*

(see index for correct answer)

- a. Savi Technology
- b. Dispatch
- c. Bucket brigade
- d. Logistics

Guidance: level 1

:: Marketing ::

_____ is based on a marketing concept which can be adopted by an organization as a strategy for business expansion. Where implemented, a franchisor licenses its know-how, procedures, intellectual property, use of its business model, brand, and rights to sell its branded products and services to a franchisee. In return the franchisee pays certain fees and agrees to comply with certain obligations, typically set out in a Franchise Agreement.

Exam Probability: **High**

49. *Answer choices:*

(see index for correct answer)

- a. Discounts and allowances
- b. Discounting

- c. Marketing automation
- d. Franchising

Guidance: level 1

:: Production and manufacturing ::

_____ consists of organization-wide efforts to "install and make permanent climate where employees continuously improve their ability to provide on demand products and services that customers will find of particular value." "Total" emphasizes that departments in addition to production are obligated to improve their operations; "management" emphasizes that executives are obligated to actively manage quality through funding, training, staffing, and goal setting. While there is no widely agreed-upon approach, TQM efforts typically draw heavily on the previously developed tools and techniques of quality control. TQM enjoyed widespread attention during the late 1980s and early 1990s before being overshadowed by ISO 9000, Lean manufacturing, and Six Sigma.

Exam Probability: **Low**

50. *Answer choices:*

(see index for correct answer)

- a. Total quality management
- b. Accelerated aging
- c. Six Sigma
- d. Production equipment control

Guidance: level 1

:: Management ::

In organizational studies, _____ is the efficient and effective development of an organization's resources when they are needed. Such resources may include financial resources, inventory, human skills, production resources, or information technology and natural resources.

Exam Probability: **High**

51. *Answer choices:*

(see index for correct answer)

- a. Resource management
- b. Allegiance
- c. Backsourcing
- d. Best practice

Guidance: level 1

:: Financial crises ::

A _____ is any of a broad variety of situations in which some financial assets suddenly lose a large part of their nominal value. In the 19th and early 20th centuries, many financial crises were associated with banking panics, and many recessions coincided with these panics. Other situations that are often called financial crises include stock market crashes and the bursting of other financial bubbles, currency crises, and sovereign defaults. Financial crises directly result in a loss of paper wealth but do not necessarily result in significant changes in the real economy.

Exam Probability: **Low**

52. *Answer choices:*

(see index for correct answer)

- a. Environmental credit crunch
- b. United Copper
- c. Financial crisis
- d. Credit crisis of 1772

Guidance: level 1

:: Infographics ::

A _____ is a graphical representation of data, in which "the data is represented by symbols, such as bars in a bar _____, lines in a line _____, or slices in a pie _____". A _____ can represent tabular numeric data, functions or some kinds of qualitative structure and provides different info.

Exam Probability: **High**

53. *Answer choices:*

(see index for correct answer)

- a. Bumper sticker
- b. The Way Things Work
- c. Visual analytics
- d. Chart

Guidance: level 1

:: Credit cards ::

A _____ is a payment card issued to users to enable the cardholder to pay a merchant for goods and services based on the cardholder's promise to the card issuer to pay them for the amounts plus the other agreed charges. The card issuer creates a revolving account and grants a line of credit to the cardholder, from which the cardholder can borrow money for payment to a merchant or as a cash advance.

Exam Probability: **Medium**

54. *Answer choices:*

(see index for correct answer)

- a. Barclaycard
- b. Japan Credit Bureau

- c. Medi Script
- d. Credit card

Guidance: level 1

:: Banking ::

A _____ is a financial institution that accepts deposits from the public and creates credit. Lending activities can be performed either directly or indirectly through capital markets. Due to their importance in the financial stability of a country, _____ s are highly regulated in most countries. Most nations have institutionalized a system known as fractional reserve _____ ing under which _____ s hold liquid assets equal to only a portion of their current liabilities. In addition to other regulations intended to ensure liquidity, _____ s are generally subject to minimum capital requirements based on an international set of capital standards, known as the Basel Accords.

Exam Probability: **Medium**

55. *Answer choices:*
(see index for correct answer)

- a. Direct bank
- b. Asset-based lending
- c. Joint account
- d. Intermediation

Guidance: level 1

:: Rhetoric ::

_____ is the pattern of narrative development that aims to make vivid a place, object, character, or group. _____ is one of four rhetorical modes, along with exposition, argumentation, and narration. In practice it would be difficult to write literature that drew on just one of the four basic modes.

Exam Probability: **Low**

56. *Answer choices:*
(see index for correct answer)

- a. Dialogus de oratoribus
- b. Rhetrickery
- c. Aporia
- d. Description

Guidance: level 1

:: Critical thinking ::

An _____ is a set of statements usually constructed to describe a set of facts which clarifies the causes, context, and consequences of those facts. This description of the facts et cetera may establish rules or laws, and may clarify the existing rules or laws in relation to any objects, or phenomena examined. The components of an _____ can be implicit, and interwoven with one another.

Exam Probability: **Low**

57. *Answer choices:*
(see index for correct answer)

- a. Explanation
- b. SEE-I
- c. Ad hoc hypothesis
- d. Topical logic

Guidance: level 1

:: Customs duties ::

A _____ is a tax on imports or exports between sovereign states. It is a form of regulation of foreign trade and a policy that taxes foreign products to encourage or safeguard domestic industry. _____ s are the simplest and oldest instrument of trade policy. Traditionally, states have used them as a source of income. Now, they are among the most widely used instruments of protection, along with import and export quotas.

Exam Probability: **High**

58. *Answer choices:*

(see index for correct answer)

- a. Customs racketeering
- b. Duty-free shop
- c. Tariff-rate quota
- d. Court of Exchequer

Guidance: level 1

:: Project management ::

_____ is the right to exercise power, which can be formalized by a state and exercised by way of judges, appointed executives of government, or the ecclesiastical or priestly appointed representatives of a God or other deities.

Exam Probability: **Low**

59. *Answer choices:*

(see index for correct answer)

- a. Project Management South Africa
- b. Responsibility assignment matrix
- c. Authority

- d. Student syndrome

Guidance: level 1

Management

Management is the administration of an organization, whether it is a business, a not-for-profit organization, or government body. Management includes the activities of setting the strategy of an organization and coordinating the efforts of its employees (or of volunteers) to accomplish its objectives through the application of available resources, such as financial, natural, technological, and human resources.

:: Management occupations ::

_____ is the process of designing, launching and running a new business, which is often initially a small business. The people who create these businesses are called entrepreneurs.

Exam Probability: **Low**

1. *Answer choices:*

(see index for correct answer)

- a. Chief gaming officer
- b. Financial secretary
- c. Entrepreneurship
- d. Chief sustainability officer

Guidance: level 1

:: Marketing ::

A _____ is an overall experience of a customer that distinguishes an organization or product from its rivals in the eyes of the customer. _____ s are used in business, marketing, and advertising. Name _____ s are sometimes distinguished from generic or store _____ s.

Exam Probability: **Medium**

2. *Answer choices:*

(see index for correct answer)

- a. Book of business
- b. Content Curation Marketing
- c. Brand
- d. Effie Award

Guidance: level 1

:: ::

_____ is the amount of time someone works beyond normal working hours. The term is also used for the pay received for this time. Normal hours may be determined in several ways.

Exam Probability: **Medium**

3. *Answer choices:*

(see index for correct answer)

- a. surface-level diversity
- b. hierarchical
- c. Overtime
- d. hierarchical perspective

Guidance: level 1

:: Labor ::

The workforce or labour force is the labour pool in employment. It is generally used to describe those working for a single company or industry, but can also apply to a geographic region like a city, state, or country. Within a company, its value can be labelled as its "Workforce in Place". The workforce of a country includes both the employed and the unemployed. The labour force participation rate, LFPR, is the ratio between the labour force and the overall size of their cohort. The term generally excludes the employers or management, and can imply those involved in manual labour. It may also mean all those who are available for work.

Exam Probability: **Low**

4. *Answer choices:*

(see index for correct answer)

- a. Company man
- b. Labor force
- c. Surplus labour
- d. Bought priesthood

Guidance: level 1

:: Labour relations ::

_____ is a field of study that can have different meanings depending on the context in which it is used. In an international context, it is a subfield of labor history that studies the human relations with regard to work – in its broadest sense – and how this connects to questions of social inequality. It explicitly encompasses unregulated, historical, and non-Western forms of labor. Here, _____ define "for or with whom one works and under what rules. These rules determine the type of work, type and amount of remuneration, working hours, degrees of physical and psychological strain, as well as the degree of freedom and autonomy associated with the work."

Exam Probability: **Low**

5. *Answer choices:*

(see index for correct answer)

- a. Negotiated cartelism
- b. Open shop
- c. Review Body
- d. Labor relations

Guidance: level 1

:: Business law ::

A _____ is an arrangement where parties, known as partners, agree to cooperate to advance their mutual interests. The partners in a _____ may be individuals, businesses, interest-based organizations, schools, governments or combinations. Organizations may partner to increase the likelihood of each achieving their mission and to amplify their reach. A _____ may result in issuing and holding equity or may be only governed by a contract.

Exam Probability: **High**

6. *Answer choices:*

(see index for correct answer)

- a. Financial Security Law of France
- b. Partnership
- c. Companies Acts
- d. Turnkey

Guidance: level 1

:: Regression analysis ::

A _____ often refers to a set of documented requirements to be satisfied by a material, design, product, or service. A _____ is often a type of technical standard.

Exam Probability: **High**

7. Answer choices:

(see index for correct answer)

- a. Ordinal regression
- b. Specification
- c. Residual sum of squares
- d. Principal component regression

Guidance: level 1

:: Management accounting ::

In economics, _____ s, indirect costs or overheads are business expenses that are not dependent on the level of goods or services produced by the business. They tend to be time-related, such as interest or rents being paid per month, and are often referred to as overhead costs. This is in contrast to variable costs, which are volume-related and unknown at the beginning of the accounting year. For a simple example, such as a bakery, the monthly rent for the baking facilities, and the monthly payments for the security system and basic phone line are _____ s, as they do not change according to how much bread the bakery produces and sells. On the other hand, the wage costs of the bakery are variable, as the bakery will have to hire more workers if the production of bread increases. Economists reckon _____ as a entry barrier for new entrepreneurs.

Exam Probability: **Medium**

8. Answer choices:

(see index for correct answer)

- a. Fixed cost
- b. activity based costing
- c. Corporate travel management
- d. Extended cost

Guidance: level 1

:: Critical thinking ::

In psychology, _____ is regarded as the cognitive process resulting in the selection of a belief or a course of action among several alternative possibilities. Every _____ process produces a final choice, which may or may not prompt action.

Exam Probability: **Medium**

9. *Answer choices:*
(see index for correct answer)

- a. Practical syllogism
- b. Adviser
- c. Rhetoric
- d. Decision-making

Guidance: level 1

:: Business process ::

A _____ or business method is a collection of related, structured activities or tasks by people or equipment which in a specific sequence produce a service or product for a particular customer or customers. _____ es occur at all organizational levels and may or may not be visible to the customers. A _____ may often be visualized as a flowchart of a sequence of activities with interleaving decision points or as a process matrix of a sequence of activities with relevance rules based on data in the process. The benefits of using _____ es include improved customer satisfaction and improved agility for reacting to rapid market change. Process-oriented organizations break down the barriers of structural departments and try to avoid functional silos.

Exam Probability: **High**

10. *Answer choices:*

(see index for correct answer)

- a. Business process
- b. Extended Enterprise Modeling Language
- c. Process capital
- d. Outsourced document processing

Guidance: level 1

:: Monopoly (economics) ::

_____ is a category of property that includes intangible creations of the human intellect. _____ encompasses two types of rights: industrial property rights and copyright. It was not until the 19th century that the term "_____" began to be used, and not until the late 20th century that it became commonplace in the majority of the world.

Exam Probability: **High**

11. *Answer choices:*

(see index for correct answer)

- a. Intellectual property
- b. Motion Picture Patents Company
- c. Coercive monopoly
- d. Concentration ratio

Guidance: level 1

:: Industrial relations ::

_____ or employee satisfaction is a measure of workers' contentedness with their job, whether or not they like the job or individual aspects or facets of jobs, such as nature of work or supervision. _____ can be measured in cognitive, affective, and behavioral components. Researchers have also noted that _____ measures vary in the extent to which they measure feelings about the job, or cognitions about the job.

Exam Probability: **High**

12. Answer choices:

(see index for correct answer)

- a. Industrial violence
- b. European Journal of Industrial Relations
- c. Job satisfaction
- d. Injury prevention

Guidance: level 1

:: Outsourcing ::

_____ is the relocation of a business process from one country to another—typically an operational process, such as manufacturing, or supporting processes, such as accounting. Typically this refers to a company business, although state governments may also employ _____ . More recently, technical and administrative services have been offshored.

Exam Probability: **High**

13. Answer choices:

(see index for correct answer)

- a. Affiliated Computer Services
- b. Selfsourcing
- c. Toronto-Dominion Bank
- d. Offshoring

Guidance: level 1

:: Stochastic processes ::

_____ is a system of rules that are created and enforced through social or governmental institutions to regulate behavior. It has been defined both as "the Science of Justice" and "the Art of Justice". _____ is a system that regulates and ensures that individuals or a community adhere to the will of the state. State-enforced _____ s can be made by a collective legislature or by a single legislator, resulting in statutes, by the executive through decrees and regulations, or established by judges through precedent, normally in common _____ jurisdictions. Private individuals can create legally binding contracts, including arbitration agreements that may elect to accept alternative arbitration to the normal court process. The formation of _____ s themselves may be influenced by a constitution, written or tacit, and the rights encoded therein. The _____ shapes politics, economics, history and society in various ways and serves as a mediator of relations between people.

Exam Probability: **Low**

14. *Answer choices:*
(see index for correct answer)

- a. Law
- b. Reflected Brownian motion
- c. Life-time of correlation
- d. Nuisance variable

Guidance: level 1

:: Hospitality management ::

A _____ is an establishment that provides paid lodging on a short-term basis. Facilities provided may range from a modest-quality mattress in a small room to large suites with bigger, higher-quality beds, a dresser, a refrigerator and other kitchen facilities, upholstered chairs, a flat screen television, and en-suite bathrooms. Small, lower-priced _____ s may offer only the most basic guest services and facilities. Larger, higher-priced _____ s may provide additional guest facilities such as a swimming pool, business centre, childcare, conference and event facilities, tennis or basketball courts, gymnasium, restaurants, day spa, and social function services. _____ rooms are usually numbered to allow guests to identify their room. Some boutique, high-end _____ s have custom decorated rooms. Some _____ s offer meals as part of a room and board arrangement. In the United Kingdom, a _____ is required by law to serve food and drinks to all guests within certain stated hours. In Japan, capsule _____ s provide a tiny room suitable only for sleeping and shared bathroom facilities.

Exam Probability: **Low**

15. *Answer choices:*
(see index for correct answer)

- a. Swiss Hotel Schools Association
- b. BSc. HCM
- c. IHM Pusa
- d. Group booking

Guidance: level 1

:: ::

In production, research, retail, and accounting, a _____ is the value of money that has been used up to produce something or deliver a service, and hence is not available for use anymore. In business, the _____ may be one of acquisition, in which case the amount of money expended to acquire it is counted as _____ . In this case, money is the input that is gone in order to acquire the thing. This acquisition _____ may be the sum of the _____ of production as incurred by the original producer, and further _____ s of transaction as incurred by the acquirer over and above the price paid to the producer. Usually, the price also includes a mark-up for profit over the _____ of production.

Exam Probability: **Medium**

16. *Answer choices:*

(see index for correct answer)

- a. deep-level diversity
- b. Sarbanes-Oxley act of 2002
- c. Cost
- d. interpersonal communication

Guidance: level 1

:: Industrial agreements ::

_____ is a process of negotiation between employers and a group of employees aimed at agreements to regulate working salaries, working conditions, benefits, and other aspects of workers' compensation and rights for workers. The interests of the employees are commonly presented by representatives of a trade union to which the employees belong. The collective agreements reached by these negotiations usually set out wage scales, working hours, training, health and safety, overtime, grievance mechanisms, and rights to participate in workplace or company affairs.

Exam Probability: **High**

17. *Answer choices:*

(see index for correct answer)

- a. Federal Labor Relations Act
- b. WorkChoices
- c. Court of Arbitration
- d. Collaborative bargaining

Guidance: level 1

:: Teams ::

A _____ usually refers to a group of individuals who work together from different geographic locations and rely on communication technology such as email, FAX, and video or voice conferencing services in order to collaborate. The term can also refer to groups or teams that work together asynchronously or across organizational levels. Powell, Piccoli and Ives define _____ s as "groups of geographically, organizationally and/or time dispersed workers brought together by information and telecommunication technologies to accomplish one or more organizational tasks." According to Ale Ebrahim et. al. , _____ s can also be defined as "small temporary groups of geographically, organizationally and/or time dispersed knowledge workers who coordinate their work predominantly with electronic information and communication technologies in order to accomplish one or more organization tasks."

Exam Probability: **Medium**

18. *Answer choices:*

(see index for correct answer)

- a. Team-building
- b. team composition

Guidance: level 1

:: Psychometrics ::

_____ is a dynamic, structured, interactive process where a neutral third party assists disputing parties in resolving conflict through the use of specialized communication and negotiation techniques. All participants in _____ are encouraged to actively participate in the process. _____ is a "party-centered" process in that it is focused primarily upon the needs, rights, and interests of the parties. The mediator uses a wide variety of techniques to guide the process in a constructive direction and to help the parties find their optimal solution. A mediator is facilitative in that she/he manages the interaction between parties and facilitates open communication. _____ is also evaluative in that the mediator analyzes issues and relevant norms, while refraining from providing prescriptive advice to the parties.

Exam Probability: **Low**

19. *Answer choices:*

(see index for correct answer)

- a. Perceptual mapping
- b. Mediation
- c. Theory of conjoint measurement
- d. Reproducibility

Guidance: level 1

:: ::

_____ is the stock of habits, knowledge, social and personality attributes embodied in the ability to perform labor so as to produce economic value.

Exam Probability: **Medium**

20. *Answer choices:*

(see index for correct answer)

- a. hierarchical perspective
- b. interpersonal communication
- c. deep-level diversity
- d. empathy

Guidance: level 1

:: ::

_____ is the capacity of consciously making sense of things, establishing and verifying facts, applying logic, and changing or justifying practices, institutions, and beliefs based on new or existing information. It is closely associated with such characteristically human activities as philosophy, science, language, mathematics and art, and is normally considered to be a distinguishing ability possessed by humans. _____ , or an aspect of it, is sometimes referred to as rationality.

Exam Probability: **High**

21. *Answer choices:*

(see index for correct answer)

- a. Reason

- b. deep-level diversity
- c. surface-level diversity
- d. co-culture

Guidance: level 1

:: E-commerce ::

> _____ is the activity of buying or selling of products on online services or over the Internet. Electronic commerce draws on technologies such as mobile commerce, electronic funds transfer, supply chain management, Internet marketing, online transaction processing, electronic data interchange , inventory management systems, and automated data collection systems.

Exam Probability: **High**

22. *Answer choices:*

(see index for correct answer)

- a. Cleaning card
- b. Government-to-citizen
- c. AS 2805
- d. Triton

Guidance: level 1

:: Summary statistics ::

_____ is the number of occurrences of a repeating event per unit of time. It is also referred to as temporal _____, which emphasizes the contrast to spatial _____ and angular _____. The period is the duration of time of one cycle in a repeating event, so the period is the reciprocal of the _____. For example: if a newborn baby's heart beats at a _____ of 120 times a minute, its period—the time interval between beats—is half a second. _____ is an important parameter used in science and engineering to specify the rate of oscillatory and vibratory phenomena, such as mechanical vibrations, audio signals, radio waves, and light.

Exam Probability: **High**

23. *Answer choices:*

(see index for correct answer)

- a. Quantile
- b. Frequency
- c. Percentile
- d. Generalized entropy index

Guidance: level 1

:: ::

A _____ is a problem offering two possibilities, neither of which is unambiguously acceptable or preferable. The possibilities are termed the horns of the _____ , a clichéd usage, but distinguishing the _____ from other kinds of predicament as a matter of usage.

Exam Probability: **Low**

24. *Answer choices:*

(see index for correct answer)

- a. information systems assessment
- b. surface-level diversity
- c. hierarchical perspective
- d. Dilemma

Guidance: level 1

:: Income ::

In business and accounting, net income is an entity's income minus cost of goods sold, expenses and taxes for an accounting period. It is computed as the residual of all revenues and gains over all expenses and losses for the period, and has also been defined as the net increase in shareholders' equity that results from a company's operations. In the context of the presentation of financial statements, the IFRS Foundation defines net income as synonymous with profit and loss. The difference between revenue and the cost of making a product or providing a service, before deducting overheads, payroll, taxation, and interest payments. This is different from operating income .

Exam Probability: **Medium**

25. *Answer choices:*

(see index for correct answer)

- a. Return of investment
- b. Revenue management
- c. Creative real estate investing
- d. Bottom line

Guidance: level 1

:: ::

_____ s and acquisitions are transactions in which the ownership of companies, other business organizations, or their operating units are transferred or consolidated with other entities. As an aspect of strategic management, M&A can allow enterprises to grow or downsize, and change the nature of their business or competitive position.

Exam Probability: **Medium**

26. *Answer choices:*

(see index for correct answer)

- a. Merger
- b. functional perspective

- c. cultural
- d. interpersonal communication

Guidance: level 1

:: Legal terms ::

_____ , a form of alternative dispute resolution , is a way to resolve disputes outside the courts. The dispute will be decided by one or more persons , which renders the "_____ award". An _____ award is legally binding on both sides and enforceable in the courts.

Exam Probability: **Medium**

27. *Answer choices:*

(see index for correct answer)

- a. Antedated
- b. Fair competition
- c. Arbitration
- d. Appearance

Guidance: level 1

:: Lean manufacturing ::

_____ is the Sino-Japanese word for "improvement". In business, _____ refers to activities that continuously improve all functions and involve all employees from the CEO to the assembly line workers. It also applies to processes, such as purchasing and logistics, that cross organizational boundaries into the supply chain. It has been applied in healthcare, psychotherapy, life-coaching, government, and banking.

Exam Probability: **High**

28. *Answer choices:*

(see index for correct answer)

- a. Kaizen
- b. Statistical thinking
- c. Muri
- d. Lean software development

Guidance: level 1

:: Leadership ::

_____/Management is a part of a style of leadership that focuses on supervision, organization, and performance; it is an integral part of the Full Range Leadership Model. _____ is a style of leadership in which leaders promote compliance by followers through both rewards and punishments. Through a rewards and punishments system, transactional leaders are able to keep followers motivated for the short-term. Unlike transformational leaders, those using the transactional approach are not looking to change the future, they look to keep things the same. Leaders using _____ as a model pay attention to followers' work in order to find faults and deviations.

Exam Probability: **Low**

29. *Answer choices:*

(see index for correct answer)

- a. Evolutionary leadership theory
- b. The Saint, the Surfer, and the CEO
- c. Transactional leadership
- d. Leadership analysis

Guidance: level 1

:: ::

_____ Corporation was an American energy, commodities, and services company based in Houston, Texas. It was founded in 1985 as a merger between Houston Natural Gas and InterNorth, both relatively small regional companies. Before its bankruptcy on December 3, 2001, _____ employed approximately 29,000 staff and was a major electricity, natural gas, communications and pulp and paper company, with claimed revenues of nearly $101 billion during 2000. Fortune named _____ "America's Most Innovative Company" for six consecutive years.

Exam Probability: **High**

30. *Answer choices:*

(see index for correct answer)

- a. information systems assessment
- b. open system
- c. similarity-attraction theory
- d. Enron

Guidance: level 1

:: Costs ::

In economics, _____ is the total economic cost of production and is made up of variable cost, which varies according to the quantity of a good produced and includes inputs such as labour and raw materials, plus fixed cost, which is independent of the quantity of a good produced and includes inputs that cannot be varied in the short term: fixed costs such as buildings and machinery, including sunk costs if any. Since cost is measured per unit of time, it is a flow variable.

Exam Probability: **High**

31. *Answer choices:*

(see index for correct answer)

- a. Search cost
- b. Flyaway cost
- c. Implicit cost
- d. Opportunity cost

Guidance: level 1

:: Management accounting ::

_____ s are costs that change as the quantity of the good or service that a business produces changes. _____ s are the sum of marginal costs over all units produced. They can also be considered normal costs. Fixed costs and _____ s make up the two components of total cost. Direct costs are costs that can easily be associated with a particular cost object. However, not all _____ s are direct costs. For example, variable manufacturing overhead costs are _____ s that are indirect costs, not direct costs. _____ s are sometimes called unit-level costs as they vary with the number of units produced.

Exam Probability: **Low**

32. *Answer choices:*

(see index for correct answer)

- a. Indirect costs
- b. Target income sales
- c. Direct material price variance
- d. Profit center

Guidance: level 1

:: ::

The _____ is a political and economic union of 28 member states that are located primarily in Europe. It has an area of 4,475,757 km2 and an estimated population of about 513 million. The EU has developed an internal single market through a standardised system of laws that apply in all member states in those matters, and only those matters, where members have agreed to act as one. EU policies aim to ensure the free movement of people, goods, services and capital within the internal market, enact legislation in justice and home affairs and maintain common policies on trade, agriculture, fisheries and regional development. For travel within the Schengen Area, passport controls have been abolished. A monetary union was established in 1999 and came into full force in 2002 and is composed of 19 EU member states which use the euro currency.

Exam Probability: **Medium**

33. *Answer choices:*

(see index for correct answer)

- a. Character
- b. empathy
- c. hierarchical perspective
- d. personal values

Guidance: level 1

:: Production and manufacturing ::

An _____ is a manufacturing process in which parts are added as the semi-finished assembly moves from workstation to workstation where the parts are added in sequence until the final assembly is produced. By mechanically moving the parts to the assembly work and moving the semi-finished assembly from work station to work station, a finished product can be assembled faster and with less labor than by having workers carry parts to a stationary piece for assembly.

Exam Probability: **Medium**

34. *Answer choices:*

(see index for correct answer)

- a. Zero Defects
- b. Economic region of production
- c. Assembly line
- d. LPA512

Guidance: level 1

:: Customs duties ::

A _____ is a tax on imports or exports between sovereign states. It is a form of regulation of foreign trade and a policy that taxes foreign products to encourage or safeguard domestic industry. _____ s are the simplest and oldest instrument of trade policy. Traditionally, states have used them as a source of income. Now, they are among the most widely used instruments of protection, along with import and export quotas.

Exam Probability: **Low**

35. *Answer choices:*

(see index for correct answer)

- a. Cochin Duty Free
- b. Carnet de Passages
- c. Canada Corn Act
- d. Tariff

Guidance: level 1

:: Asset ::

In financial accounting, an _____ is any resource owned by the business. Anything tangible or intangible that can be owned or controlled to produce value and that is held by a company to produce positive economic value is an _____ . Simply stated, _____ s represent value of ownership that can be converted into cash . The balance sheet of a firm records the monetary value of the _____ s owned by that firm. It covers money and other valuables belonging to an individual or to a business.

Exam Probability: **Medium**

36. *Answer choices:*

(see index for correct answer)

- a. Fixed asset

- b. Current asset

Guidance: level 1

:: ::

_____ is the moral stance, political philosophy, ideology, or social outlook that emphasizes the moral worth of the individual. Individualists promote the exercise of one's goals and desires and so value independence and self-reliance and advocate that interests of the individual should achieve precedence over the state or a social group, while opposing external interference upon one's own interests by society or institutions such as the government. _____ is often defined in contrast to totalitarianism, collectivism, and more corporate social forms.

Exam Probability: **Medium**

37. *Answer choices:*
(see index for correct answer)

- a. hierarchical perspective
- b. interpersonal communication
- c. Individualism
- d. functional perspective

Guidance: level 1

:: ::

The business environment is a marketing term and refers to factors and forces that affect a firm's ability to build and maintain successful customer relationships. The business environment has been defined as "the totality of physical and social factors that are taken directly into consideration in the decision-making behaviour of individuals in the organisation."

Exam Probability: **Medium**

38. *Answer choices:*
(see index for correct answer)

- a. personal values
- b. Character
- c. Environmental scanning
- d. co-culture

Guidance: level 1

:: Occupations ::

An _____ is a person who has a position of authority in a hierarchical organization. The term derives from the late Latin from officiarius, meaning "official".

Exam Probability: **Low**

39. *Answer choices:*

(see index for correct answer)

- a. Nuclear gypsy
- b. Officer
- c. Drawing-in frame
- d. Commissionaire

Guidance: level 1

:: Quality management ::

A _____ or quality control circle is a group of workers who do the same or similar work, who meet regularly to identify, analyze and solve work-related problems. Normally small in size, the group is usually led by a supervisor or manager and presents its solutions to management; where possible, workers implement the solutions themselves in order to improve the performance of the organization and motivate employees. _____ s were at their most popular during the 1980s, but continue to exist in the form of Kaizen groups and similar worker participation schemes.

Exam Probability: **Low**

40. *Answer choices:*

(see index for correct answer)

- a. Quality management system
- b. Common Assessment Framework

- c. E-TQM College
- d. Germanischer Lloyd

Guidance: level 1

:: Logistics ::

_____ is generally the detailed organization and implementation of a complex operation. In a general business sense, _____ is the management of the flow of things between the point of origin and the point of consumption in order to meet requirements of customers or corporations. The resources managed in _____ may include tangible goods such as materials, equipment, and supplies, as well as food and other consumable items. The _____ of physical items usually involves the integration of information flow, materials handling, production, packaging, inventory, transportation, warehousing, and often security.

Exam Probability: **Low**

41. *Answer choices:*

(see index for correct answer)

- a. Ground Parachute Extraction System
- b. Liquid logistics
- c. G-Log
- d. Logistics

Guidance: level 1

:: Discrimination ::

In social psychology, a _____ is an over-generalized belief about a particular category of people. _____s are generalized because one assumes that the _____ is true for each individual person in the category. While such generalizations may be useful when making quick decisions, they may be erroneous when applied to particular individuals. _____s encourage prejudice and may arise for a number of reasons.

Exam Probability: **Medium**

42. *Answer choices:*

(see index for correct answer)

- a. Anti-Americanism
- b. Elitism
- c. Economic discrimination

Guidance: level 1

:: Marketing ::

_____ or stock control can be broadly defined as "the activity of checking a shop's stock." However, a more focused definition takes into account the more science-based, methodical practice of not only verifying a business' inventory but also focusing on the many related facets of inventory management "within an organisation to meet the demand placed upon that business economically." Other facets of _____ include supply chain management, production control, financial flexibility, and customer satisfaction. At the root of _____ , however, is the _____ problem, which involves determining when to order, how much to order, and the logistics of those decisions.

Exam Probability: **Medium**

43. *Answer choices:*

(see index for correct answer)

- a. Global Center for Health Innovation
- b. Brandweek
- c. Double bottom line
- d. Inventory control

Guidance: level 1

:: Information systems ::

_____ is the process of creating, sharing, using and managing the knowledge and information of an organisation. It refers to a multidisciplinary approach to achieving organisational objectives by making the best use of knowledge.

Exam Probability: **High**

44. *Answer choices:*

(see index for correct answer)

- a. Automated information system
- b. Knowledge management
- c. Event stream processing
- d. Preference elicitation

Guidance: level 1

:: Product management ::

_____ s, also known as Shewhart charts or process-behavior charts, are a statistical process control tool used to determine if a manufacturing or business process is in a state of control.

Exam Probability: **High**

45. *Answer choices:*

(see index for correct answer)

- a. Brand equity
- b. Technology acceptance model
- c. Brand extension
- d. Diffusion of innovations

Guidance: level 1

:: Human resource management ::

_____ , also known as management by results, was first popularized by Peter Drucker in his 1954 book The Practice of Management. _____ is the process of defining specific objectives within an organization that management can convey to organization members, then deciding on how to achieve each objective in sequence. This process allows managers to take work that needs to be done one step at a time to allow for a calm, yet productive work environment. This process also helps organization members to see their accomplishments as they achieve each objective, which reinforces a positive work environment and a sense of achievement. An important part of MBO is the measurement and comparison of an employee's actual performance with the standards set. Ideally, when employees themselves have been involved with the goal-setting and choosing the course of action to be followed by them, they are more likely to fulfill their responsibilities. According to George S. Odiorne, the system of _____ can be described as a process whereby the superior and subordinate jointly identify common goals, define each individual's major areas of responsibility in terms of the results expected of him or her, and use these measures as guides for operating the unit and assessing the contribution of each of its members.

Exam Probability: **High**

46. *Answer choices:*

(see index for correct answer)

- a. Training and development
- b. Open-book management
- c. Workforce management

- d. Management by objectives

Guidance: level 1

:: Behaviorism ::

In behavioral psychology, _____ is a consequence applied that will strengthen an organism's future behavior whenever that behavior is preceded by a specific antecedent stimulus. This strengthening effect may be measured as a higher frequency of behavior, longer duration, greater magnitude, or shorter latency. There are two types of _____, known as positive _____ and negative _____; positive is where by a reward is offered on expression of the wanted behaviour and negative is taking away an undesirable element in the persons environment whenever the desired behaviour is achieved.

Exam Probability: **Low**

47. *Answer choices:*
(see index for correct answer)

- a. Reinforcement
- b. Matching Law
- c. Systematic desensitization
- d. chaining

Guidance: level 1

:: Problem solving ::

A _____ is a unit or formation established to work on a single defined task or activity. Originally introduced by the United States Navy, the term has now caught on for general usage and is a standard part of NATO terminology. Many non-military organizations now create " _____ s" or task groups for temporary activities that might have once been performed by ad hoc committees.

Exam Probability: **Medium**

48. *Answer choices:*

(see index for correct answer)

- a. Task force
- b. Thinking outside the box
- c. Failure analysis
- d. Nursing process

Guidance: level 1

:: ::

In sales, commerce and economics, a _____ is the recipient of a good, service, product or an idea - obtained from a seller, vendor, or supplier via a financial transaction or exchange for money or some other valuable consideration.

Exam Probability: **Medium**

49. *Answer choices:*

(see index for correct answer)

- a. surface-level diversity
- b. Character
- c. similarity-attraction theory
- d. personal values

Guidance: level 1

:: Project management ::

_____ is a process of setting goals, planning and/or controlling the organizing and leading the execution of any type of activity, such as.

Exam Probability: **Low**

50. *Answer choices:*

(see index for correct answer)

- a. Management process
- b. Jeff Sutherland
- c. Case competition
- d. Grandfather principle

Guidance: level 1

:: Production economics ::

_____ is the joint use of a resource or space. It is also the process of dividing and distributing. In its narrow sense, it refers to joint or alternating use of inherently finite goods, such as a common pasture or a shared residence. Still more loosely, "_____" can actually mean giving something as an outright gift: for example, to "share" one's food really means to give some of it as a gift. _____ is a basic component of human interaction, and is responsible for strengthening social ties and ensuring a person's well-being.

Exam Probability: **High**

51. *Answer choices:*
(see index for correct answer)

- a. Learning-by-doing
- b. Choice of techniques
- c. Industrial production index
- d. Diseconomies of scale

Guidance: level 1

:: ::

The _____ is an intergovernmental organization that is concerned with the regulation of international trade between nations. The WTO officially commenced on 1 January 1995 under the Marrakesh Agreement, signed by 124 nations on 15 April 1994, replacing the General Agreement on Tariffs and Trade , which commenced in 1948. It is the largest international economic organization in the world.

Exam Probability: **Low**

52. *Answer choices:*

(see index for correct answer)

- a. co-culture
- b. levels of analysis
- c. interpersonal communication
- d. cultural

Guidance: level 1

:: ::

_____ is the process of two or more people or organizations working together to complete a task or achieve a goal. _____ is similar to cooperation. Most _____ requires leadership, although the form of leadership can be social within a decentralized and egalitarian group. Teams that work collaboratively often access greater resources, recognition and rewards when facing competition for finite resources.

Exam Probability: **High**

53. *Answer choices:*

(see index for correct answer)

- a. information systems assessment
- b. open system
- c. functional perspective
- d. interpersonal communication

Guidance: level 1

:: ::

_____ or haggling is a type of negotiation in which the buyer and seller of a good or service debate the price and exact nature of a transaction. If the _____ produces agreement on terms, the transaction takes place. _____ is an alternative pricing strategy to fixed prices. Optimally, if it costs the retailer nothing to engage and allow _____ , s/he can divine the buyer's willingness to spend. It allows for capturing more consumer surplus as it allows price discrimination, a process whereby a seller can charge a higher price to one buyer who is more eager . Haggling has largely disappeared in parts of the world where the cost to haggle exceeds the gain to retailers for most common retail items. However, for expensive goods sold to uninformed buyers such as automobiles, _____ can remain commonplace.

Exam Probability: **Low**

54. *Answer choices:*

(see index for correct answer)

- a. Bargaining
- b. process perspective
- c. similarity-attraction theory
- d. information systems assessment

Guidance: level 1

:: Information science ::

_____ is the resolution of uncertainty; it is that which answers the question of "what an entity is" and thus defines both its essence and nature of its characteristics. _____ relates to both data and knowledge, as data is meaningful _____ representing values attributed to parameters, and knowledge signifies understanding of a concept. _____ is uncoupled from an observer, which is an entity that can access _____ and thus discern what it specifies; _____ exists beyond an event horizon for example. In the case of knowledge, the _____ itself requires a cognitive observer to be obtained.

Exam Probability: **High**

55. *Answer choices:*
(see index for correct answer)

- a. Knowledge Organization Systems
- b. Information school
- c. Conceptions of Library and Information Science

- d. Information

Guidance: level 1

:: Supply chain management terms ::

In business and finance, _____ is a system of organizations, people, activities, information, and resources involved in moving a product or service from supplier to customer. _____ activities involve the transformation of natural resources, raw materials, and components into a finished product that is delivered to the end customer. In sophisticated _____ systems, used products may re-enter the _____ at any point where residual value is recyclable. _____ s link value chains.

Exam Probability: **Low**

56. *Answer choices:*

(see index for correct answer)

- a. Widget
- b. Most valuable customers
- c. Supply chain
- d. Consumables

Guidance: level 1

:: Analysis ::

_____ is the process of breaking a complex topic or substance into smaller parts in order to gain a better understanding of it. The technique has been applied in the study of mathematics and logic since before Aristotle, though _____ as a formal concept is a relatively recent development.

Exam Probability: **Medium**

57. *Answer choices:*

(see index for correct answer)

- a. DESTEP
- b. Paradox of analysis
- c. Analysis
- d. Analytical quality control

Guidance: level 1

:: Management ::

A _____ is an idea of the future or desired result that a person or a group of people envisions, plans and commits to achieve. People endeavor to reach _____ s within a finite time by setting deadlines.

Exam Probability: **Medium**

58. *Answer choices:*

(see index for correct answer)

- a. IT performance management
- b. Goal
- c. Preparation
- d. Process capability

Guidance: level 1

:: Organizational theory ::

_____ is the process of groups of organisms working or acting together for common, mutual, or some underlying benefit, as opposed to working in competition for selfish benefit. Many animal and plant species cooperate both with other members of their own species and with members of other species.

Exam Probability: **High**

59. *Answer choices:*
(see index for correct answer)

- a. Cooperation
- b. resource dependence
- c. Organizational effectiveness
- d. Smart city

Guidance: level 1

Business law

Corporate law (also known as business law) is the body of law governing the rights, relations, and conduct of persons, companies, organizations and businesses. It refers to the legal practice relating to, or the theory of corporations. Corporate law often describes the law relating to matters which derive directly from the life-cycle of a corporation. It thus encompasses the formation, funding, governance, and death of a corporation.

:: Statutory law ::

_____ or statute law is written law set down by a body of legislature or by a singular legislator . This is as opposed to oral or customary law; or regulatory law promulgated by the executive or common law of the judiciary. Statutes may originate with national, state legislatures or local municipalities.

Exam Probability: **Low**

1. *Answer choices:*

(see index for correct answer)

- a. ratification
- b. incorporation by reference
- c. Statute of repose
- d. Statutory Law

Guidance: level 1

:: Legal terms ::

_____ is the set of laws that governs how members of a society are to behave. It is contrasted with procedural law, which is the set of procedures for making, administering, and enforcing _____ . _____ defines rights and responsibilities in civil law, and crimes and punishments in criminal law. It may be codified in statutes or exist through precedent in common law.

Exam Probability: **Low**

2. *Answer choices:*

(see index for correct answer)

- a. Substantive law
- b. Innominate jury
- c. Mischief
- d. Competent authority

Guidance: level 1

:: Money market instruments ::

_____ , in the global financial market, is an unsecured promissory note with a fixed maturity of not more than 270 days.

Exam Probability: **Low**

3. *Answer choices:*
(see index for correct answer)

- a. Banker's acceptance
- b. Commercial Paper

Guidance: level 1

:: ::

_____ is the collection of mechanisms, processes and relations by which corporations are controlled and operated. Governance structures and principles identify the distribution of rights and responsibilities among different participants in the corporation and include the rules and procedures for making decisions in corporate affairs. _____ is necessary because of the possibility of conflicts of interests between stakeholders, primarily between shareholders and upper management or among shareholders.

Exam Probability: **High**

4. *Answer choices:*

(see index for correct answer)

- a. Character
- b. similarity-attraction theory
- c. open system
- d. Corporate governance

Guidance: level 1

:: Criminal procedure ::

_____ is the adjudication process of the criminal law. While _____ differs dramatically by jurisdiction, the process generally begins with a formal criminal charge with the person on trial either being free on bail or incarcerated, and results in the conviction or acquittal of the defendant. _____ can be either in form of inquisitorial or adversarial _____ .

Exam Probability: **Medium**

5. *Answer choices:*

(see index for correct answer)

- a. directed verdict
- b. Criminal procedure

Guidance: level 1

:: Legal doctrines and principles ::

The _____ rule is a rule in the Anglo-American common law that governs what kinds of evidence parties to a contract dispute can introduce when trying to determine the specific terms of a contract. The rule also prevents parties who have reduced their agreement to a final written document from later introducing other evidence, such as the content of oral discussions from earlier in the negotiation process, as evidence of a different intent as to the terms of the contract. The rule provides that "extrinsic evidence is inadmissible to vary a written contract". The term "parol" derives from the Anglo-Norman French parol or parole, meaning "word of mouth" or "verbal", and in medieval times referred to oral pleadings in a court case.

Exam Probability: **Low**

6. *Answer choices:*

(see index for correct answer)

- a. Parol evidence
- b. Attractive nuisance
- c. Acquiescence
- d. Exclusionary rule

Guidance: level 1

:: Commercial item transport and distribution ::

A _____ is a commitment or expectation to perform some action in general or if certain circumstances arise. A _____ may arise from a system of ethics or morality, especially in an honor culture. Many duties are created by law, sometimes including a codified punishment or liability for non-performance. Performing one's _____ may require some sacrifice of self-interest.

Exam Probability: **High**

7. *Answer choices:*

(see index for correct answer)

- a. Truck
- b. Incoterms
- c. Straddle carrier
- d. Duty

Guidance: level 1

:: Mereology ::

_____, in the abstract, is what belongs to or with something, whether as an attribute or as a component of said thing. In the context of this article, it is one or more components, whether physical or incorporeal, of a person's estate; or so belonging to, as in being owned by, a person or jointly a group of people or a legal entity like a corporation or even a society. Depending on the nature of the _____, an owner of _____ has the right to consume, alter, share, redefine, rent, mortgage, pawn, sell, exchange, transfer, give away or destroy it, or to exclude others from doing these things, as well as to perhaps abandon it; whereas regardless of the nature of the _____, the owner thereof has the right to properly use it, or at the very least exclusively keep it.

Exam Probability: **High**

8. *Answer choices:*

(see index for correct answer)

- a. Property
- b. Mereological essentialism
- c. Gunk
- d. Meronomy

Guidance: level 1

_____, often abbreviated cert. in the United States, is a process for seeking judicial review and a writ issued by a court that agrees to review. A _____ is issued by a superior court, directing an inferior court, tribunal, or other public authority to send the record of a proceeding for review.

Exam Probability: **Low**

9. *Answer choices:*

(see index for correct answer)

- a. interpersonal communication
- b. Certiorari
- c. similarity-attraction theory
- d. Character

Guidance: level 1

:: Project management ::

A _____ is a source or supply from which a benefit is produced and it has some utility. _____ s can broadly be classified upon their availability—they are classified into renewable and non-renewable _____ s.Examples of non renewable _____ s are coal ,crude oil natural gas nuclear energy etc. Examples of renewable _____ s are air,water,wind,solar energy etc. They can also be classified as actual and potential on the basis of level of development and use, on the basis of origin they can be classified as biotic and abiotic, and on the basis of their distribution, as ubiquitous and localized . An item becomes a _____ with time and developing technology. Typically, _____ s are materials, energy, services, staff, knowledge, or other assets that are transformed to produce benefit and in the process may be consumed or made unavailable. Benefits of _____ utilization may include increased wealth, proper functioning of a system, or enhanced well-being. From a human perspective a natural _____ is anything obtained from the environment to satisfy human needs and wants. From a broader biological or ecological perspective a _____ satisfies the needs of a living organism .

Exam Probability: **High**

10. *Answer choices:*

(see index for correct answer)

- a. Changes clause
- b. The Practice Standard for Scheduling
- c. Punch list
- d. Axelos

Guidance: level 1

:: ::

The _____ is the central philosophical concept in the deontological moral philosophy of Immanuel Kant. Introduced in Kant's 1785 Groundwork of the Metaphysics of Morals, it may be defined as a way of evaluating motivations for action.

Exam Probability: **Medium**

11. *Answer choices:*

(see index for correct answer)

- a. Sarbanes-Oxley act of 2002
- b. open system
- c. Categorical imperative
- d. corporate values

Guidance: level 1

:: ::

A contract is a legally-binding agreement which recognises and governs the rights and duties of the parties to the agreement. A contract is legally enforceable because it meets the requirements and approval of the law. An agreement typically involves the exchange of goods, services, money, or promises of any of those. In the event of breach of contract, the law awards the injured party access to legal remedies such as damages and cancellation.

Exam Probability: **Low**

12. Answer choices:

(see index for correct answer)

- a. co-culture
- b. surface-level diversity
- c. Contract law
- d. process perspective

Guidance: level 1

:: Real estate ::

_____, real estate, realty, or immovable property In English common law refers to landed properties belonging to some person. It include all structures, crops, buildings, machinery, wells, dams, ponds, mines, canals, and roads, among other things. The term is historic, arising from the now-discontinued form of action, which distinguish between _____ disputes and personal property disputes. Personal property was, and continues to refer to all properties that are not real properties.

Exam Probability: **Low**

13. Answer choices:

(see index for correct answer)

- a. Common area maintenance charges
- b. ReOS
- c. Real property

- d. Cul-de-sac

Guidance: level 1

:: Contract law ::

In contract law, a _____ is a promise which is not a condition of the contract or an innominate term: it is a term "not going to the root of the contract", and which only entitles the innocent party to damages if it is breached: i.e. the _____ is not true or the defaulting party does not perform the contract in accordance with the terms of the _____. A _____ is not guarantee. It is a mere promise. It may be enforced if it is breached by an award for the legal remedy of damages.

Exam Probability: **High**

14. *Answer choices:*

(see index for correct answer)

- a. Performance Based Contracting
- b. Offeror
- c. Warranty
- d. ConsensusDOCS

Guidance: level 1

:: Fair use ::

_____ is a doctrine in the law of the United States that permits limited use of copyrighted material without having to first acquire permission from the copyright holder. _____ is one of the limitations to copyright intended to balance the interests of copyright holders with the public interest in the wider distribution and use of creative works by allowing as a defense to copyright infringement claims certain limited uses that might otherwise be considered infringement.

Exam Probability: **Medium**

15. *Answer choices:*

(see index for correct answer)

- a. Fair use
- b. FAIR USE Act
- c. Nominative use
- d. Fair Use Project

Guidance: level 1

:: ::

_____, or auditory perception, is the ability to perceive sounds by detecting vibrations, changes in the pressure of the surrounding medium through time, through an organ such as the ear. The academic field concerned with _____ is auditory science.

Exam Probability: **Low**

16. Answer choices:

(see index for correct answer)

- a. imperative
- b. information systems assessment
- c. Hearing
- d. Character

Guidance: level 1

:: ::

The _____ of 1933, also known as the 1933 Act, the _____, the Truth in _____, the Federal _____, and the `33 Act, was enacted by the United States Congress on May 27, 1933, during the Great Depression, after the stock market crash of 1929. Legislated pursuant to the Interstate Commerce Clause of the Constitution, it requires every offer or sale of securities that uses the means and instrumentalities of interstate commerce to be registered with the SEC pursuant to the 1933 Act, unless an exemption from registration exists under the law. The term "means and instrumentalities of interstate commerce" is extremely broad and it is virtually impossible to avoid the operation of the statute by attempting to offer or sell a security without using an "instrumentality" of interstate commerce. Any use of a telephone, for example, or the mails would probably be enough to subject the transaction to the statute.

Exam Probability: **Low**

17. Answer choices:

(see index for correct answer)

- a. hierarchical
- b. Securities Act
- c. Sarbanes-Oxley act of 2002
- d. functional perspective

Guidance: level 1

:: Euthenics ::

_____ is an ethical framework and suggests that an entity, be it an organization or individual, has an obligation to act for the benefit of society at large. _____ is a duty every individual has to perform so as to maintain a balance between the economy and the ecosystems. A trade-off may exist between economic development, in the material sense, and the welfare of the society and environment, though this has been challenged by many reports over the past decade. _____ means sustaining the equilibrium between the two. It pertains not only to business organizations but also to everyone whose any action impacts the environment. This responsibility can be passive, by avoiding engaging in socially harmful acts, or active, by performing activities that directly advance social goals. _____ must be intergenerational since the actions of one generation have consequences on those following.

Exam Probability: **Low**

18. *Answer choices:*

(see index for correct answer)

- a. Social responsibility
- b. Home economics

- c. Family and consumer science
- d. Euthenics

Guidance: level 1

:: ::

_____ is an insurance that covers the whole or a part of the risk of a person incurring medical expenses, spreading the risk over a large number of persons. By estimating the overall risk of health care and health system expenses over the risk pool, an insurer can develop a routine finance structure, such as a monthly premium or payroll tax, to provide the money to pay for the health care benefits specified in the insurance agreement. The benefit is administered by a central organization such as a government agency, private business, or not-for-profit entity.

Exam Probability: **High**

19. *Answer choices:*

(see index for correct answer)

- a. imperative
- b. similarity-attraction theory
- c. Health insurance
- d. levels of analysis

Guidance: level 1

:: ::

_____ is the practical authority granted to a legal body to administer justice within a defined field of responsibility, e.g., Michigan tax law. In federations like the United States, areas of _____ apply to local, state, and federal levels; e.g. the court has _____ to apply federal law.

Exam Probability: **Medium**

20. *Answer choices:*

(see index for correct answer)

- a. personal values
- b. cultural
- c. Jurisdiction
- d. process perspective

Guidance: level 1

:: Labour relations ::

_____ is a field of study that can have different meanings depending on the context in which it is used. In an international context, it is a subfield of labor history that studies the human relations with regard to work – in its broadest sense – and how this connects to questions of social inequality. It explicitly encompasses unregulated, historical, and non-Western forms of labor. Here, _____ define "for or with whom one works and under what rules. These rules determine the type of work, type and amount of remuneration, working hours, degrees of physical and psychological strain, as well as the degree of freedom and autonomy associated with the work."

Exam Probability: **Low**

21. *Answer choices:*

(see index for correct answer)

- a. Merit shop
- b. Eurocadres
- c. Social dialogue
- d. Picketing

Guidance: level 1

:: United States federal public corruption crime ::

Mail fraud and _____ are federal crimes in the United States that involve mailing or electronically transmitting something associated with fraud. Jurisdiction is claimed by the federal government if the illegal activity crosses interstate or international borders.

Exam Probability: **Low**

22. *Answer choices:*

(see index for correct answer)

- a. Racketeer Influenced and Corrupt Organizations Act
- b. Wire fraud

Guidance: level 1

:: ::

A _____ is any person who contracts to acquire an asset in return for some form of consideration.

Exam Probability: **High**

23. *Answer choices:*

(see index for correct answer)

- a. functional perspective
- b. Buyer
- c. Character
- d. open system

Guidance: level 1

:: Legal terms ::

_____, or exemplary damages, are damages assessed in order to punish the defendant for outrageous conduct and/or to reform or deter the defendant and others from engaging in conduct similar to that which formed the basis of the lawsuit. Although the purpose of _____ is not to compensate the plaintiff, the plaintiff will receive all or some of the _____ award.

Exam Probability: **Low**

24. *Answer choices:*
(see index for correct answer)

- a. Punitive damages
- b. Appropriation
- c. Multiplepoinding
- d. Chain of title

Guidance: level 1

:: Legal terms ::

_____s may be governments, corporations or investment trusts. _____s are legally responsible for the obligations of the issue and for reporting financial conditions, material developments and any other operational activities as required by the regulations of their jurisdictions.

Exam Probability: **High**

25. *Answer choices:*

(see index for correct answer)

- a. Bifurcation
- b. Generally recognized as safe and effective
- c. Door tenant
- d. Issuer

Guidance: level 1

:: Contract law ::

A _____ is a contract in which one party agrees to supply as much of a good or service as is required by the other party, and in exchange the other party expressly or implicitly promises that it will obtain its goods or services exclusively from the first party. For example, a grocery store might enter into a contract with the farmer who grows oranges under which the farmer would supply the grocery store with as many oranges as the store could sell. The farmer could sue for breach of contract if the store were thereafter to purchase oranges for this purpose from any other party. The converse of this situation is an output contract, in which one buyer agrees to purchase however much of a good or service the seller is able to produce.

Exam Probability: **Low**

26. *Answer choices:*

(see index for correct answer)

- a. Requirements contract
- b. Mirror image rule
- c. Indian contract law
- d. Terms of service

Guidance: level 1

:: Progressive Era in the United States ::

The Clayton Antitrust Act of 1914, was a part of United States antitrust law with the goal of adding further substance to the U.S. antitrust law regime; the _____ sought to prevent anticompetitive practices in their incipiency. That regime started with the Sherman Antitrust Act of 1890, the first Federal law outlawing practices considered harmful to consumers. The _____ specified particular prohibited conduct, the three-level enforcement scheme, the exemptions, and the remedial measures.

Exam Probability: **Medium**

27. *Answer choices:*

(see index for correct answer)

- a. pragmatism
- b. Clayton Act
- c. Mann Act

Guidance: level 1

:: Business law ::

A _____ is an offer that will remain open for a certain period or until a certain time or occurrence of a certain event, during which it is incapable of being revoked. As a general rule, all offers are revocable at any time prior to acceptance, even those offers that purport to be irrevocable on their face.

Exam Probability: **Medium**

28. *Answer choices:*

(see index for correct answer)

- a. De facto corporation and corporation by estoppel
- b. Firm offer
- c. Power harassment
- d. Double ticketing

Guidance: level 1

:: Manufactured goods ::

A _____ or final good is any commodity that is produced or consumed by the consumer to satisfy current wants or needs. _____ s are ultimately consumed, rather than used in the production of another good. For example, a microwave oven or a bicycle that is sold to a consumer is a final good or _____ , but the components that are sold to be used in those goods are intermediate goods. For example, textiles or transistors can be used to make some further goods.

Exam Probability: **High**

29. *Answer choices:*

(see index for correct answer)

- a. Final good
- b. Consumer Good
- c. Tarpaulin
- d. Household goods

Guidance: level 1

:: ::

The _____ to the United States Constitution prevents the government from making laws which respect an establishment of religion, prohibit the free exercise of religion, or abridge the freedom of speech, the freedom of the press, the right to peaceably assemble, or the right to petition the government for redress of grievances. It was adopted on December 15, 1791, as one of the ten amendments that constitute the Bill of Rights.

Exam Probability: **Low**

30. *Answer choices:*

(see index for correct answer)

- a. First Amendment
- b. process perspective

- c. similarity-attraction theory
- d. empathy

Guidance: level 1

:: ::

In English law, a _____ or _____ absolute is an estate in land, a form of freehold ownership. It is a way that real estate and land may be owned in common law countries, and is the highest possible ownership interest that can be held in real property. Allodial title is reserved to governments under a civil law structure. The rights of the _____ owner are limited by government powers of taxation, compulsory purchase, police power, and escheat, and it could also be limited further by certain encumbrances or conditions in the deed, such as, for example, a condition that required the land to be used as a public park, with a reversion interest in the grantor if the condition fails; this is a _____ conditional.

Exam Probability: **Medium**

31. *Answer choices:*

(see index for correct answer)

- a. information systems assessment
- b. Fee simple
- c. empathy
- d. personal values

Guidance: level 1

:: Business law ::

An _____ is an agreement in which a producer agrees to sell his or her entire production to the buyer, who in turn agrees to purchase the entire output. Example: an almond grower enters into an _____ with an almond packer: thus the producer has a "home" for output of nuts, and the packer of nuts is happy to try the particular product. The converse of this situation is a requirements contract, under which a seller agrees to supply the buyer with as much of a good or service as the buyer wants, in exchange for the buyer's agreement not to buy that good or service elsewhere.

Exam Probability: **High**

32. Answer choices:

(see index for correct answer)

- a. Ladenschlussgesetz
- b. Output contract
- c. Consumer privacy
- d. Power harassment

Guidance: level 1

:: ::

An _____ is the production of goods or related services within an economy. The major source of revenue of a group or company is the indicator of its relevant _____. When a large group has multiple sources of revenue generation, it is considered to be working in different industries. Manufacturing _____ became a key sector of production and labour in European and North American countries during the Industrial Revolution, upsetting previous mercantile and feudal economies. This came through many successive rapid advances in technology, such as the production of steel and coal.

Exam Probability: **Low**

33. *Answer choices:*

(see index for correct answer)

- a. Industry
- b. interpersonal communication
- c. empathy
- d. cultural

Guidance: level 1

:: Criminal law ::

_____ is the body of law that relates to crime. It proscribes conduct perceived as threatening, harmful, or otherwise endangering to the property, health, safety, and moral welfare of people inclusive of one's self. Most _____ is established by statute, which is to say that the laws are enacted by a legislature. _____ includes the punishment and rehabilitation of people who violate such laws. _____ varies according to jurisdiction, and differs from civil law, where emphasis is more on dispute resolution and victim compensation, rather than on punishment or rehabilitation. Criminal procedure is a formalized official activity that authenticates the fact of commission of a crime and authorizes punitive or rehabilitative treatment of the offender.

Exam Probability: **Medium**

34. *Answer choices:*

(see index for correct answer)

- a. Mala prohibita
- b. mitigating factor
- c. Mala in se
- d. Criminal law

Guidance: level 1

:: Marketing ::

A _____ is an overall experience of a customer that distinguishes an organization or product from its rivals in the eyes of the customer. _____ s are used in business, marketing, and advertising. Name _____ s are sometimes distinguished from generic or store _____ s.

Exam Probability: **High**

35. *Answer choices:*

(see index for correct answer)

- a. Analyst relations
- b. Engagement marketing
- c. Marchitecture
- d. Brand

Guidance: level 1

:: Contract law ::

_____ is a legal cause of action and a type of civil wrong, in which a binding agreement or bargained-for exchange is not honored by one or more of the parties to the contract by non-performance or interference with the other party's performance. Breach occurs when a party to a contract fails to fulfill its obligation as described in the contract, or communicates an intent to fail the obligation or otherwise appears not to be able to perform its obligation under the contract. Where there is _____ , the resulting damages will have to be paid by the party breaching the contract to the aggrieved party.

Exam Probability: **High**

36. *Answer choices:*

(see index for correct answer)

- a. Requirements contract
- b. Verbal contract
- c. Breach of contract
- d. English clause

Guidance: level 1

:: ::

In law, a _____ is a coming together of parties to a dispute, to present information in a tribunal, a formal setting with the authority to adjudicate claims or disputes. One form of tribunal is a court. The tribunal, which may occur before a judge, jury, or other designated trier of fact, aims to achieve a resolution to their dispute.

Exam Probability: **High**

37. *Answer choices:*

(see index for correct answer)

- a. corporate values
- b. information systems assessment
- c. surface-level diversity
- d. Trial

Guidance: level 1

:: ::

_____ , also referred to as orthostasis, is a human position in which the body is held in an upright position and supported only by the feet.

Exam Probability: **High**

38. *Answer choices:*

(see index for correct answer)

- a. information systems assessment
- b. interpersonal communication
- c. levels of analysis
- d. Character

Guidance: level 1

:: Insurance law ::

_____ exists when an insured person derives a financial or other kind of benefit from the continuous existence, without repairment or damage, of the insured object. A person has an _____ in something when loss of or damage to that thing would cause the person to suffer a financial or other kind of loss. Normally, _____ is established by ownership, possession, or direct relationship. For example, people have _____ s in their own homes and vehicles, but not in their neighbors' homes and vehicles, and almost certainly not those of strangers.

Exam Probability: **Medium**

39. *Answer choices:*

(see index for correct answer)

- a. Insurance regulatory law
- b. Commissioner v. First Security Bank of Utah, N.A.
- c. Insurable interest
- d. Motor vehicle insurance law in India

Guidance: level 1

:: Business law ::

A _____ is a legal right granted by a debtor to a creditor over the debtor's property which enables the creditor to have recourse to the property if the debtor defaults in making payment or otherwise performing the secured obligations. One of the most common examples of a _____ is a mortgage: When person, by the action of an expressed conveyance, pledges by a promise to pay a certain sum of money, with certain conditions, on a said date or dates for a said period, that action on the page with wet ink applied on the part of the one wishing the exchange creates the original funds and negotiable Instrument. That action of pledging conveys a promise binding upon the mortgagee which creates a face value upon the Instrument of the amount of currency being asked for in exchange. It is therein in good faith offered to the Bank in exchange for local currency from the Bank to buy a house. The particular country's Bank Acts usually requires the Banks to deliver such fund bearing negotiable instruments to the Countries Main Bank such as is the case in Canada. This creates a _____ in the land the house sits on for the Bank and they file a caveat at land titles on the house as evidence of that _____. If the mortgagee fails to pay defaulting in his promise to repay the exchange, the bank then applies to the court to for-close on your property to eventually sell the house and apply the proceeds to the outstanding exchange.

Exam Probability: **High**

40. *Answer choices:*

(see index for correct answer)

- a. Partnership
- b. Recharacterisation
- c. Security interest
- d. United Kingdom commercial law

Guidance: level 1

The _____ is an independent agency of the Federal government of the United States with responsibilities for enforcing U.S. labor law in relation to collective bargaining and unfair labor practices. Under the National Labor Relations Act of 1935 it supervises elections for labor union representation and can investigate and remedy unfair labor practices. Unfair labor practices may involve union-related situations or instances of protected concerted activity. The NLRB is governed by a five-person board and a General Counsel, all of whom are appointed by the President with the consent of the Senate. Board members are appointed to five-year terms and the General Counsel is appointed to a four-year term. The General Counsel acts as a prosecutor and the Board acts as an appellate quasi-judicial body from decisions of administrative law judges.

Exam Probability: **Medium**

41. *Answer choices:*

(see index for correct answer)

- a. National Labor Relations Board
- b. Character
- c. corporate values
- d. open system

Guidance: level 1

_____ is a concept of English common law and is a necessity for simple contracts but not for special contracts. The concept has been adopted by other common law jurisdictions, including the US.

Exam Probability: **Medium**

42. *Answer choices:*

(see index for correct answer)

- a. hierarchical
- b. open system
- c. Consideration
- d. process perspective

Guidance: level 1

:: Debt ::

A _____ is a party that has a claim on the services of a second party. It is a person or institution to whom money is owed. The first party, in general, has provided some property or service to the second party under the assumption that the second party will return an equivalent property and service. The second party is frequently called a debtor or borrower. The first party is called the _____, which is the lender of property, service, or money.

Exam Probability: **Low**

43. Answer choices:

(see index for correct answer)

- a. Cessio bonorum
- b. Recourse debt
- c. Internal debt
- d. Debit commission

Guidance: level 1

:: Writs ::

In common law, a _____ is a formal _____ ten order issued by a body with administrative or judicial jurisdiction; in modern usage, this body is generally a court. Warrants, prerogative _____ s, and subpoenas are common types of _____, but many forms exist and have existed.

Exam Probability: **High**

44. Answer choices:

(see index for correct answer)

- a. Qui tam
- b. Writ
- c. Writ of assistance

Guidance: level 1

:: Business law ::

A _____ is a group of people who jointly supervise the activities of an organization, which can be either a for-profit business, nonprofit organization, or a government agency. Such a board's powers, duties, and responsibilities are determined by government regulations and the organization's own constitution and bylaws. These authorities may specify the number of members of the board, how they are to be chosen, and how often they are to meet.

Exam Probability: **Low**

45. *Answer choices:*
(see index for correct answer)

- a. Economic torts
- b. Starting a Business Index
- c. Corporation by estoppel
- d. Security interest

Guidance: level 1

:: Decision theory ::

Within economics the concept of _____ is used to model worth or value, but its usage has evolved significantly over time. The term was introduced initially as a measure of pleasure or satisfaction within the theory of utilitarianism by moral philosophers such as Jeremy Bentham and John Stuart Mill. But the term has been adapted and reapplied within neoclassical economics, which dominates modern economic theory, as a _____ function that represents a consumer's preference ordering over a choice set. As such, it is devoid of its original interpretation as a measurement of the pleasure or satisfaction obtained by the consumer from that choice.

Exam Probability: **Medium**

46. *Answer choices:*

(see index for correct answer)

- a. Utility
- b. Rete algorithm
- c. Normative model of decision-making
- d. Mental accounting

Guidance: level 1

:: Legal doctrines and principles ::

_____ is a doctrine that a party is responsible for acts of their agents. For example, in the United States, there are circumstances when an employer is liable for acts of employees performed within the course of their employment. This rule is also called the master-servant rule, recognized in both common law and civil law jurisdictions.

Exam Probability: **Low**

47. *Answer choices:*

(see index for correct answer)

- a. Duty to rescue
- b. Mutual assent
- c. Respondeat superior
- d. Eminent domain

Guidance: level 1

:: Business law ::

A _____ is a form of security interest granted over an item of property to secure the payment of a debt or performance of some other obligation. The owner of the property, who grants the _____ , is referred to as the _____ ee and the person who has the benefit of the _____ is referred to as the _____ or or _____ holder.

Exam Probability: **Low**

48. *Answer choices:*

(see index for correct answer)

- a. Power harassment
- b. Independent contractor

- c. Lien
- d. Companies law

Guidance: level 1

:: Contract law ::

A _____ is a legally-binding agreement which recognises and governs the rights and duties of the parties to the agreement. A _____ is legally enforceable because it meets the requirements and approval of the law. An agreement typically involves the exchange of goods, services, money, or promises of any of those. In the event of breach of _____ , the law awards the injured party access to legal remedies such as damages and cancellation.

Exam Probability: **Medium**

49. *Answer choices:*

(see index for correct answer)

- a. Contract
- b. Implied warranty
- c. Specific performance
- d. Terms of service

Guidance: level 1

:: ::

A lawsuit is a proceeding by a party or parties against another in the civil court of law. The archaic term "suit in law" is found in only a small number of laws still in effect today. The term "lawsuit" is used in reference to a civil action brought in a court of law in which a plaintiff, a party who claims to have incurred loss as a result of a defendant's actions, demands a legal or equitable remedy. The defendant is required to respond to the plaintiff's complaint. If the plaintiff is successful, judgment is in the plaintiff's favor, and a variety of court orders may be issued to enforce a right, award damages, or impose a temporary or permanent injunction to prevent an act or compel an act. A declaratory judgment may be issued to prevent future legal disputes.

Exam Probability: **Low**

50. *Answer choices:*

(see index for correct answer)

- a. levels of analysis
- b. empathy
- c. interpersonal communication
- d. Litigation

Guidance: level 1

:: Communication of falsehoods ::

_____, calumny, vilification, or traducement is the communication of a false statement that harms the reputation of, depending on the law of the country, an individual, business, product, group, government, religion, or nation.

Exam Probability: **Low**

51. *Answer choices:*

(see index for correct answer)

- a. Defamation
- b. Malingering
- c. Liar paradox
- d. Erratum

Guidance: level 1

:: Legal procedure ::

An _____ is generally the first occasion that the trier of fact has to hear from a lawyer in a trial, aside possibly from questioning during voir dire. The _____ is generally constructed to serve as a "road map" for the fact-finder. This is especially essential, in many jury trials, since jurors know nothing at all about the case before the trial, . Though such statements may be dramatic and vivid, they must be limited to the evidence reasonably expected to be presented during the trial. Attorneys generally conclude _____ s with a reminder that at the conclusion of evidence, the attorney will return to ask the fact-finder to find in his or her client's favor.

Exam Probability: **Medium**

52. *Answer choices:*

(see index for correct answer)

- a. Opening statement
- b. appellate
- c. Procedural law
- d. civil procedure

Guidance: level 1

:: Types of business entity ::

> A _____, the basic form of partnership under common law, is in most countries an association of persons or an unincorporated company with the following major features.

Exam Probability: **High**

53. *Answer choices:*

(see index for correct answer)

- a. Intermediary corporation
- b. Holding company
- c. General partnership
- d. Limited liability partnership

Guidance: level 1

:: Legal doctrines and principles ::

In some common law jurisdictions, _____ is a defense to a tort claim based on negligence. If it is available, the defense completely bars plaintiffs from any recovery if they contribute to their own injury through their own negligence.

Exam Probability: **Low**

54. *Answer choices:*

(see index for correct answer)

- a. Acquiescence
- b. compulsory acquisition
- c. Contributory negligence
- d. compulsory purchase

Guidance: level 1

:: Jurisdiction ::

In United States law, _____ jurisdiction is the subject-matter jurisdiction of United States federal courts to hear a civil case because the plaintiff has alleged a violation of the United States Constitution, federal law, or a treaty to which the United States is a party.

Exam Probability: **Low**

55. *Answer choices:*

(see index for correct answer)

- a. Federal question
- b. Removal jurisdiction
- c. Federal question jurisdiction
- d. Appellate jurisdiction

Guidance: level 1

:: ::

An _____ , commonly called an appeals court, court of appeals , appeal court , court of second instance or second instance court, is any court of law that is empowered to hear an appeal of a trial court or other lower tribunal. In most jurisdictions, the court system is divided into at least three levels: the trial court, which initially hears cases and reviews evidence and testimony to determine the facts of the case; at least one intermediate _____ ; and a supreme court which primarily reviews the decisions of the intermediate courts. A jurisdiction's supreme court is that jurisdiction's highest _____ . _____ s nationwide can operate under varying rules.

Exam Probability: **High**

56. *Answer choices:*

(see index for correct answer)

- a. co-culture
- b. Appellate Court
- c. similarity-attraction theory
- d. hierarchical

Guidance: level 1

:: ::

> In contract law, rescission is an equitable remedy which allows a contractual party to cancel the contract. Parties may _____ if they are the victims of a vitiating factor, such as misrepresentation, mistake, duress, or undue influence. Rescission is the unwinding of a transaction. This is done to bring the parties, as far as possible, back to the position in which they were before they entered into a contract.

Exam Probability: **High**

57. *Answer choices:*

(see index for correct answer)

- a. similarity-attraction theory
- b. personal values

- c. Rescind
- d. deep-level diversity

Guidance: level 1

:: Criminal procedure ::

> In law, a verdict is the formal finding of fact made by a jury on matters or questions submitted to the jury by a judge. In a bench trial, the judge's decision near the end of the trial is simply referred to as a finding. In England and Wales, a coroner's findings are called verdicts .

Exam Probability: **Low**

58. *Answer choices:*
(see index for correct answer)

- a. Directed verdict
- b. Exoneration

Guidance: level 1

:: ::

An _____ is a criminal accusation that a person has committed a crime. In jurisdictions that use the concept of felonies, the most serious criminal offence is a felony; jurisdictions that do not use the felonies concept often use that of an indictable offence, an offence that requires an _____.

Exam Probability: **High**

59. *Answer choices:*

(see index for correct answer)

- a. similarity-attraction theory
- b. personal values
- c. open system
- d. Indictment

Guidance: level 1

Finance

Finance is a field that is concerned with the allocation (investment) of assets and liabilities over space and time, often under conditions of risk or uncertainty. Finance can also be defined as the science of money management. Participants in the market aim to price assets based on their risk level, fundamental value, and their expected rate of return. Finance can be split into three sub-categories: public finance, corporate finance and personal finance.

In business, economics or investment, market _____ is a market's feature whereby an individual or firm can quickly purchase or sell an asset without causing a drastic change in the asset's price. _____ is about how big the trade-off is between the speed of the sale and the price it can be sold for. In a liquid market, the trade-off is mild: selling quickly will not reduce the price much. In a relatively illiquid market, selling it quickly will require cutting its price by some amount.

Exam Probability: **High**

1. *Answer choices:*

(see index for correct answer)

- a. hierarchical
- b. Sarbanes-Oxley act of 2002
- c. Liquidity
- d. deep-level diversity

Guidance: level 1

:: Inventory ::

In business and accounting/accountancy, _____ or continuous inventory describes systems of inventory where information on inventory quantity and availability is updated on a continuous basis as a function of doing business. Generally this is accomplished by connecting the inventory system with order entry and in retail the point of sale system. In this case, book inventory would be exactly the same as, or almost the same, as the real inventory.

Exam Probability: **Low**

2. *Answer choices:*

(see index for correct answer)

- a. just-in-time manufacturing
- b. Perpetual inventory
- c. Order picking
- d. Reorder point

Guidance: level 1

:: Funds ::

_____ value is the value of an entity's assets minus the value of its liabilities, often in relation to open-end or mutual funds, since shares of such funds registered with the U.S. Securities and Exchange Commission are redeemed at their _____ value. It is also a key figure with regard to hedge funds and venture capital funds when calculating the value of the underlying investments in these funds by investors. This may also be the same as the book value or the equity value of a business. _____ value may represent the value of the total equity, or it may be divided by the number of shares outstanding held by investors, thereby representing the _____ value per share.

Exam Probability: **Medium**

3. *Answer choices:*

(see index for correct answer)

- a. China-Africa Development Fund
- b. Anglo-Swedish Literary Foundation
- c. Global macro
- d. Social Enterprise Investment Fund

Guidance: level 1

:: Project management ::

Some scenarios associate "this kind of planning" with learning "life skills". _____s are necessary, or at least useful, in situations where individuals need to know what time they must be at a specific location to receive a specific service, and where people need to accomplish a set of goals within a set time period.

Exam Probability: **High**

4. *Answer choices:*
(see index for correct answer)

- a. Site survey
- b. Expected commercial value
- c. Project management triangle
- d. Scope creep

Guidance: level 1

:: Business economics ::

In finance, _____ is the risk of losses caused by interest rate changes. The prices of most financial instruments, such as stocks and bonds move inversely with interest rates, so investors are subject to capital loss when rates rise.

Exam Probability: **Medium**

5. *Answer choices:*

(see index for correct answer)

- a. Productivity model
- b. Gross operating surplus
- c. Average daily rate
- d. Units of transportation measurement

Guidance: level 1

:: Marketing ::

A _____ is the quantity of payment or compensation given by one party to another in return for one unit of goods or services.. A _____ is influenced by both production costs and demand for the product. A _____ may be determined by a monopolist or may be imposed on the firm by market conditions.

Exam Probability: **Medium**

6. *Answer choices:*

(see index for correct answer)

- a. Mobile marketing research
- b. Next-best-action marketing
- c. Multichannel marketing
- d. Lingerie party

Guidance: level 1

:: Competition (economics) ::

_____ arises whenever at least two parties strive for a goal which cannot be shared: where one's gain is the other's loss .

Exam Probability: **Medium**

7. *Answer choices:*

(see index for correct answer)

- a. Tax competition
- b. Leapfrogging
- c. Blindspots analysis
- d. Regulatory competition

Guidance: level 1

:: ::

An _____ is an asset that lacks physical substance. It is defined in opposition to physical assets such as machinery and buildings. An _____ is usually very hard to evaluate. Patents, copyrights, franchises, goodwill, trademarks, and trade names. The general interpretation also includes software and other intangible computer based assets are all examples of _____ s. _____ s generally—though not necessarily—suffer from typical market failures of non-rivalry and non-excludability.

Exam Probability: **High**

8. *Answer choices:*

(see index for correct answer)

- a. levels of analysis
- b. surface-level diversity
- c. Intangible asset
- d. imperative

Guidance: level 1

:: Financial markets ::

In economics and finance, _____ is the practice of taking advantage of a price difference between two or more markets: striking a combination of matching deals that capitalize upon the imbalance, the profit being the difference between the market prices. When used by academics, an _____ is a transaction that involves no negative cash flow at any probabilistic or temporal state and a positive cash flow in at least one state; in simple terms, it is the possibility of a risk-free profit after transaction costs. For example, an _____ opportunity is present when there is the opportunity to instantaneously buy something for a low price and sell it for a higher price.

Exam Probability: **High**

9. *Answer choices:*

(see index for correct answer)

- a. Market maker
- b. Head fake
- c. Arbitrage
- d. Consolidated Tape System

Guidance: level 1

:: ::

An _____, for United States federal income tax, is a closely held corporation that makes a valid election to be taxed under Subchapter S of Chapter 1 of the Internal Revenue Code. In general, _____s do not pay any income taxes. Instead, the corporation's income or losses are divided among and passed through to its shareholders. The shareholders must then report the income or loss on their own individual income tax returns.

Exam Probability: **Low**

10. *Answer choices:*

(see index for correct answer)

- a. hierarchical perspective
- b. Character
- c. deep-level diversity
- d. empathy

Guidance: level 1

:: Manufacturing ::

_____s are goods that have completed the manufacturing process but have not yet been sold or distributed to the end user.

Exam Probability: **Medium**

11. *Answer choices:*

(see index for correct answer)

- a. Industrial Valley
- b. Parts cleaning
- c. Finished good
- d. Air bearing

Guidance: level 1

:: Financial markets ::

A _____ is a financial market in which long-term debt or equity-backed securities are bought and sold. _____ s channel the wealth of savers to those who can put it to long-term productive use, such as companies or governments making long-term investments. Financial regulators like the Bank of England and the U.S. Securities and Exchange Commission oversee _____ s to protect investors against fraud, among other duties.

Exam Probability: **Medium**

12. *Answer choices:*

(see index for correct answer)

- a. Private equity fund
- b. Global Financial Centres Index
- c. Head fake
- d. Capital market

Guidance: level 1

:: ::

A tax is a compulsory financial charge or some other type of levy imposed upon a taxpayer by a governmental organization in order to fund various public expenditures. A failure to pay, along with evasion of or resistance to _____ , is punishable by law. Taxes consist of direct or indirect taxes and may be paid in money or as its labour equivalent.

Exam Probability: **Low**

13. *Answer choices:*

(see index for correct answer)

- a. similarity-attraction theory
- b. process perspective
- c. Character
- d. empathy

Guidance: level 1

:: Accounting terminology ::

_____ is money owed by a business to its suppliers shown as a liability on a company's balance sheet. It is distinct from notes payable liabilities, which are debts created by formal legal instrument documents.

Exam Probability: **Low**

14. *Answer choices:*

(see index for correct answer)

- a. Accounts payable
- b. Accounting equation
- c. Statement of financial position
- d. Share premium

Guidance: level 1

:: Financial markets ::

For an individual, a _____ is the minimum amount of money by which the expected return on a risky asset must exceed the known return on a risk-free asset in order to induce an individual to hold the risky asset rather than the risk-free asset. It is positive if the person is risk averse. Thus it is the minimum willingness to accept compensation for the risk.

Exam Probability: **Low**

15. *Answer choices:*

(see index for correct answer)

- a. dark pool
- b. Long/short equity
- c. Stock correlation network
- d. Risk premium

Guidance: level 1

:: Accounting terminology ::

In accounting/accountancy, _____ are journal entries usually made at the end of an accounting period to allocate income and expenditure to the period in which they actually occurred. The revenue recognition principle is the basis of making _____ that pertain to unearned and accrued revenues under accrual-basis accounting. They are sometimes called Balance Day adjustments because they are made on balance day.

Exam Probability: **Low**

16. *Answer choices:*

(see index for correct answer)

- a. Basis of accounting
- b. Adjusting entries
- c. profit and loss statement
- d. Chart of accounts

Guidance: level 1

:: Accounting source documents ::

A _____ or account statement is a summary of financial transactions which have occurred over a given period on a bank account held by a person or business with a financial institution.

Exam Probability: **High**

17. *Answer choices:*

(see index for correct answer)

- a. Bank statement
- b. Parcel audit
- c. Air waybill
- d. Superbill

Guidance: level 1

:: Accounting terminology ::

_____ of something is, in finance, the adding together of interest or different investments over a period of time. It holds specific meanings in accounting, where it can refer to accounts on a balance sheet that represent liabilities and non-cash-based assets used in _____ -based accounting. These types of accounts include, among others, accounts payable, accounts receivable, goodwill, deferred tax liability and future interest expense.

Exam Probability: **Low**

18. *Answer choices:*
(see index for correct answer)

- a. profit and loss statement
- b. Capital appreciation
- c. Accrual
- d. Adjusting entries

Guidance: level 1

:: Fixed income market ::

In finance, the _____ is a curve showing several yields or interest rates across different contract lengths for a similar debt contract. The curve shows the relation between the interest rate and the time to maturity, known as the "term", of the debt for a given borrower in a given currency. For example, the U.S. dollar interest rates paid on U.S. Treasury securities for various maturities are closely watched by many traders, and are commonly plotted on a graph such as the one on the right which is informally called "the _____". More formal mathematical descriptions of this relation are often called the term structure of interest rates.

Exam Probability: **Low**

19. *Answer choices:*

(see index for correct answer)

- a. Fixed income
- b. Basis point
- c. Yield curve
- d. Fixed-income attribution

Guidance: level 1

:: Manufacturing ::

_____ costs are all manufacturing costs that are related to the cost object but cannot be traced to that cost object in an economically feasible way.

Exam Probability: **Medium**

20. *Answer choices:*

(see index for correct answer)

- a. Motoman
- b. Flexible manufacturing
- c. Manufacturing overhead
- d. Ppc cycle

Guidance: level 1

:: Cash flow ::

In corporate finance, _____ or _____ to firm is a way of looking at a business's cash flow to see what is available for distribution among all the securities holders of a corporate entity. This may be useful to parties such as equity holders, debt holders, preferred stock holders, and convertible security holders when they want to see how much cash can be extracted from a company without causing issues to its operations.

Exam Probability: **Medium**

21. *Answer choices:*

(see index for correct answer)

- a. Invoice discounting
- b. First Chicago Method

- c. Discounted payback period
- d. Propequity

Guidance: level 1

:: ::

The _____ is a private, non-profit organization standard-setting body whose primary purpose is to establish and improve Generally Accepted Accounting Principles within the United States in the public's interest. The Securities and Exchange Commission designated the FASB as the organization responsible for setting accounting standards for public companies in the US. The FASB replaced the American Institute of Certified Public Accountants' Accounting Principles Board on July 1, 1973.

Exam Probability: **Low**

22. *Answer choices:*

(see index for correct answer)

- a. similarity-attraction theory
- b. hierarchical
- c. functional perspective
- d. Financial Accounting Standards Board

Guidance: level 1

:: Actuarial science ::

_____ services are provided by some large financial institutions, such as banks, or insurance or investment houses, whereby they guarantee payment in case of damage or financial loss and accept the financial risk for liability arising from such guarantee. An _____ arrangement may be created in a number of situations including insurance, issue of securities in a public offering, and bank lending, among others. The person or institution that agrees to sell a minimum number of securities of the company for commission is called the underwriter.

Exam Probability: **Low**

23. *Answer choices:*

(see index for correct answer)

- a. Reliability theory
- b. Ogden tables
- c. Underwriting
- d. John Graunt

Guidance: level 1

:: ::

_____ is the process of making predictions of the future based on past and present data and most commonly by analysis of trends. A commonplace example might be estimation of some variable of interest at some specified future date. Prediction is a similar, but more general term. Both might refer to formal statistical methods employing time series, cross-sectional or longitudinal data, or alternatively to less formal judgmental methods. Usage can differ between areas of application: for example, in hydrology the terms "forecast" and "_____" are sometimes reserved for estimates of values at certain specific future times, while the term "prediction" is used for more general estimates, such as the number of times floods will occur over a long period.

Exam Probability: **Low**

24. *Answer choices:*

(see index for correct answer)

- a. similarity-attraction theory
- b. hierarchical
- c. Forecasting
- d. functional perspective

Guidance: level 1

:: Marketing ::

A _____ is an overall experience of a customer that distinguishes an organization or product from its rivals in the eyes of the customer. _____ s are used in business, marketing, and advertising. Name _____ s are sometimes distinguished from generic or store _____ s.

Exam Probability: **Low**

25. *Answer choices:*

(see index for correct answer)

- a. Next-best-action marketing
- b. Channel conflict
- c. Brand
- d. Place branding

Guidance: level 1

:: Financial accounting ::

_____ is the value of all the non-financial and financial assets owned by an institutional unit or sector minus the value of all its outstanding liabilities. Since financial assets minus outstanding liabilities equal net financial assets, _____ can also be conveniently expressed as non-financial assets plus net financial assets. _____ can apply to companies, individuals, governments or economic sectors such as the sector of financial corporations or to entire countries.

Exam Probability: **Medium**

26. *Answer choices:*

(see index for correct answer)

- a. Accelerated depreciation

- b. Asset swap
- c. Book value
- d. Net worth

Guidance: level 1

:: ::

_____ is the concept of one topic being connected to another topic in a way that makes it useful to consider the second topic when considering the first. The concept of _____ is studied in many different fields, including cognitive sciences, logic, and library and information science. Most fundamentally, however, it is studied in epistemology. Different theories of knowledge have different implications for what is considered relevant and these fundamental views have implications for all other fields as well.

Exam Probability: **Medium**

27. *Answer choices:*
(see index for correct answer)

- a. corporate values
- b. information systems assessment
- c. Character
- d. hierarchical

Guidance: level 1

:: Leasing ::

A finance lease is a type of lease in which a finance company is typically the legal owner of the asset for the duration of the lease, while the lessee not only has operating control over the asset, but also has a some share of the economic risks and returns from the change in the valuation of the underlying asset.

Exam Probability: **Low**

28. *Answer choices:*
(see index for correct answer)

- a. Synthetic lease
- b. Farmout agreement

Guidance: level 1

:: ::

_____ is the process whereby a business sets the price at which it will sell its products and services, and may be part of the business's marketing plan. In setting prices, the business will take into account the price at which it could acquire the goods, the manufacturing cost, the market place, competition, market condition, brand, and quality of product.

Exam Probability: **High**

29. *Answer choices:*

(see index for correct answer)

- a. Pricing
- b. process perspective
- c. corporate values
- d. co-culture

Guidance: level 1

:: Generally Accepted Accounting Principles ::

_____ , or non-current liabilities, are liabilities that are due beyond a year or the normal operation period of the company. The normal operation period is the amount of time it takes for a company to turn inventory into cash. On a classified balance sheet, liabilities are separated between current and _____ to help users assess the company's financial standing in short-term and long-term periods. _____ give users more information about the long-term prosperity of the company, while current liabilities inform the user of debt that the company owes in the current period. On a balance sheet, accounts are listed in order of liquidity, so _____ come after current liabilities. In addition, the specific long-term liability accounts are listed on the balance sheet in order of liquidity. Therefore, an account due within eighteen months would be listed before an account due within twenty-four months. Examples of _____ are bonds payable, long-term loans, capital leases, pension liabilities, post-retirement healthcare liabilities, deferred compensation, deferred revenues, deferred income taxes, and derivative liabilities.

Exam Probability: **Low**

30. *Answer choices:*

(see index for correct answer)

- a. Net income
- b. French generally accepted accounting principles
- c. Treasury stock
- d. Construction in progress

Guidance: level 1

:: Separation of investment and commercial banking ::

A _____ is a type of bank that provides services such as accepting deposits, making business loans, and offering basic investment products that is operated as a business for profit.

Exam Probability: **Medium**

31. *Answer choices:*

(see index for correct answer)

- a. Merchant bank
- b. Volcker Rule
- c. Bancassurance
- d. Commercial bank

Guidance: level 1

:: Financial ratios ::

The _____ is a financial ratio indicating the relative proportion of shareholders' equity and debt used to finance a company's assets. Closely related to leveraging, the ratio is also known as risk, gearing or leverage. The two components are often taken from the firm's balance sheet or statement of financial position , but the ratio may also be calculated using market values for both, if the company's debt and equity are publicly traded, or using a combination of book value for debt and market value for equity financially.

Exam Probability: **Low**

32. *Answer choices:*

(see index for correct answer)

- a. Return on assets
- b. Implied multiple
- c. Debt-to-equity ratio
- d. Information ratio

Guidance: level 1

:: Generally Accepted Accounting Principles ::

In accounting, _____, gross margin, sales profit, or credit sales is the difference between revenue and the cost of making a product or providing a service, before deducting overheads, payroll, taxation, and interest payments. This is different from operating profit. Gross margin is the term normally used in the U.S., while _____ is the more common usage in the UK and Australia.

Exam Probability: **Medium**

33. *Answer choices:*

(see index for correct answer)

- a. deferred revenue
- b. Gross profit
- c. Financial position of the United States
- d. Engagement letter

Guidance: level 1

:: Bonds (finance) ::

An _____ is a legal contract that reflects or covers a debt or purchase obligation. It specifically refers to two types of practices: in historical usage, an _____ d servant status, and in modern usage, it is an instrument used for commercial debt or real estate transaction.

Exam Probability: **High**

34. *Answer choices:*

(see index for correct answer)

- a. Clean price
- b. Kimchi bond
- c. Current yield
- d. Indenture

Guidance: level 1

:: Portfolio theories ::

In finance, the _____ is a model used to determine a theoretically appropriate required rate of return of an asset, to make decisions about adding assets to a well-diversified portfolio.

Exam Probability: **High**

35. *Answer choices:*

(see index for correct answer)

- a. Tail risk parity
- b. Efficient frontier
- c. Intertemporal portfolio choice
- d. Behavioral portfolio theory

Guidance: level 1

:: Capital gains taxes ::

A _____ refers to profit that results from a sale of a capital asset, such as stock, bond or real estate, where the sale price exceeds the purchase price. The gain is the difference between a higher selling price and a lower purchase price. Conversely, a capital loss arises if the proceeds from the sale of a capital asset are less than the purchase price.

Exam Probability: **Low**

36. *Answer choices:*

(see index for correct answer)

- a. Capital Cost Allowance
- b. Capital gain
- c. Capital cost tax factor

Guidance: level 1

:: Generally Accepted Accounting Principles ::

_____ , also referred to as the bottom line, net income, or net earnings is a measure of the profitability of a venture after accounting for all costs and taxes. It is the actual profit, and includes the operating expenses that are excluded from gross profit.

Exam Probability: **Medium**

37. *Answer choices:*

(see index for correct answer)

- a. Income statement
- b. Expense
- c. Deprival value
- d. Profit

Guidance: level 1

:: Scheduling (computing) ::

Ageing or _____ is the process of becoming older. The term refers especially to human beings, many animals, and fungi, whereas for example bacteria, perennial plants and some simple animals are potentially biologically immortal. In the broader sense, ageing can refer to single cells within an organism which have ceased dividing or to the population of a species.

Exam Probability: **Medium**

38. *Answer choices:*

(see index for correct answer)

- a. Aging
- b. Adaptive partition scheduler

- c. Affinity mask
- d. Kernel preemption

Guidance: level 1

:: Financial accounting ::

In accounting, _____ is the value of an asset according to its balance sheet account balance. For assets, the value is based on the original cost of the asset less any depreciation, amortization or impairment costs made against the asset. Traditionally, a company's _____ is its total assets minus intangible assets and liabilities. However, in practice, depending on the source of the calculation, _____ may variably include goodwill, intangible assets, or both. The value inherent in its workforce, part of the intellectual capital of a company, is always ignored. When intangible assets and goodwill are explicitly excluded, the metric is often specified to be "tangible _____".

Exam Probability: **High**

39. *Answer choices:*
(see index for correct answer)

- a. Book value
- b. Convenience translation
- c. Asset recovery
- d. Commuted cash value

Guidance: level 1

_____ is a means of protection from financial loss. It is a form of risk management, primarily used to hedge against the risk of a contingent or uncertain loss

Exam Probability: **High**

40. *Answer choices:*

(see index for correct answer)

- a. hierarchical
- b. Insurance
- c. deep-level diversity
- d. Sarbanes-Oxley act of 2002

Guidance: level 1

_____ or accountancy is the measurement, processing, and communication of financial information about economic entities such as businesses and corporations. The modern field was established by the Italian mathematician Luca Pacioli in 1494. _____, which has been called the "language of business", measures the results of an organization's economic activities and conveys this information to a variety of users, including investors, creditors, management, and regulators. Practitioners of _____ are known as accountants. The terms "_____" and "financial reporting" are often used as synonyms.

Exam Probability: **High**

41. *Answer choices:*

(see index for correct answer)

- a. functional perspective
- b. open system
- c. interpersonal communication
- d. Accounting

Guidance: level 1

A _____ is a fund into which a sum of money is added during an employee's employment years, and from which payments are drawn to support the person's retirement from work in the form of periodic payments. A _____ may be a "defined benefit plan" where a fixed sum is paid regularly to a person, or a "defined contribution plan" under which a fixed sum is invested and then becomes available at retirement age. _____ s should not be confused with severance pay; the former is usually paid in regular installments for life after retirement, while the latter is typically paid as a fixed amount after involuntary termination of employment prior to retirement.

Exam Probability: **Medium**

42. *Answer choices:*

(see index for correct answer)

- a. Pension
- b. hierarchical
- c. corporate values
- d. co-culture

Guidance: level 1

:: ::

_____ officially refers to an administrative area of the Principality of Monaco, specifically the ward of _____ /Spélugues, where the _____ Casino is located. Informally the name also refers to a larger district, the _____ Quarter, which besides _____ /Spélugues also includes the wards of La Rousse/Saint Roman, Larvotto/Bas Moulins, and Saint Michel. The permanent population of the ward of _____ is about 3,500, while that of the quarter is about 15,000. Monaco has four traditional quarters. From west to east they are: Fontvieille, Monaco-Ville, La Condamine, and _____ .

Exam Probability: **High**

43. *Answer choices:*

(see index for correct answer)

- a. cultural
- b. functional perspective
- c. Sarbanes-Oxley act of 2002
- d. Character

Guidance: level 1

:: ::

An _____ is the production of goods or related services within an economy. The major source of revenue of a group or company is the indicator of its relevant _____. When a large group has multiple sources of revenue generation, it is considered to be working in different industries. Manufacturing _____ became a key sector of production and labour in European and North American countries during the Industrial Revolution, upsetting previous mercantile and feudal economies. This came through many successive rapid advances in technology, such as the production of steel and coal.

Exam Probability: **High**

44. *Answer choices:*

(see index for correct answer)

- a. process perspective
- b. information systems assessment
- c. hierarchical
- d. similarity-attraction theory

Guidance: level 1

:: ::

_____ is a political and social philosophy promoting traditional social institutions in the context of culture and civilization. The central tenets of _____ include tradition, human imperfection, organic society, hierarchy, authority, and property rights. Conservatives seek to preserve a range of institutions such as religion, parliamentary government, and property rights, with the aim of emphasizing social stability and continuity. The more traditional elements—reactionaries—oppose modernism and seek a return to "the way things were".

Exam Probability: **Low**

45. *Answer choices:*

(see index for correct answer)

- a. empathy
- b. levels of analysis
- c. corporate values
- d. co-culture

Guidance: level 1

:: Bonds (finance) ::

A _____ is a type of bond that allows the issuer of the bond to retain the privilege of redeeming the bond at some point before the bond reaches its date of maturity. In other words, on the call date, the issuer has the right, but not the obligation, to buy back the bonds from the bond holders at a defined call price. Technically speaking, the bonds are not really bought and held by the issuer but are instead cancelled immediately.

Exam Probability: **High**

46. *Answer choices:*

(see index for correct answer)

- a. Bullet strategy
- b. Original issue discount
- c. Convertible bond
- d. Callable bond

Guidance: level 1

:: Generally Accepted Accounting Principles ::

A _____ , in accrual accounting, is any account where the asset or liability is not realized until a future date , e.g. annuities, charges, taxes, income, etc. The deferred item may be carried, dependent on type of _____ , as either an asset or liability. See also accrual.

Exam Probability: **Low**

47. *Answer choices:*

(see index for correct answer)

- a. Revenue recognition
- b. Treasury stock
- c. Contributed capital

- d. Deferral

Guidance: level 1

:: Stock market ::

_____ is freedom from, or resilience against, potential harm caused by others. Beneficiaries of _____ may be of persons and social groups, objects and institutions, ecosystems or any other entity or phenomenon vulnerable to unwanted change by its environment.

Exam Probability: **High**

48. *Answer choices:*

(see index for correct answer)

- a. Follow-on offering
- b. Market moving information
- c. Security
- d. All or none

Guidance: level 1

:: Accounting systems ::

In bookkeeping, a _____ statement is a process that explains the difference on a specified date between the bank balance shown in an organization's bank statement, as supplied by the bank and the corresponding amount shown in the organization's own accounting records.

Exam Probability: **High**

49. *Answer choices:*

(see index for correct answer)

- a. Bank reconciliation
- b. Momentum accounting and triple-entry bookkeeping
- c. Single-entry bookkeeping
- d. Off-balance sheet

Guidance: level 1

:: Loans ::

In finance, a _____ is the lending of money by one or more individuals, organizations, or other entities to other individuals, organizations etc. The recipient incurs a debt, and is usually liable to pay interest on that debt until it is repaid, and also to repay the principal amount borrowed.

Exam Probability: **High**

50. *Answer choices:*

(see index for correct answer)

- a. Loan servicing
- b. Loan covenant
- c. Asset-based loan
- d. SGE Loans

Guidance: level 1

:: Real estate ::

Amortisation is paying off an amount owed over time by making planned, incremental payments of principal and interest. To amortise a loan means "to kill it off". In accounting, amortisation refers to charging or writing off an intangible asset's cost as an operational expense over its estimated useful life to reduce a company's taxable income.

Exam Probability: **Low**

51. *Answer choices:*

(see index for correct answer)

- a. Home inspection
- b. Amortization
- c. Rent control
- d. AMP Technologies

Guidance: level 1

:: Corporate finance ::

_____ in corporate finance is the way a corporation finances its assets through some combination of equity, debt, or hybrid securities.

Exam Probability: **High**

52. *Answer choices:*
(see index for correct answer)

- a. Capital structure
- b. Management buy-in
- c. Accord and satisfaction
- d. Managerial finance

Guidance: level 1

:: ::

A _____, in the word's original meaning, is a sheet of paper on which one performs work. They come in many forms, most commonly associated with children's school work assignments, tax forms, and accounting or other business environments. Software is increasingly taking over the paper-based _____ .

Exam Probability: **Medium**

53. *Answer choices:*

(see index for correct answer)

- a. process perspective
- b. Worksheet
- c. empathy
- d. functional perspective

Guidance: level 1

:: ::

A _____ is any person who contracts to acquire an asset in return for some form of consideration.

Exam Probability: **Medium**

54. *Answer choices:*

(see index for correct answer)

- a. functional perspective
- b. information systems assessment
- c. empathy
- d. Sarbanes-Oxley act of 2002

Guidance: level 1

:: Commerce ::

A _____ , is a document acknowledging that a person has received money or property in payment following a sale or other transfer of goods or provision of a service. All _____ s must have the date of purchase on them. If the recipient of the payment is legally required to collect sales tax or VAT from the customer, the amount would be added to the _____ and the collection would be deemed to have been on behalf of the relevant tax authority. In many countries, a retailer is required to include the sales tax or VAT in the displayed price of goods sold, from which the tax amount would be calculated at point of sale and remitted to the tax authorities in due course. Similarly, amounts may be deducted from amounts payable, as in the case of wage withholding taxes. On the other hand, tips or other gratuities given by a customer, for example in a restaurant, would not form part of the payment amount or appear on the _____ .

Exam Probability: **Low**

55. *Answer choices:*
(see index for correct answer)

- a. Receipt
- b. Trade in services statistics
- c. Global Commerce Initiative
- d. Bill of sale

Guidance: level 1

:: Financial ratios ::

The _____ or dividend-price ratio of a share is the dividend per share, divided by the price per share. It is also a company's total annual dividend payments divided by its market capitalization, assuming the number of shares is constant. It is often expressed as a percentage.

Exam Probability: **Medium**

56. *Answer choices:*

(see index for correct answer)

- a. Days sales outstanding
- b. Debtor collection period
- c. Dividend yield
- d. Capital employed

Guidance: level 1

:: Mathematical finance ::

_____ is the value of an asset at a specific date. It measures the nominal future sum of money that a given sum of money is "worth" at a specified time in the future assuming a certain interest rate, or more generally, rate of return; it is the present value multiplied by the accumulation function. The value does not include corrections for inflation or other factors that affect the true value of money in the future. This is used in time value of money calculations.

Exam Probability: **Medium**

57. *Answer choices:*

(see index for correct answer)

- a. Index arbitrage
- b. Weighted average cost of capital
- c. Stochastic discount factor
- d. ExMark

Guidance: level 1

:: Mutualism (movement) ::

A _____ is a professionally managed investment fund that pools money from many investors to purchase securities. These investors may be retail or institutional in nature.

Exam Probability: **Medium**

58. *Answer choices:*

(see index for correct answer)

- a. Co-buying
- b. ICA Group
- c. Mutual fund
- d. Communal work

Guidance: level 1

:: Income taxes ::

An _____ is a tax imposed on individuals or entities that varies with respective income or profits. _____ generally is computed as the product of a tax rate times taxable income. Taxation rates may vary by type or characteristics of the taxpayer.

Exam Probability: **High**

59. *Answer choices:*

(see index for correct answer)

- a. Income and Corporation Taxes Act 1970
- b. Income tax
- c. Shome Panel
- d. Income tax in Singapore

Guidance: level 1

Human resource management

Human resource (HR) management is the strategic approach to the effective management of organization workers so that they help the business gain a competitive advantage. It is designed to maximize employee performance in service of an employer's strategic objectives. HR is primarily concerned with the management of people within organizations, focusing on policies and on systems. HR departments are responsible for overseeing employee-benefits design, employee recruitment, training and development, performance appraisal, and rewarding (e.g., managing pay and benefit systems). HR also concerns itself with organizational change and industrial relations, that is, the balancing of organizational practices with requirements arising from collective bargaining and from governmental laws.

:: Asset ::

In financial accounting, an _____ is any resource owned by the business. Anything tangible or intangible that can be owned or controlled to produce value and that is held by a company to produce positive economic value is an _____ . Simply stated, _____ s represent value of ownership that can be converted into cash . The balance sheet of a firm records the monetary value of the _____ s owned by that firm. It covers money and other valuables belonging to an individual or to a business.

Exam Probability: **Medium**

1. *Answer choices:*

(see index for correct answer)

- a. Asset
- b. Current asset

Guidance: level 1

:: ::

A trade union is an association of workers forming a legal unit or legal personhood, usually called a "bargaining unit", which acts as bargaining agent and legal representative for a unit of employees in all matters of law or right arising from or in the administration of a collective agreement. Labour unions typically fund the formal organisation, head office, and legal team functions of the labour union through regular fees or union dues. The delegate staff of the labour union representation in the workforce are made up of workplace volunteers who are appointed by members in democratic elections.

Exam Probability: **High**

2. *Answer choices:*

(see index for correct answer)

- a. co-culture
- b. Labor union
- c. functional perspective
- d. hierarchical

Guidance: level 1

:: Occupational safety and health ::

Note: Parts of this article are written from the perspective of aircraft safety analysis techniques and definitions; these may not represent current best practice and the article needs to be updated to represent a more generic description of _____ and discussion of more modern standards and techniques.

Exam Probability: **High**

3. *Answer choices:*

(see index for correct answer)

- a. Global road safety for workers
- b. Animal lead poisoning

- c. Lead safe work practices
- d. Hazard analysis

Guidance: level 1

:: Income ::

In business and accounting, net income is an entity's income minus cost of goods sold, expenses and taxes for an accounting period. It is computed as the residual of all revenues and gains over all expenses and losses for the period, and has also been defined as the net increase in shareholders' equity that results from a company's operations. In the context of the presentation of financial statements, the IFRS Foundation defines net income as synonymous with profit and loss. The difference between revenue and the cost of making a product or providing a service, before deducting overheads, payroll, taxation, and interest payments. This is different from operating income .

Exam Probability: **High**

4. *Answer choices:*

(see index for correct answer)

- a. Gratuity
- b. Bottom line
- c. Return on investment
- d. Per capita income

Guidance: level 1

:: Cognitive biases ::

The _____ is a type of immediate judgement discrepancy, or cognitive bias, where a person making an initial assessment of another person, place, or thing will assume ambiguous information based upon concrete information. A simplified example of the _____ is when an individual noticing that the person in the photograph is attractive, well groomed, and properly attired, assumes, using a mental heuristic, that the person in the photograph is a good person based upon the rules of that individual's social concept. This constant error in judgment is reflective of the individual's preferences, prejudices, ideology, aspirations, and social perception. The _____ is an evaluation by an individual and can affect the perception of a decision, action, idea, business, person, group, entity, or other whenever concrete data is generalized or influences ambiguous information.

Exam Probability: **High**

5. *Answer choices:*
(see index for correct answer)

- a. Halo effect
- b. Self-defeating prophecy
- c. Wishful thinking
- d. Restraint bias

Guidance: level 1

:: Industrial engineering ::

_____ is the formal process that sits alongside Requirements analysis and focuses on the human elements of the requirements.

Exam Probability: **Low**

6. *Answer choices:*

(see index for correct answer)

- a. Response surface methodology
- b. Material flow
- c. Standard data system
- d. Needs analysis

Guidance: level 1

:: Recruitment ::

_____ is a tool companies and organizations use as a way to communicate the good and the bad characteristics of the job during the hiring process of new employees, or as a tool to reestablish job specificity for existing employees. _____ s should provide the individuals with a well-rounded description that details what obligations the individual can expect to perform while working for that specific company. Descriptions may include, but are not limited to, work environment, expectations, and Company policies.

Exam Probability: **Medium**

7. Answer choices:

(see index for correct answer)

- a. Realistic job preview
- b. S.I.R. Method of Recruiting
- c. Haigui
- d. INGRADA

Guidance: level 1

:: ::

An _____ is a period of work experience offered by an organization for a limited period of time. Once confined to medical graduates, the term is now used for a wide range of placements in businesses, non-profit organizations and government agencies. They are typically undertaken by students and graduates looking to gain relevant skills and experience in a particular field. Employers benefit from these placements because they often recruit employees from their best interns, who have known capabilities, thus saving time and money in the long run. _____ s are usually arranged by third-party organizations which recruit interns on behalf of industry groups. Rules vary from country to country about when interns should be regarded as employees. The system can be open to exploitation by unscrupulous employers.

Exam Probability: **Low**

8. Answer choices:

(see index for correct answer)

- a. corporate values
- b. hierarchical perspective
- c. Internship
- d. co-culture

Guidance: level 1

:: ::

A _____ contract is a form of employment that carries fewer hours per week than a full-time job. They work in shifts. The shifts are often rotational. Workers are considered to be _____ if they commonly work fewer than 30 hours per week. According to the International Labour Organization, the number of _____ workers has increased from one-fourth to a half in the past 20 years in most developed countries, excluding the United States. There are many reasons for working _____, including the desire to do so, having one's hours cut back by an employer and being unable to find a full-time job. The International Labour Organisation Convention 175 requires that _____ workers be treated no less favourably than full-time workers.

Exam Probability: **High**

9. *Answer choices:*

(see index for correct answer)

- a. empathy
- b. Part-time
- c. personal values

- d. surface-level diversity

Guidance: level 1

:: ::

Educational technology is "the study and ethical practice of facilitating learning and improving performance by creating, using, and managing appropriate technological processes and resources".

Exam Probability: **Medium**

10. *Answer choices:*

(see index for correct answer)

- a. cultural
- b. levels of analysis
- c. surface-level diversity
- d. E-learning

Guidance: level 1

:: Employment of foreign-born ::

_____ refers to the international labor pool of workers, including those employed by multinational companies and connected through a global system of networking and production, immigrant workers, transient migrant workers, telecommuting workers, those in export-oriented employment, contingent work or other precarious employment. As of 2012, the global labor pool consisted of approximately 3 billion workers, around 200 million unemployed.

Exam Probability: **Medium**

11. *Answer choices:*

(see index for correct answer)

- a. Human capital flight
- b. H-2B visa
- c. L-1 visa
- d. Global workforce

Guidance: level 1

:: Recruitment ::

_____ , also known as Recruitment communications and Recruitment agency, includes all communications used by an organization to attract talent to work within it. Recruitment advertisements may be the first impression of a company for many job seekers. In turn, the strength of employer branding in job postings can directly impact interest in job openings.

Exam Probability: **Medium**

12. Answer choices:

(see index for correct answer)

- a. Recession-proof job
- b. Purple squirrel
- c. Employment discrimination against persons with criminal records
- d. Recruitment advertising

Guidance: level 1

:: Labour relations ::

> _____ is a form of protest in which people congregate outside a place of work or location where an event is taking place. Often, this is done in an attempt to dissuade others from going in, but it can also be done to draw public attention to a cause. Picketers normally endeavor to be non-violent. It can have a number of aims, but is generally to put pressure on the party targeted to meet particular demands or cease operations. This pressure is achieved by harming the business through loss of customers and negative publicity, or by discouraging or preventing workers or customers from entering the site and thereby preventing the business from operating normally.

Exam Probability: **High**

13. Answer choices:

(see index for correct answer)

- a. Picketing
- b. Jesse Simons

- c. Review Body
- d. Negotiated cartelism

Guidance: level 1

:: ::

_____ is the amount of time someone works beyond normal working hours. The term is also used for the pay received for this time. Normal hours may be determined in several ways.

Exam Probability: **High**

14. *Answer choices:*

(see index for correct answer)

- a. deep-level diversity
- b. Overtime
- c. corporate values
- d. Character

Guidance: level 1

:: Employment compensation ::

_____s and benefits in kind include various types of non-wage compensation provided to employees in addition to their normal wages or salaries. Instances where an employee exchanges wages for some other form of benefit is generally referred to as a "salary packaging" or "salary exchange" arrangement. In most countries, most kinds of _____ s are taxable to at least some degree. Examples of these benefits include: housing furnished or not, with or without free utilities; group insurance ; disability income protection; retirement benefits; daycare; tuition reimbursement; sick leave; vacation ; social security; profit sharing; employer student loan contributions; conveyancing; domestic help ; and other specialized benefits.

Exam Probability: **Low**

15. *Answer choices:*

(see index for correct answer)

- a. Wages for housework
- b. Spiff
- c. Employee benefit
- d. Broodfonds

Guidance: level 1

:: Management ::

A _____ is a method or technique that has been generally accepted as superior to any alternatives because it produces results that are superior to those achieved by other means or because it has become a standard way of doing things, e.g., a standard way of complying with legal or ethical requirements.

Exam Probability: **High**

16. *Answer choices:*

(see index for correct answer)

- a. Virtual customer environment
- b. Strategic management
- c. Enterprise smart grid
- d. Best practice

Guidance: level 1

:: Financial accounting ::

_____ is the intangible value of a business, covering its people, the value relating to its relationships, and everything that is left when the employees go home, of which intellectual property is but one component. It is the sum of everything everybody in a company knows that gives it a competitive edge. The term is used in academia in an attempt to account for the value of intangible assets not listed explicitly on a company's balance sheets. On a national level _____ refers to national intangible capital, NIC. A second meaning that is used in academia and was adopted in large corporations is focused on the recycling of knowledge via knowledge management and _____ management. Creating, shaping and updating the stock of _____ requires the formulation of a strategic vision, which blends together all three dimensions of _____ within the organisational context through exploration, exploitation, measurement, and disclosure. _____ is used in the context of assessing the wealth of organizations. A metric for the value of _____ is the amount by which the enterprise value of a firm exceeds the value of its tangible assets. Directly visible on corporate books is capital embodied in its physical assets and financial capital; however all three make up the value of an enterprise. Measuring the real value and the total performance of _____'s components is a critical part of running a company in the knowledge economy and Information Age. Understanding the _____ in an enterprise allows leveraging of its intellectual assets. For a corporation, the result will optimize its stock price.

Exam Probability: **Medium**

17. *Answer choices:*

(see index for correct answer)

- a. Finance charge
- b. Accelerated depreciation
- c. Intellectual capital
- d. Asset swap

Guidance: level 1

:: Employment compensation ::

Employee stock ownership, or employee share ownership, is an ownership interest in a company held by the company's workforce. The ownership interest may be facilitated by the company as part of employees' remuneration or incentive compensation for work performed, or the company itself may be employee owned.

Exam Probability: **High**

18. *Answer choices:*

(see index for correct answer)

- a. Real wage
- b. Employee stock ownership plan
- c. Workers Compensation Act 1987
- d. Fringe benefits tax

Guidance: level 1

:: ::

In organizational behavior and industrial/organizational psychology, proactivity or _____ behavior by individuals refers to anticipatory, change-oriented and self-initiated behavior in situations. _____ behavior involves acting in advance of a future situation, rather than just reacting. It means taking control and making things happen rather than just adjusting to a situation or waiting for something to happen. _____ employees generally do not need to be asked to act, nor do they require detailed instructions.

Exam Probability: **Medium**

19. *Answer choices:*

(see index for correct answer)

- a. interpersonal communication
- b. process perspective
- c. levels of analysis
- d. Proactive

Guidance: level 1

:: Organizational behavior ::

_____ is the state or fact of exclusive rights and control over property, which may be an object, land/real estate or intellectual property. _____ involves multiple rights, collectively referred to as title, which may be separated and held by different parties.

Exam Probability: **Medium**

20. *Answer choices:*

(see index for correct answer)

- a. Achievement Motivation Inventory
- b. Counterproductive norms
- c. Affective events theory
- d. Ownership

Guidance: level 1

_____ is an important topic of Human Resource Management. It helps develop the career of the individual and the prosperous growth of the organization. On the job training is a form of training provided at the workplace. During the training, employees are familiarized with the working environment they will become part of. Employees also get a hands-on experience using machinery, equipment, tools, materials, etc. Part of is to face the challenges that occur during the performance of the job. An experienced employee or a manager are executing the role of the mentor who through written, or verbal instructions and demonstrations are passing on his/her knowledge and company-specific skills to the new employee. Executing the training on at the job location, rather than the classroom, creates a stress-free environment for the employees. _____ is the most popular method of training not only in the United States but in most of the developed countries, such as the United Kingdom, China, Russia, etc. Its effectiveness is based on the use of existing workplace tools, machines, documents and equipment, and the knowledge of specialists who are working in this field. _____ is easy to arrange and manage and it simplifies the process of adapting to the new workplace. OJT is highly used for practical tasks. It is inexpensive, and it doesn't require special equipment that is normally used for a specific job. Upon satisfaction of completion of the training, the employer is expected to retain participants as regular employees.

Exam Probability: **Low**

21. *Answer choices:*

(see index for correct answer)

- a. surface-level diversity
- b. On-the-job training
- c. open system
- d. Character

Guidance: level 1

:: Employment compensation ::

Compensation and benefits is a sub-discipline of human resources, focused on employee compensation and benefits policy-making. While compensation and benefits are tangible, there are intangible rewards such as recognition, work-life and development. Combined, these are referred to as _____ s . The term "compensation and benefits" refers to the discipline as well as the rewards themselves.

Exam Probability: **Low**

22. *Answer choices:*

(see index for correct answer)

- a. Prevailing wage
- b. Corporate child care
- c. Explanation of benefits
- d. Reservation wage

Guidance: level 1

:: United Kingdom labour law ::

The _____ was a series of programs, public work projects, financial reforms, and regulations enacted by President Franklin D. Roosevelt in the United States between 1933 and 1936. It responded to needs for relief, reform, and recovery from the Great Depression. Major federal programs included the Civilian Conservation Corps, the Civil Works Administration, the Farm Security Administration, the National Industrial Recovery Act of 1933 and the Social Security Administration. They provided support for farmers, the unemployed, youth and the elderly. The _____ included new constraints and safeguards on the banking industry and efforts to re-inflate the economy after prices had fallen sharply. _____ programs included both laws passed by Congress as well as presidential executive orders during the first term of the presidency of Franklin D. Roosevelt.

Exam Probability: **Low**

23. *Answer choices:*

(see index for correct answer)

- a. New Deal
- b. Criminal Law Amendment Act 1871
- c. Contracts of Employment Act 1963
- d. United Kingdom agency worker law

Guidance: level 1

:: Management ::

_____ or executive pay is composed of the financial compensation and other non-financial awards received by an executive from their firm for their service to the organization. It is typically a mixture of salary, bonuses, shares of or call options on the company stock, benefits, and perquisites, ideally configured to take into account government regulations, tax law, the desires of the organization and the executive, and rewards for performance.

Exam Probability: **High**

24. *Answer choices:*

(see index for correct answer)

- a. Millennium software
- b. Executive compensation
- c. Middle management
- d. Business-oriented architecture

Guidance: level 1

:: Recruitment ::

A _____, also referred commonly as a career fair or career expo, is an event in which employers, recruiters, and schools give information to potential employees. Job seekers attend these while trying to make a good impression to potential coworkers by speaking face-to-face with one another, filling out résumés, and asking questions in attempt to get a good feel on the work needed. Likewise, online _____ s are held, giving job seekers another way to get in contact with probable employers using the internet.

Exam Probability: **Medium**

25. *Answer choices:*

(see index for correct answer)

- a. Employee referral
- b. Job fair
- c. Association of Graduate Recruiters
- d. Online job fair

Guidance: level 1

:: ::

In educational development, _____ provides a person, often a student, focus for selecting a career or subject to undertake in the future. Often educational institutions provide career counsellors to assist students with their educational development.

Exam Probability: **Medium**

26. *Answer choices:*

(see index for correct answer)

- a. empathy
- b. hierarchical
- c. Character

- d. process perspective

Guidance: level 1

:: Majority–minority relations ::

_____ , also known as reservation in India and Nepal, positive discrimination / action in the United Kingdom, and employment equity in Canada and South Africa, is the policy of promoting the education and employment of members of groups that are known to have previously suffered from discrimination. Historically and internationally, support for _____ has sought to achieve goals such as bridging inequalities in employment and pay, increasing access to education, promoting diversity, and redressing apparent past wrongs, harms, or hindrances.

Exam Probability: **Low**

27. *Answer choices:*
(see index for correct answer)

- a. cultural dissonance
- b. Affirmative action
- c. cultural Relativism

Guidance: level 1

:: Production and manufacturing ::

_____ is a theory of management that analyzes and synthesizes workflows. Its main objective is improving economic efficiency, especially labor productivity. It was one of the earliest attempts to apply science to the engineering of processes and to management. _____ is sometimes known as Taylorism after its founder, Frederick Winslow Taylor.

Exam Probability: **High**

28. *Answer choices:*

(see index for correct answer)

- a. Highly accelerated life test
- b. Scientific management
- c. Value engineering
- d. PA512

Guidance: level 1

:: Employment compensation ::

The _____ has been successfully used by a variety of public and private companies for many decades. These plans combine leadership, total workforce education, and widespread employee participation with a reward system linked to organization performance. The _____ is a gainsharing program in which employees share in pre-established cost savings, based upon employee effort. Formal employee participation is necessary with the _____, as well as periodic progress reporting and an incentive formula.

Exam Probability: **High**

29. *Answer choices:*

(see index for correct answer)

- a. Medical Care and Sickness Benefits Convention, 1969
- b. Dearness allowance
- c. Federal Wage System
- d. Scanlon plan

Guidance: level 1

:: United States employment discrimination case law ::

_____, 524 U.S. 775, is a US labor law case of the United States Supreme Court in which the Court identified the circumstances under which an employer may be held liable under Title VII of the Civil Rights Act of 1964 for the acts of a supervisory employee whose sexual harassment of subordinates has created a hostile work environment amounting to employment discrimination. The court held that "an employer is vicariously liable for actionable discrimination caused by a supervisor, but subject to an affirmative defense looking to the reasonableness of the employer's conduct as well as that of a plaintiff victim."

Exam Probability: **Low**

30. *Answer choices:*

(see index for correct answer)

- a. New York City Transit Authority v. Beazer
- b. Shyamala Rajender v. University of Minnesota
- c. Ricci v. DeStefano
- d. Faragher v. City of Boca Raton

Guidance: level 1

:: Employment compensation ::

> _____ refers to various incentive plans introduced by businesses that provide direct or indirect payments to employees that depend on company's profitability in addition to employees' regular salary and bonuses. In publicly traded companies these plans typically amount to allocation of shares to employees. One of the earliest pioneers of _____ was Englishman Theodore Cooke Taylor, who is known to have introduced the practice in his woollen mills during the late 1800s .

Exam Probability: **Medium**

31. *Answer choices:*

(see index for correct answer)

- a. Living wage
- b. Agency Workers Regulations 2010
- c. Holidays with Pay Convention, 1936
- d. Compa-ratio

Guidance: level 1

:: Television terminology ::

Distance education or long-_____ is the education of students who may not always be physically present at a school. Traditionally, this usually involved correspondence courses wherein the student corresponded with the school via post. Today it involves online education. Courses that are conducted are either hybrid, blended or 100% _____ . Massive open online courses , offering large-scale interactive participation and open access through the World Wide Web or other network technologies, are recent developments in distance education. A number of other terms are used roughly synonymously with distance education.

Exam Probability: **Medium**

32. *Answer choices:*

(see index for correct answer)

- a. Distance learning
- b. multiplexing
- c. Satellite television
- d. not-for-profit

Guidance: level 1

:: Trade unions ::

A _____ , in North America, or union branch , in the United Kingdom and other countries, is a local branch of a usually national trade union. The terms used for sub-branches of _____ s vary from country to country and include "shop committee", "shop floor committee", "board of control", "chapel", and others.

Exam Probability: **Medium**

33. *Answer choices:*

(see index for correct answer)

- a. Local union
- b. Bump
- c. Union democracy
- d. Global Labour University

Guidance: level 1

:: Business models ::

A _____ is a diagram that is used to document the primary strategic goals being pursued by an organization or management team. It is an element of the documentation associated with the Balanced Scorecard, and in particular is characteristic of the second generation of Balanced Scorecard designs that first appeared during the mid-1990s. The first diagrams of this type appeared in the early 1990s, and the idea of using this type of diagram to help document Balanced Scorecard was discussed in a paper by Drs. Robert S. Kaplan and David P. Norton in 1996.

Exam Probability: **Medium**

34. *Answer choices:*

(see index for correct answer)

- a. Strategy map
- b. Small business
- c. Home business
- d. Subsidiary

Guidance: level 1

:: Job interview ::

An _____ is a survey conducted with an individual who is separating from an organization or relationship. Most commonly, this occurs between an employee and an organization, a student and an educational institution, or a member and an association. An organization can use the information gained from an _____ to assess what should be improved, changed, or remain intact. More so, an organization can use the results from _____ s to reduce employee, student, or member turnover and increase productivity and engagement, thus reducing the high costs associated with turnover. Some examples of the value of conducting _____ s include shortening the recruiting and hiring process, reducing absenteeism, improving innovation, sustaining performance, and reducing possible litigation if issues mentioned in the _____ are addressed. It is important for each organization to customize its own _____ in order to maintain the highest levels of survey validity and reliability.

Exam Probability: **High**

35. *Answer choices:*

(see index for correct answer)

- a. Programming interview
- b. Exit interview
- c. Mock interview
- d. SOARA

Guidance: level 1

:: Human resource management ::

_____ assesses whether a person performs a job well. _____, studied academically as part of industrial and organizational psychology, also forms a part of human resources management. Performance is an important criterion for organizational outcomes and success. John P. Campbell describes _____ as an individual-level variable, or something a single person does. This differentiates it from more encompassing constructs such as organizational performance or national performance, which are higher-level variables.

Exam Probability: **Medium**

36. *Answer choices:*

(see index for correct answer)

- a. Occupational burnout
- b. Job performance
- c. Flextime

- d. Management by observation

Guidance: level 1

:: Lean manufacturing ::

> _____ is the Sino-Japanese word for "improvement". In business, _____ refers to activities that continuously improve all functions and involve all employees from the CEO to the assembly line workers. It also applies to processes, such as purchasing and logistics, that cross organizational boundaries into the supply chain. It has been applied in healthcare, psychotherapy, life-coaching, government, and banking.

Exam Probability: **High**

37. *Answer choices:*
(see index for correct answer)

- a. Kanban
- b. Kaizen
- c. Lean product development
- d. Manufacturing supermarket

Guidance: level 1

:: Human resource management ::

_____ is a process for identifying and developing new leaders who can replace old leaders when they leave, retire or die. _____ increases the availability of experienced and capable employees that are prepared to assume these roles as they become available. Taken narrowly, "replacement planning" for key roles is the heart of _____ .

Exam Probability: **Low**

38. *Answer choices:*

(see index for correct answer)

- a. Vendor on premises
- b. Succession planning
- c. Restructuring
- d. Recruitment process outsourcing

Guidance: level 1

:: Human resource management ::

_____ refers to the anticipation of required human capital for an organization and the planning to meet those needs. The field increased in popularity after McKinsey's 1997 research and the 2001 book on The War for Talent. _____ in this context does not refer to the management of entertainers.

Exam Probability: **Low**

39. *Answer choices:*

(see index for correct answer)

- a. Job sharing
- b. Talent management
- c. Senior management
- d. Compensation and benefits

Guidance: level 1

:: Recruitment ::

A _____ or background investigation is the process of looking up and compiling criminal records, commercial records, and financial records of an individual or an organization. The frequency, purpose, and legitimacy of _____ s varies between countries, industries, and individuals. A variety of methods are used to complete such a check, from comprehensive data base search to personal references.

Exam Probability: **Low**

40. *Answer choices:*

(see index for correct answer)

- a. HResume
- b. contract of employment
- c. Overqualification
- d. Background check

Guidance: level 1

:: ::

A _____ is the ability to carry out a task with determined results often within a given amount of time, energy, or both. _____s can often be divided into domain-general and domain-specific _____s. For example, in the domain of work, some general _____s would include time management, teamwork and leadership, self-motivation and others, whereas domain-specific _____s would be used only for a certain job. _____ usually requires certain environmental stimuli and situations to assess the level of _____ being shown and used.

Exam Probability: **Low**

41. *Answer choices:*

(see index for correct answer)

- a. deep-level diversity
- b. open system
- c. functional perspective
- d. Skill

Guidance: level 1

:: Free market ::

Piece work is any type of employment in which a worker is paid a fixed _____ for each unit produced or action performed regardless of time.

Exam Probability: **High**

42. *Answer choices:*

(see index for correct answer)

- a. Regulated market
- b. Piece rate

Guidance: level 1

:: ::

From an accounting perspective, _____ is crucial because _____ and _____ taxes considerably affect the net income of most companies and because they are subject to laws and regulations.

Exam Probability: **Low**

43. *Answer choices:*

(see index for correct answer)

- a. surface-level diversity
- b. imperative

- c. deep-level diversity
- d. interpersonal communication

Guidance: level 1

:: Telecommuting ::

_____ , also called telework, teleworking, working from home, mobile work, remote work, and flexible workplace, is a work arrangement in which employees do not commute or travel to a central place of work, such as an office building, warehouse, or store. Teleworkers in the 21st century often use mobile telecommunications technology such as Wi-Fi-equipped laptop or tablet computers and smartphones to work from coffee shops; others may use a desktop computer and a landline phone at their home. According to a Reuters poll, approximately "one in five workers around the globe, particularly employees in the Middle East, Latin America and Asia, telecommute frequently and nearly 10 percent work from home every day." In the 2000s, annual leave or vacation in some organizations was seen as absence from the workplace rather than ceasing work, and some office employees used telework to continue to check work e-mails while on vacation.

Exam Probability: **Medium**

44. *Answer choices:*

(see index for correct answer)

- a. OmNovia Technologies
- b. Home Work Convention, 1996
- c. IvanAnywhere
- d. Remote office center

Guidance: level 1

:: Legal terms ::

_____ , a form of alternative dispute resolution , is a way to resolve disputes outside the courts. The dispute will be decided by one or more persons , which renders the " _____ award". An _____ award is legally binding on both sides and enforceable in the courts.

Exam Probability: **Medium**

45. *Answer choices:*

(see index for correct answer)

- a. Arbitration
- b. Collateral estoppel
- c. Long cause
- d. Exclusion clause

Guidance: level 1

:: Power (social and political) ::

In a notable study of power conducted by social psychologists John R. P. French and Bertram Raven in 1959, power is divided into five separate and distinct forms. In 1965 Raven revised this model to include a sixth form by separating the informational power base as distinct from the _____ base.

Exam Probability: **Low**

46. *Answer choices:*

(see index for correct answer)

- a. Hard power
- b. need for power
- c. Expert power

Guidance: level 1

:: Termination of employment ::

The _____ of 1988 is a US labor law which protects employees, their families, and communities by requiring most employers with 100 or more employees to provide 60 calendar-day advance notification of plant closings and mass layoffs of employees, as defined in the Act. In 2001, there were about 2,000 mass layoffs and plant closures which were subject to WARN advance notice requirements and which affected about 660,000 employees.

Exam Probability: **Medium**

47. *Answer choices:*

(see index for correct answer)

- a. Notice period
- b. Pink slip
- c. Worker Adjustment and Retraining Notification Act
- d. Termination of Employment Convention, 1982

Guidance: level 1

:: Teams ::

A _____ usually refers to a group of individuals who work together from different geographic locations and rely on communication technology such as email, FAX, and video or voice conferencing services in order to collaborate. The term can also refer to groups or teams that work together asynchronously or across organizational levels. Powell, Piccoli and Ives define _____ s as "groups of geographically, organizationally and/or time dispersed workers brought together by information and telecommunication technologies to accomplish one or more organizational tasks." According to Ale Ebrahim et. al. , _____ s can also be defined as "small temporary groups of geographically, organizationally and/or time dispersed knowledge workers who coordinate their work predominantly with electronic information and communication technologies in order to accomplish one or more organization tasks."

Exam Probability: **Low**

48. *Answer choices:*

(see index for correct answer)

- a. team composition
- b. Team-building

Guidance: level 1

:: ::

In business strategy, _____ is establishing a competitive advantage by having the lowest cost of operation in the industry. _____ is often driven by company efficiency, size, scale, scope and cumulative experience. A _____ strategy aims to exploit scale of production, well-defined scope and other economies, producing highly standardized products, using advanced technology. In recent years, more and more companies have chosen a strategic mix to achieve market leadership. These patterns consist of simultaneous _____, superior customer service and product leadership. Walmart has succeeded across the world due to its _____ strategy. The company has cut down on exesses at every point of production and thus are able to provide the consumers with quality products at low prices.

Exam Probability: **High**

49. *Answer choices:*

(see index for correct answer)

- a. open system
- b. information systems assessment
- c. co-culture
- d. personal values

Guidance: level 1

:: Project management ::

_____ is a name for various theories of human motivation built on Douglas McGregor's Theory X and Theory Y. Theories X, Y and various versions of Z have been used in human resource management, organizational behavior, organizational communication and organizational development.

Exam Probability: **High**

50. *Answer choices:*

(see index for correct answer)

- a. Theory Z
- b. Total project control
- c. Scope statement
- d. Small-scale project management

Guidance: level 1

:: Production and manufacturing ::

_____ is a set of techniques and tools for process improvement. Though as a shortened form it may be found written as 6S, it should not be confused with the methodology known as 6S.

Exam Probability: **High**

51. *Answer choices:*

(see index for correct answer)

- a. Screw conveyor
- b. Product lifecycle management
- c. Transfer line
- d. Accelerated aging

Guidance: level 1

:: ::

_____ was the plaintiff in the American employment discrimination case Ledbetter v. Goodyear Tire & Rubber Co. Congress passed a fair pay act in her name, the _____ Fair Pay Act of 2009. She has since become a women's equality activist, public speaker, and author. In 2011, Ledbetter was inducted into the National Women's Hall of Fame.

Exam Probability: **Low**

52. *Answer choices:*

(see index for correct answer)

- a. hierarchical perspective
- b. interpersonal communication
- c. process perspective
- d. Lilly Ledbetter

Guidance: level 1

:: ::

_____ is the process of gathering and measuring information on targeted variables in an established system, which then enables one to answer relevant questions and evaluate outcomes. _____ is a component of research in all fields of study including physical and social sciences, humanities, and business. While methods vary by discipline, the emphasis on ensuring accurate and honest collection remains the same. The goal for all _____ is to capture quality evidence that allows analysis to lead to the formulation of convincing and credible answers to the questions that have been posed.

Exam Probability: **Low**

53. *Answer choices:*

(see index for correct answer)

- a. hierarchical
- b. imperative
- c. deep-level diversity

- d. functional perspective

Guidance: level 1

:: Labour law ::

A _____ is a legal contract that is meant to limit the liability of an employer whose employees are romantically involved. An employer may choose to require a _____ when a romantic relationship within the company becomes known, in order to indemnify the company in case the employees' romantic relationship fails, primarily so that one party can't bring a sexual harassment lawsuit against the company. To that end, the _____ states that the relationship is consensual, and both parties of the relationship must sign it. The _____ may also stipulate rules for acceptable romantic behavior in the workplace.

Exam Probability: **Low**

54. *Answer choices:*

(see index for correct answer)

- a. Greenfield agreement
- b. Love contract
- c. Non-compete clause
- d. Loudermill letter

Guidance: level 1

:: Employment discrimination ::

A _____ is a metaphor used to represent an invisible barrier that keeps a given demographic from rising beyond a certain level in a hierarchy.

Exam Probability: **Low**

55. *Answer choices:*

(see index for correct answer)

- a. Glass ceiling
- b. LGBT employment discrimination in the United States
- c. New South Wales selection bias
- d. Employment discrimination

Guidance: level 1

:: Training ::

A _____ is commonly known as an individual taking part in a _____ program or a graduate program within a company after having graduated from university or college.

Exam Probability: **Low**

56. *Answer choices:*

(see index for correct answer)

- a. Overlearning
- b. Practicum
- c. Trainee
- d. Discipline

Guidance: level 1

:: ::

The causes of _____ are heavily debated. Classical economics, new classical economics, and the Austrian School of economics argued that market mechanisms are reliable means of resolving _____ . These theories argue against interventions imposed on the labor market from the outside, such as unionization, bureaucratic work rules, minimum wage laws, taxes, and other regulations that they claim discourage the hiring of workers. Keynesian economics emphasizes the cyclical nature of _____ and recommends government interventions in the economy that it claims will reduce _____ during recessions. This theory focuses on recurrent shocks that suddenly reduce aggregate demand for goods and services and thus reduce demand for workers. Keynesian models recommend government interventions designed to increase demand for workers; these can include financial stimuli, publicly funded job creation, and expansionist monetary policies. Its namesake economist, John Maynard Keynes, believed that the root cause of _____ is the desire of investors to receive more money rather than produce more products, which is not possible without public bodies producing new money. A third group of theories emphasize the need for a stable supply of capital and investment to maintain full employment. On this view, government should guarantee full employment through fiscal policy, monetary policy and trade policy as stated, for example, in the US Employment Act of 1946, by counteracting private sector or trade investment volatility, and reducing inequality.

Exam Probability: **Medium**

57. *Answer choices:*

(see index for correct answer)

- a. levels of analysis
- b. Unemployment
- c. functional perspective
- d. Sarbanes-Oxley act of 2002

Guidance: level 1

:: Belief ::

_____ is an umbrella term of influence. _____ can attempt to influence a person's beliefs, attitudes, intentions, motivations, or behaviors. In business, _____ is a process aimed at changing a person's attitude or behavior toward some event, idea, object, or other person, by using written, spoken words or visual tools to convey information, feelings, or reasoning, or a combination thereof. _____ is also an often used tool in the pursuit of personal gain, such as election campaigning, giving a sales pitch, or in trial advocacy. _____ can also be interpreted as using one's personal or positional resources to change people's behaviors or attitudes. Systematic _____ is the process through which attitudes or beliefs are leveraged by appeals to logic and reason. Heuristic _____ on the other hand is the process through which attitudes or beliefs are leveraged by appeals to habit or emotion.

Exam Probability: **High**

58. *Answer choices:*

(see index for correct answer)

- a. Sententia fidei proxima
- b. Persuasion
- c. Ideological assumption
- d. Popular belief

Guidance: level 1

:: Evaluation methods ::

In social psychology, _____ is the process of looking at oneself in order to assess aspects that are important to one's identity. It is one of the motives that drive self-evaluation, along with self-verification and self-enhancement. Sedikides suggests that the _____ motive will prompt people to seek information to confirm their uncertain self-concept rather than their certain self-concept and at the same time people use _____ to enhance their certainty of their own self-knowledge. However, the _____ motive could be seen as quite different from the other two self-evaluation motives. Unlike the other two motives through _____ people are interested in the accuracy of their current self view, rather than improving their self-view. This makes _____ the only self-evaluative motive that may cause a person's self-esteem to be damaged.

Exam Probability: **Medium**

59. *Answer choices:*

(see index for correct answer)

- a. Advanced Concept Technology Demonstration
- b. Logic model
- c. Gender evaluation methodology
- d. Moral statistics

Guidance: level 1

Information systems

Information systems (IS) are formal, sociotechnical, organizational systems designed to collect, process, store, and distribute information. In a sociotechnical perspective Information Systems are composed by four components: technology, process, people and organizational structure.

:: Business models ::

_____ , a portmanteau of the words "free" and "premium", is a pricing strategy by which a product or service is provided free of charge, but money is charged for additional features, services, or virtual or physical goods. The business model has been in use by the software industry since the 1980s as a licensing scheme. A subset of this model used by the video game industry is called free-to-play.

Exam Probability: **Medium**

1. *Answer choices:*

(see index for correct answer)

- a. Lawyers on Demand
- b. Blended value
- c. The Community Company
- d. Freemium

Guidance: level 1

:: Knowledge engineering ::

The _____ is an extension of the World Wide Web through standards by the World Wide Web Consortium . The standards promote common data formats and exchange protocols on the Web, most fundamentally the Resource Description Framework . According to the W3C, "The _____ provides a common framework that allows data to be shared and reused across application, enterprise, and community boundaries". The _____ is therefore regarded as an integrator across different content, information applications and systems.

Exam Probability: **Low**

2. *Answer choices:*

(see index for correct answer)

- a. Knowledge engineer

- b. Subject-matter expert
- c. Semantic Web
- d. Knowledge engineering

Guidance: level 1

:: Telecommunications engineering ::

A _____ is a computer processor that incorporates the functions of a central processing unit on a single integrated circuit , or at most a few integrated circuits. The _____ is a multipurpose, clock driven, register based, digital integrated circuit that accepts binary data as input, processes it according to instructions stored in its memory and provides results as output. _____ s contain both combinational logic and sequential digital logic. _____ s operate on numbers and symbols represented in the binary number system.

Exam Probability: **High**

3. *Answer choices:*

(see index for correct answer)

- a. network architecture
- b. Computer network

Guidance: level 1

:: ::

_____ is software designed to provide a platform for other software. Examples of _____ include operating systems like macOS, Ubuntu and Microsoft Windows, computational science software, game engines, industrial automation, and software as a service applications.

Exam Probability: **High**

4. *Answer choices:*

(see index for correct answer)

- a. interpersonal communication
- b. System software
- c. open system
- d. surface-level diversity

Guidance: level 1

:: Business process ::

Business process re-engineering is a business management strategy, originally pioneered in the early 1990s, focusing on the analysis and design of workflows and business processes within an organization. BPR aimed to help organizations fundamentally rethink how they do their work in order to improve customer service, cut operational costs, and become world-class competitors.

Exam Probability: **High**

5. *Answer choices:*

(see index for correct answer)

- a. Social BPM
- b. Intention mining
- c. Business process reengineering
- d. Communication-enabled business process

Guidance: level 1

:: Payment systems ::

An _____ is an electronic telecommunications device that enables customers of financial institutions to perform financial transactions, such as cash withdrawals, deposits, transfer funds, or obtaining account information, at any time and without the need for direct interaction with bank staff.

Exam Probability: **Medium**

6. *Answer choices:*

(see index for correct answer)

- a. SADAD Payment System
- b. Freedompay
- c. Automated teller machine

- d. K-CASH

Guidance: level 1

:: ::

_____ is a brand name associated with the development of the _____ web browser. It is now owned by Verizon Media, a subsidiary of Verizon. The brand belonged to the _____ Communications Corporation, an independent American computer services company, whose headquarters were in Mountain View, California, and later Dulles, Virginia. The browser was once dominant but lost to Internet Explorer and other competitors after the so-called first browser war, its market share falling from more than 90 percent in the mid-1990s to less than 1 percent in 2006.

Exam Probability: **High**

7. *Answer choices:*

(see index for correct answer)

- a. surface-level diversity
- b. interpersonal communication
- c. empathy
- d. deep-level diversity

Guidance: level 1

:: Industrial design ::

In physics and mathematics, the _____ of a mathematical space is informally defined as the minimum number of coordinates needed to specify any point within it. Thus a line has a _____ of one because only one coordinate is needed to specify a point on it for example, the point at 5 on a number line. A surface such as a plane or the surface of a cylinder or sphere has a _____ of two because two coordinates are needed to specify a point on it for example, both a latitude and longitude are required to locate a point on the surface of a sphere. The inside of a cube, a cylinder or a sphere is three-_____al because three coordinates are needed to locate a point within these spaces.

Exam Probability: **Low**

8. *Answer choices:*

(see index for correct answer)

- a. Vertical form fill sealing machine
- b. Design and Technology
- c. Snow White design language
- d. Dimension

Guidance: level 1

:: Intelligence (information gathering) ::

_____ comprises the strategies and technologies used by enterprises for the data analysis of business information. BI technologies provide historical, current and predictive views of business operations. Common functions of _____ technologies include reporting, online analytical processing, analytics, data mining, process mining, complex event processing, business performance management, benchmarking, text mining, predictive analytics and prescriptive analytics. BI technologies can handle large amounts of structured and sometimes unstructured data to help identify, develop and otherwise create new strategic business opportunities. They aim to allow for the easy interpretation of these big data. Identifying new opportunities and implementing an effective strategy based on insights can provide businesses with a competitive market advantage and long-term stability.

Exam Probability: **Medium**

9. *Answer choices:*

(see index for correct answer)

- a. Titan traffic database
- b. Central media
- c. spying
- d. Geophysical MASINT

Guidance: level 1

:: E-commerce ::

_____ is a subset of electronic commerce that involves social media, online media that supports social interaction, and user contributions to assist online buying and selling of products and services.

Exam Probability: **Low**

10. *Answer choices:*

(see index for correct answer)

- a. Debit card
- b. Trust seal
- c. EPAS
- d. IDEAL

Guidance: level 1

:: Information technology management ::

_____ is a collective term for all approaches to prepare, support and help individuals, teams, and organizations in making organizational change. The most common change drivers include: technological evolution, process reviews, crisis, and consumer habit changes; pressure from new business entrants, acquisitions, mergers, and organizational restructuring. It includes methods that redirect or redefine the use of resources, business process, budget allocations, or other modes of operation that significantly change a company or organization. Organizational _____ considers the full organization and what needs to change, while _____ may be used solely to refer to how people and teams are affected by such organizational transition. It deals with many different disciplines, from behavioral and social sciences to information technology and business solutions.

Exam Probability: **Medium**

11. *Answer choices:*

(see index for correct answer)

- a. DevOps
- b. Web commerce
- c. Cherwell Software
- d. Change management

Guidance: level 1

:: Information systems ::

_____ , Chief Digital Information Officer or Information Technology Director, is a job title commonly given to the most senior executive in an enterprise who works for the traditional information technology and computer systems that support enterprise goals.

Exam Probability: **Medium**

12. *Answer choices:*

(see index for correct answer)

- a. European Research Center for Information Systems
- b. Value sensitive design
- c. Hybrid Data Infrastructure
- d. Connectionist expert system

Guidance: level 1

:: Data management ::

Data aggregation is the compiling of information from databases with intent to prepare combined datasets for data processing.

Exam Probability: **Low**

13. *Answer choices:*

(see index for correct answer)

- a. Transaction data
- b. Single source publishing
- c. Hybrid array
- d. Distributed database

Guidance: level 1

:: Marketing by medium ::

_____, also called online marketing or Internet advertising or web advertising, is a form of marketing and advertising which uses the Internet to deliver promotional marketing messages to consumers. Many consumers find _____ disruptive and have increasingly turned to ad blocking for a variety of reasons. When software is used to do the purchasing, it is known as programmatic advertising.

Exam Probability: **High**

14. *Answer choices:*
(see index for correct answer)

- a. Social video marketing
- b. Digital marketing
- c. Social intelligence architect
- d. Social marketing intelligence

Guidance: level 1

:: Strategic management ::

In marketing strategy, first-mover advantage is the advantage gained by the initial significant occupant of a market segment. First-mover advantage may be gained by technological leadership, or early purchase of resources.

Exam Probability: **Low**

15. *Answer choices:*
(see index for correct answer)

- a. strategy implementation
- b. Cluster development
- c. Keiretsu
- d. Complexity management

Guidance: level 1

:: Geographic information systems ::

_____ is the computational process of transforming a physical address description to a location on the Earth's surface. Reverse _____, on the other hand, converts geographic coordinates to a description of a location, usually the name of a place or an addressable location. _____ relies on a computer representation of address points, the street / road network, together with postal and administrative boundaries.

Exam Probability: **Low**

16. *Answer choices:*

(see index for correct answer)

- a. David Mark
- b. Toponym Resolution
- c. Geocoding
- d. Buffer

Guidance: level 1

:: ::

Sustainability is the process of people maintaining change in a balanced environment, in which the exploitation of resources, the direction of investments, the orientation of technological development and institutional change are all in harmony and enhance both current and future potential to meet human needs and aspirations. For many in the field, sustainability is defined through the following interconnected domains or pillars: environment, economic and social, which according to Fritjof Capra is based on the principles of Systems Thinking. Sub-domains of _____ development have been considered also: cultural, technological and political. While _____ development may be the organizing principle for sustainability for some, for others, the two terms are paradoxical . _____ development is the development that meets the needs of the present without compromising the ability of future generations to meet their own needs. Brundtland Report for the World Commission on Environment and Development introduced the term of _____ development.

Exam Probability: **Medium**

17. *Answer choices:*

(see index for correct answer)

- a. corporate values
- b. process perspective
- c. empathy
- d. Sustainable

Guidance: level 1

:: Human–machine interaction ::

In electrical engineering, a _____ is an electrical component that can "make" or "break" an electrical circuit, interrupting the current or diverting it from one conductor to another. The mechanism of a _____ removes or restores the conducting path in a circuit when it is operated. It may be operated manually, for example, a light _____ or a keyboard button, may be operated by a moving object such as a door, or may be operated by some sensing element for pressure, temperature or flow. A _____ will have one or more sets of contacts, which may operate simultaneously, sequentially, or alternately. _____ es in high-powered circuits must operate rapidly to prevent destructive arcing, and may include special features to assist in rapidly interrupting a heavy current. Multiple forms of actuators are used for operation by hand or to sense position, level, temperature or flow. Special types are used, for example, for control of machinery, to reverse electric motors, or to sense liquid level. Many specialized forms exist. A common use is control of lighting, where multiple _____ es may be wired into one circuit to allow convenient control of light fixtures.

Exam Probability: **Low**

18. *Answer choices:*

(see index for correct answer)

- a. Switch
- b. Pistol grip
- c. Telegraph key
- d. Emotions in virtual communication

Guidance: level 1

:: Commercial item transport and distribution ::

In commerce, supply-chain management, the management of the flow of goods and services, involves the movement and storage of raw materials, of work-in-process inventory, and of finished goods from point of origin to point of consumption. Interconnected or interlinked networks, channels and node businesses combine in the provision of products and services required by end customers in a supply chain. Supply-chain management has been defined as the "design, planning, execution, control, and monitoring of supply-chain activities with the objective of creating net value, building a competitive infrastructure, leveraging worldwide logistics, synchronizing supply with demand and measuring performance globally."SCM practice draws heavily from the areas of industrial engineering, systems engineering, operations management, logistics, procurement, information technology, and marketing and strives for an integrated approach. Marketing channels play an important role in supply-chain management. Current research in supply-chain management is concerned with topics related to sustainability and risk management, among others. Some suggest that the "people dimension" of SCM, ethical issues, internal integration, transparency/visibility, and human capital/talent management are topics that have, so far, been underrepresented on the research agenda.

Exam Probability: **Medium**

19. *Answer choices:*

(see index for correct answer)

- a. Trade facilitation
- b. Zeppelin
- c. Wholesale
- d. Supply chain management

Guidance: level 1

:: Internet marketing ::

_____ is the measurement, collection, analysis and reporting of web data for purposes of understanding and optimizing web usage. However, _____ is not just a process for measuring web traffic but can be used as a tool for business and market research, and to assess and improve the effectiveness of a website. _____ applications can also help companies measure the results of traditional print or broadcast advertising campaigns. It helps one to estimate how traffic to a website changes after the launch of a new advertising campaign. _____ provides information about the number of visitors to a website and the number of page views. It helps gauge traffic and popularity trends which is useful for market research.

Exam Probability: **Medium**

20. *Answer choices:*

(see index for correct answer)

- a. Yesmail
- b. App store optimization
- c. Golden Triangle
- d. Ad text optimization

Guidance: level 1

:: Statistical laws ::

In statistics and business, a _____ of some distributions of numbers is the portion of the distribution having a large number of occurrences far from the "head" or central part of the distribution. The distribution could involve popularities, random numbers of occurrences of events with various probabilities, etc. The term is often used loosely, with no definition or arbitrary definition, but precise definitions are possible.

Exam Probability: **Medium**

21. *Answer choices:*

(see index for correct answer)

- a. Long tail
- b. Law of the unconscious statistician
- c. Law of total expectation
- d. Law of total cumulance

Guidance: level 1

In communications and information processing, _____ is a system of rules to convert information—such as a letter, word, sound, image, or gesture—into another form or representation, sometimes shortened or secret, for communication through a communication channel or storage in a storage medium. An early example is the invention of language, which enabled a person, through speech, to communicate what they saw, heard, felt, or thought to others. But speech limits the range of communication to the distance a voice can carry, and limits the audience to those present when the speech is uttered. The invention of writing, which converted spoken language into visual symbols, extended the range of communication across space and time.

Exam Probability: **Medium**

22. *Answer choices:*

(see index for correct answer)

- a. imperative
- b. hierarchical
- c. functional perspective
- d. Code

Guidance: level 1

_____ Holdings, Inc. is an American company operating a worldwide online payments system that supports online money transfers and serves as an electronic alternative to traditional paper methods like checks and money orders. The company operates as a payment processor for online vendors, auction sites, and many other commercial users, for which it charges a fee in exchange for benefits such as one-click transactions and password memory. _____'s payment system, also called _____, is considered a type of payment rail.

Exam Probability: **High**

23. *Answer choices:*

(see index for correct answer)

- a. open system
- b. cultural
- c. PayPal
- d. personal values

Guidance: level 1

:: ::

_____ consists of tailoring a service or a product to accommodate specific individuals, sometimes tied to groups or segments of individuals. A wide variety of organizations use _____ to improve customer satisfaction, digital sales conversion, marketing results, branding, and improved website metrics as well as for advertising. _____ is a key element in social media and recommender systems.

Exam Probability: **Low**

24. *Answer choices:*

(see index for correct answer)

- a. similarity-attraction theory
- b. process perspective
- c. Personalization
- d. empathy

Guidance: level 1

:: Google services ::

_____ is a web mapping service developed by Google. It offers satellite imagery, aerial photography, street maps, 360° panoramic views of streets, real-time traffic conditions, and route planning for traveling by foot, car, bicycle and air , or public transportation.

Exam Probability: **Low**

25. *Answer choices:*

(see index for correct answer)

- a. Google Mars
- b. Google App Engine
- c. Google Maps

- d. App Inventor for Android

Guidance: level 1

:: Marketing by medium ::

_____ or viral advertising is a business strategy that uses existing social networks to promote a product. Its name refers to how consumers spread information about a product with other people in their social networks, much in the same way that a virus spreads from one person to another. It can be delivered by word of mouth or enhanced by the network effects of the Internet and mobile networks.

Exam Probability: **High**

26. *Answer choices:*
(see index for correct answer)

- a. Brand infiltration
- b. Social video marketing
- c. Viral marketing
- d. Direct Text Marketing

Guidance: level 1

:: Management systems ::

An _____, also known as an <u>Executive support system </u>, is a type of management support system that facilitates and supports senior executive information and decision-making needs. It provides easy access to internal and external information relevant to organizational goals. It is commonly considered a specialized form of decision support system.

Exam Probability: **Low**

27. *Answer choices:*

(see index for correct answer)

- a. Intelligent enterprise
- b. Windows Management Instrumentation
- c. Service network
- d. Line function

Guidance: level 1

:: Data management ::

"_____" is a field that treats ways to analyze, systematically extract information from, or otherwise deal with data sets that are too large or complex to be dealt with by traditional data-processing application software. Data with many cases offer greater statistical power, while data with higher complexity may lead to a higher false discovery rate. _____ challenges include capturing data, data storage, data analysis, search, sharing, transfer, visualization, querying, updating, information privacy and data source. _____ was originally associated with three key concepts: volume, variety, and velocity. Other concepts later attributed with _____ are veracity and value.

Exam Probability: **High**

28. *Answer choices:*

(see index for correct answer)

- a. Data profiling
- b. Big data
- c. BBC Archives
- d. Record linkage

Guidance: level 1

:: Information technology management ::

The term _____ is used to refer to periods when a system is unavailable. _____ or outage duration refers to a period of time that a system fails to provide or perform its primary function. Reliability, availability, recovery, and unavailability are related concepts. The unavailability is the proportion of a time-span that a system is unavailable or offline. This is usually a result of the system failing to function because of an unplanned event, or because of routine maintenance.

Exam Probability: **Low**

29. *Answer choices:*

(see index for correct answer)

- a. ISO/IEC 19770
- b. Mung
- c. Downtime
- d. ESCM

Guidance: level 1

:: Data management ::

Given organizations' increasing dependency on information technology to run their operations, Business continuity planning covers the entire organization, and Disaster recovery focuses on IT.

Exam Probability: **High**

30. *Answer choices:*

(see index for correct answer)

- a. Disaster recovery plan
- b. Distributed transaction
- c. Hybrid array
- d. Novell Storage Manager

Guidance: level 1

:: Fraud ::

In law, _____ is intentional deception to secure unfair or unlawful gain, or to deprive a victim of a legal right. _____ can violate civil law, a criminal law, or it may cause no loss of money, property or legal right but still be an element of another civil or criminal wrong. The purpose of _____ may be monetary gain or other benefits, for example by obtaining a passport, travel document, or driver`s license, or mortgage _____, where the perpetrator may attempt to qualify for a mortgage by way of false statements.

Exam Probability: **Medium**

31. *Answer choices:*

(see index for correct answer)

- a. Pharma fraud
- b. 2010 Medicaid fraud

- c. Fraud
- d. Parcel mule scam

Guidance: level 1

:: Payment systems ::

> _____ is a mobile phone-based money transfer, financing and microfinancing service, launched in 2007 by Vodafone for Safaricom and Vodacom, the largest mobile network operators in Kenya and Tanzania. It has since expanded to Afghanistan, South Africa, India and in 2014 to Romania and in 2015 to Albania. _____ allows users to deposit, withdraw, transfer money and pay for goods and services easily with a mobile device.

Exam Probability: **Low**

32. *Answer choices:*

(see index for correct answer)

- a. Sri Lanka Interbank Payment System
- b. M-Pesa
- c. CurdBee
- d. Immediate Payment Service

Guidance: level 1

:: ::

_____ is the function of specifying access rights/privileges to resources, which is related to information security and computer security in general and to access control in particular. More formally, "to authorize" is to define an access policy. For example, human resources staff are normally authorized to access employee records and this policy is usually formalized as access control rules in a computer system. During operation, the system uses the access control rules to decide whether access requests from consumers shall be approved or disapproved. Resources include individual files or an item's data, computer programs, computer devices and functionality provided by computer applications. Examples of consumers are computer users, computer Software and other Hardware on the computer.

Exam Probability: **High**

33. *Answer choices:*

(see index for correct answer)

- a. Authorization
- b. open system
- c. hierarchical
- d. imperative

Guidance: level 1

:: Procurement practices ::

_____ or commercially available off-the-shelf products are packaged solutions which are then adapted to satisfy the needs of the purchasing organization, rather than the commissioning of custom-made, or bespoke, solutions. A related term, Mil-COTS, refers to COTS products for use by the U.S. military.

Exam Probability: **Medium**

34. *Answer choices:*

(see index for correct answer)

- a. Syndicated procurement
- b. Commercial off-the-shelf

Guidance: level 1

:: Network analyzers ::

A _____ , meaning "meat eater" , is an organism that derives its energy and nutrient requirements from a diet consisting mainly or exclusively of animal tissue, whether through predation or scavenging. Animals that depend solely on animal flesh for their nutrient requirements are called obligate _____ s while those that also consume non-animal food are called facultative _____ s. Omnivores also consume both animal and non-animal food, and, apart from the more general definition, there is no clearly defined ratio of plant to animal material that would distinguish a facultative _____ from an omnivore. A _____ at the top of the food chain, not preyed upon by other animals, is termed an apex predator.

Exam Probability: **Low**

35. *Answer choices:*

(see index for correct answer)

- a. Ettercap
- b. Packet generator
- c. University Toolkit
- d. Microsoft Network Monitor

Guidance: level 1

:: Computer security standards ::

The _____ for Information Technology Security Evaluation is an international standard for computer security certification. It is currently in version 3.1 revision 5.

Exam Probability: **Medium**

36. *Answer choices:*

(see index for correct answer)

- a. Blacker
- b. FIPS 140
- c. Common Criteria
- d. BS 7799

Guidance: level 1

:: Ubiquitous computing ::

A _____ , chip card, or integrated circuit card is a physical electronic authorization device, used to control access to a resource. It is typically a plastic credit card sized card with an embedded integrated circuit. Many _____ s include a pattern of metal contacts to electrically connect to the internal chip. Others are contactless, and some are both. _____ s can provide personal identification, authentication, data storage, and application processing. Applications include identification, financial, mobile phones , public transit, computer security, schools, and healthcare. _____ s may provide strong security authentication for single sign-on within organizations. Several nations have deployed _____ s throughout their populations.

Exam Probability: **Medium**

37. *Answer choices:*

(see index for correct answer)

- a. Calm technology
- b. Hyperconnectivity
- c. Smart card
- d. Wireless lock

Guidance: level 1

:: Reputation management ::

A _____ is an astronomical object consisting of a luminous spheroid of plasma held together by its own gravity. The nearest _____ to Earth is the Sun. Many other _____s are visible to the naked eye from Earth during the night, appearing as a multitude of fixed luminous points in the sky due to their immense distance from Earth. Historically, the most prominent _____s were grouped into constellations and asterisms, the brightest of which gained proper names. Astronomers have assembled _____ catalogues that identify the known _____s and provide standardized stellar designations. However, most of the estimated 300 sextillion _____s in the Universe are invisible to the naked eye from Earth, including all _____s outside our galaxy, the Milky Way.

Exam Probability: **Low**

38. *Answer choices:*

(see index for correct answer)

- a. Meta-moderation system
- b. Infamy
- c. Star
- d. Advogato

Guidance: level 1

:: Information systems ::

In artificial intelligence, an _____ is a computer system that emulates the decision-making ability of a human expert. _____ s are designed to solve complex problems by reasoning through bodies of knowledge, represented mainly as if–then rules rather than through conventional procedural code. The first _____ s were created in the 1970s and then proliferated in the 1980s. _____ s were among the first truly successful forms of artificial intelligence software. However, some experts point out that _____ s were not part of true artificial intelligence since they lack the ability to learn autonomously from external data. An _____ is divided into two subsystems: the inference engine and the knowledge base. The knowledge base represents facts and rules. The inference engine applies the rules to the known facts to deduce new facts. Inference engines can also include explanation and debugging abilities.

Exam Probability: **Medium**

39. *Answer choices:*

(see index for correct answer)

- a. Chief information officer
- b. Proactive information delivery
- c. Expert system
- d. Heritage Operations Processing System

Guidance: level 1

:: User interfaces ::

_____, keystroke biometrics, typing dynamics and lately typing biometrics, is the detailed timing information which describes exactly when each key was pressed and when it was released as a person is typing at a computer keyboard.

Exam Probability: **Low**

40. *Answer choices:*

(see index for correct answer)

- a. Virtual console
- b. Keystroke dynamics
- c. Sparsh
- d. User interface management systems

Guidance: level 1

:: Internet privacy ::

An _____ is a private network accessible only to an organization's staff. Often, a wide range of information and services are available on an organization's internal _____ that are unavailable to the public, unlike the Internet. A company-wide _____ can constitute an important focal point of internal communication and collaboration, and provide a single starting point to access internal and external resources. In its simplest form, an _____ is established with the technologies for local area networks and wide area networks . Many modern _____ s have search engines, user profiles, blogs, mobile apps with notifications, and events planning within their infrastructure.

Exam Probability: **Medium**

41. *Answer choices:*

(see index for correct answer)

- a. Intranet
- b. Internet censorship circumvention
- c. 2010 Duke University faux sex thesis controversy
- d. Cypherpunks

Guidance: level 1

:: Commerce websites ::

_____ is an American classified advertisements website with sections devoted to jobs, housing, for sale, items wanted, services, community service, gigs, résumés, and discussion forums.

Exam Probability: **Low**

42. *Answer choices:*

(see index for correct answer)

- a. Defence Discount Service
- b. WikiExperts
- c. Craigslist
- d. Best In The House Tickets

Guidance: level 1

:: Global Positioning System ::

The _____ , originally Navstar GPS, is a satellite-based radionavigation system owned by the United States government and operated by the United States Air Force. It is a global navigation satellite system that provides geolocation and time information to a GPS receiver anywhere on or near the Earth where there is an unobstructed line of sight to four or more GPS satellites. Obstacles such as mountains and buildings block the relatively weak GPS signals.

Exam Probability: **High**

43. *Answer choices:*

(see index for correct answer)

- a. Plate Boundary Observatory
- b. National Executive Committee for Space-Based Positioning, Navigation and Timing
- c. Global Positioning System
- d. Reference ellipsoid

Guidance: level 1

:: ::

A _____ is a system designed to capture, store, manipulate, analyze, manage, and present spatial or geographic data. GIS applications are tools that allow users to create interactive queries, analyze spatial information, edit data in maps, and present the results of all these operations. GIS sometimes refers to geographic information science, the science underlying geographic concepts, applications, and systems.

Exam Probability: **Low**

44. *Answer choices:*

(see index for correct answer)

- a. interpersonal communication
- b. similarity-attraction theory
- c. Geographic information system
- d. functional perspective

Guidance: level 1

:: ::

_____, Inc. is an American online social media and social networking service company based in Menlo Park, California. It was founded by Mark Zuckerberg, along with fellow Harvard College students and roommates Eduardo Saverin, Andrew McCollum, Dustin Moskovitz and Chris Hughes. It is considered one of the Big Four technology companies along with Amazon, Apple, and Google.

Exam Probability: **High**

45. Answer choices:

(see index for correct answer)

- a. information systems assessment
- b. Sarbanes-Oxley act of 2002
- c. open system
- d. Facebook

Guidance: level 1

:: Customer relationship management software ::

_____ Software Corporation is a Global Business Software company based in Austin, TX and was founded in 1972. Its products are aimed at the manufacturing, distribution, retail and services industries.

Exam Probability: **Medium**

46. Answer choices:

(see index for correct answer)

- a. Cirrus Insight
- b. 24SevenOffice
- c. Epicor
- d. CiviCRM

Guidance: level 1

:: Infographics ::

A _____ is a graphical representation of data, in which "the data is represented by symbols, such as bars in a bar _____ , lines in a line _____ , or slices in a pie _____ ". A _____ can represent tabular numeric data, functions or some kinds of qualitative structure and provides different info.

Exam Probability: **High**

47. *Answer choices:*

(see index for correct answer)

- a. Inspiration Software
- b. House sign
- c. Chart
- d. Planimetrics

Guidance: level 1

:: Strategic management ::

_____ is a management term for an element that is necessary for an organization or project to achieve its mission. Alternative terms are key result area and key success factor .

Exam Probability: **Low**

48. *Answer choices:*

(see index for correct answer)

- a. Critical success factor
- b. Complexity management
- c. Cost of operation
- d. Talent portfolio management

Guidance: level 1

:: Distribution, retailing, and wholesaling ::

_____ measures the performance of a system. Certain goals are defined and the _____ gives the percentage to which those goals should be achieved. Fill rate is different from _____ .

Exam Probability: **Low**

49. *Answer choices:*

(see index for correct answer)

- a. Service level
- b. Futura plus
- c. Teleflorist
- d. Pacific Comics

Guidance: level 1

:: ::

_____ rate is the ratio of users who click on a specific link to the number of total users who view a page, email, or advertisement. It is commonly used to measure the success of an online advertising campaign for a particular website as well as the effectiveness of email campaigns.

Exam Probability: **Medium**

50. *Answer choices:*

(see index for correct answer)

- a. Character
- b. information systems assessment
- c. Click-through
- d. similarity-attraction theory

Guidance: level 1

:: Management ::

_____ is the kind of knowledge that is difficult to transfer to another person by means of writing it down or verbalizing it. For example, that London is in the United Kingdom is a piece of explicit knowledge that can be written down, transmitted, and understood by a recipient. However, the ability to speak a language, ride a bicycle, knead dough, play a musical instrument, or design and use complex equipment requires all sorts of knowledge that is not always known explicitly, even by expert practitioners, and which is difficult or impossible to explicitly transfer to other people.

Exam Probability: **Low**

51. *Answer choices:*

(see index for correct answer)

- a. Value proposition
- b. Capability management
- c. Tacit knowledge
- d. Corporate transparency

Guidance: level 1

:: E-commerce ::

_____ is the activity of buying or selling of products on online services or over the Internet. Electronic commerce draws on technologies such as mobile commerce, electronic funds transfer, supply chain management, Internet marketing, online transaction processing, electronic data interchange , inventory management systems, and automated data collection systems.

Exam Probability: **High**

52. *Answer choices:*

(see index for correct answer)

- a. Online Shopping in Bangladesh
- b. Virtual enterprise
- c. Inventory Information Approval System
- d. Yakala.co

Guidance: level 1

:: Google services ::

Google Ads is an online advertising platform developed by Google, where advertisers pay to display brief advertisements, service offerings, product listings, video content, and generate mobile application installs within the Google ad network to web users.

Exam Probability: **High**

53. *Answer choices:*

(see index for correct answer)

- a. Google Cloud Connect
- b. Google Map Maker
- c. Google Flights

- d. AdWords

Guidance: level 1

:: Online companies ::

> _____ is a business directory service and crowd-sourced review forum, and a public company of the same name that is headquartered in San Francisco, California. The company develops, hosts and markets the _____.com website and the _____ mobile app, which publish crowd-sourced reviews about businesses. It also operates an online reservation service called _____ Reservations.

Exam Probability: **Medium**

54. *Answer choices:*

(see index for correct answer)

- a. Yelp
- b. Airbnb
- c. Tweetmyjobs
- d. Qihoo

Guidance: level 1

:: Reputation management ::

_____ refers to the influencing and controlling of an individual's or group's reputation. Originally a public relations term, the growth of the internet and social media, along with _____ companies, have made search results a core part of an individual's or group's reputation. Online _____, sometimes abbreviated as ORM, focuses on the management of product and service search website results. Ethical grey areas include mug shot removal sites, astroturfing customer review sites, censoring negative complaints, and using search engine optimization tactics to influence results.

Exam Probability: **High**

55. *Answer choices:*

(see index for correct answer)

- a. ClaimID
- b. Reputation management
- c. Raph Levien
- d. Distrust

Guidance: level 1

:: Information systems ::

A _____ is an information system that supports business or organizational decision-making activities. DSSs serve the management, operations and planning levels of an organization and help people make decisions about problems that may be rapidly changing and not easily specified in advance—i.e. unstructured and semi-structured decision problems. _____ s can be either fully computerized or human-powered, or a combination of both.

Exam Probability: **Low**

56. *Answer choices:*

(see index for correct answer)

- a. SAP Information Interchange OnDemand
- b. Decision support system
- c. Diablo Data Systems
- d. FAO GM Foods Platform

Guidance: level 1

:: Critical thinking ::

In psychology, _____ is regarded as the cognitive process resulting in the selection of a belief or a course of action among several alternative possibilities. Every _____ process produces a final choice, which may or may not prompt action.

Exam Probability: **High**

57. *Answer choices:*

(see index for correct answer)

- a. Inquiry: Critical Thinking Across the Disciplines
- b. Scientific temper
- c. Precision questioning

- d. Vagueness

Guidance: level 1

:: Data quality ::

_____ is the maintenance of, and the assurance of the accuracy and consistency of, data over its entire life-cycle, and is a critical aspect to the design, implementation and usage of any system which stores, processes, or retrieves data. The term is broad in scope and may have widely different meanings depending on the specific context even under the same general umbrella of computing. It is at times used as a proxy term for data quality, while data validation is a pre-requisite for _____ . _____ is the opposite of data corruption. The overall intent of any _____ technique is the same: ensure data is recorded exactly as intended and upon later retrieval, ensure the data is the same as it was when it was originally recorded. In short, _____ aims to prevent unintentional changes to information. _____ is not to be confused with data security, the discipline of protecting data from unauthorized parties.

Exam Probability: **Low**

58. *Answer choices:*

(see index for correct answer)

- a. Data degradation
- b. Information quality
- c. Input mask
- d. Data integrity

Guidance: level 1

:: Business process ::

_____ is a discipline in operations management in which people use various methods to discover, model, analyze, measure, improve, optimize, and automate business processes. BPM focuses on improving corporate performance by managing business processes. Any combination of methods used to manage a company's business processes is BPM. Processes can be structured and repeatable or unstructured and variable. Though not required, enabling technologies are often used with BPM.

Exam Probability: **High**

59. *Answer choices:*

(see index for correct answer)

- a. ADONIS
- b. Intention mining
- c. Leverage-point modeling
- d. Business process management

Guidance: level 1

Marketing

Marketing is the study and management of exchange relationships. Marketing is the business process of creating relationships with and satisfying customers. With its focus on the customer, marketing is one of the premier components of business management.

Marketing is defined by the American Marketing Association as "the activity, set of institutions, and processes for creating, communicating, delivering, and exchanging offerings that have value for customers, clients, partners, and society at large."

:: Product management ::

"_____" is a phrase used in the marketing industry which describes the value of having a well-known brand name, based on the idea that the owner of a well-known brand name can generate more revenue simply from brand recognition; that is from products with that brand name than from products with a less well known name, as consumers believe that a product with a well-known name is better than products with less well-known names.

Exam Probability: **Medium**

1. *Answer choices:*

(see index for correct answer)

- a. Swing tag
- b. Electronic registration mark
- c. Brand equity
- d. Scarcity Development Cycle

Guidance: level 1

:: Library science ::

_____ refers to data which is collected by someone who is someone other than the user. Common sources of _____ for social science include censuses, information collected by government departments, organizational records and data that was originally collected for other research purposes. Primary data, by contrast, are collected by the investigator conducting the research.

Exam Probability: **High**

2. *Answer choices:*

(see index for correct answer)

- a. Secondary data
- b. CiteProc
- c. Library science education in India
- d. In the Library with the Lead Pipe

Guidance: level 1

:: Marketing ::

A _____ is the people, organizations, and activities necessary to transfer the ownership of goods from the point of production to the point of consumption. It is the way products get to the end-user, the consumer; and is also known as a distribution channel. A _____ is a useful tool for management, and is crucial to creating an effective and well-planned marketing strategy.

Exam Probability: **High**

3. *Answer choices:*

(see index for correct answer)

- a. Local store marketing
- b. Marketing channel

- c. Servicescape
- d. Generic trademark

Guidance: level 1

:: Supply chain management ::

_____ is the removal of intermediaries in economics from a supply chain, or cutting out the middlemen in connection with a transaction or a series of transactions. Instead of going through traditional distribution channels, which had some type of intermediary , companies may now deal with customers directly, for example via the Internet. Hence, the use of factory direct and direct from the factory to mean the same thing.

Exam Probability: **High**

4. *Answer choices:*

(see index for correct answer)

- a. Certified Supply Chain Professional
- b. Calculating demand forecast accuracy
- c. Global supply-chain finance
- d. Enterprise resource planning

Guidance: level 1

:: Market research ::

_____ is an organized effort to gather information about target markets or customers. It is a very important component of business strategy. The term is commonly interchanged with marketing research; however, expert practitioners may wish to draw a distinction, in that marketing research is concerned specifically about marketing processes, while _____ is concerned specifically with markets.

Exam Probability: **Low**

5. *Answer choices:*

(see index for correct answer)

- a. Market research
- b. Zyfin
- c. Demographic marketer
- d. IModerate

Guidance: level 1

:: ::

_____ is change in the heritable characteristics of biological populations over successive generations. These characteristics are the expressions of genes that are passed on from parent to offspring during reproduction. Different characteristics tend to exist within any given population as a result of mutation, genetic recombination and other sources of genetic variation. _____ occurs when _____ary processes such as natural selection and genetic drift act on this variation, resulting in certain characteristics becoming more common or rare within a population. It is this process of _____ that has given rise to biodiversity at every level of biological organisation, including the levels of species, individual organisms and molecules.

Exam Probability: **High**

6. *Answer choices:*

(see index for correct answer)

- a. hierarchical perspective
- b. Character
- c. Evolution
- d. co-culture

Guidance: level 1

:: ::

In financial markets, a share is a unit used as mutual funds, limited partnerships, and real estate investment trusts. The owner of _____ in the corporation/company is a shareholder of the corporation. A share is an indivisible unit of capital, expressing the ownership relationship between the company and the shareholder. The denominated value of a share is its face value, and the total of the face value of issued _____ represent the capital of a company, which may not reflect the market value of those _____.

Exam Probability: **High**

7. *Answer choices:*

(see index for correct answer)

- a. Shares
- b. interpersonal communication
- c. cultural
- d. levels of analysis

Guidance: level 1

:: ::

Distribution is one of the four elements of the marketing mix. Distribution is the process of making a product or service available for the consumer or business user who needs it. This can be done directly by the producer or service provider, or using indirect channels with distributors or intermediaries. The other three elements of the marketing mix are product, pricing, and promotion.

Exam Probability: **Medium**

8. *Answer choices:*

(see index for correct answer)

- a. hierarchical
- b. hierarchical perspective
- c. Distribution channel
- d. deep-level diversity

Guidance: level 1

:: Industry ::

_____ describes various measures of the efficiency of production. Often, a _____ measure is expressed as the ratio of an aggregate output to a single input or an aggregate input used in a production process, i.e. output per unit of input. Most common example is the labour _____ measure, e.g., such as GDP per worker. There are many different definitions of _____ and the choice among them depends on the purpose of the _____ measurement and/or data availability. The key source of difference between various _____ measures is also usually related to how the outputs and the inputs are aggregated into scalars to obtain such a ratio-type measure of _____ .

Exam Probability: **Medium**

9. *Answer choices:*

(see index for correct answer)

- a. Tube and clamp scaffold
- b. Productivity
- c. Industrialisation
- d. International Standard Industrial Classification

Guidance: level 1

:: Market research ::

_____, an acronym for Information through Disguised Experimentation is an annual market research fair conducted by the students of IIM-Lucknow. Students create games and use various other simulated environments to capture consumers' subconscious thoughts. This innovative method of market research removes the sensitization effect that might bias peoples answers to questions. This ensures that the most truthful answers are captured to research questions. The games are designed in such a way that the observers can elicit all the required information just by observing and noting down the behaviour and the responses of the participants.

Exam Probability: **Low**

10. *Answer choices:*

(see index for correct answer)

- a. Computer-assisted personal interviewing
- b. Sectoral analysis
- c. Marketing Fair
- d. Incite

Guidance: level 1

:: Retailing ::

A _____ is a self-service shop offering a wide variety of food, beverages and household products, organized into sections and shelves. It is larger and has a wider selection than earlier grocery stores, but is smaller and more limited in the range of merchandise than a hypermarket or big-box market.

Exam Probability: **Low**

11. *Answer choices:*

(see index for correct answer)

- a. Retail Systems Research
- b. Supermarket
- c. Chocolaterie
- d. Warehouse store

Guidance: level 1

:: Marketing techniques ::

_____ is the activity of dividing a broad consumer or business market, normally consisting of existing and potential customers, into sub-groups of consumers based on some type of shared characteristics. In dividing or segmenting markets, researchers typically look for common characteristics such as shared needs, common interests, similar lifestyles or even similar demographic profiles. The overall aim of segmentation is to identify high yield segments – that is, those segments that are likely to be the most profitable or that have growth potential – so that these can be selected for special attention.

Exam Probability: **High**

12. *Answer choices:*

(see index for correct answer)

- a. SONCAS
- b. REAN
- c. Product displacement
- d. Market segmentation

Guidance: level 1

:: ::

A _____ is an organization, usually a group of people or a company, authorized to act as a single entity and recognized as such in law. Early incorporated entities were established by charter. Most jurisdictions now allow the creation of new _____ s through registration.

Exam Probability: **Medium**

13. *Answer choices:*

(see index for correct answer)

- a. similarity-attraction theory
- b. Corporation
- c. interpersonal communication
- d. surface-level diversity

Guidance: level 1

:: ::

_____ Motor Company is an American multinational automaker that has its main headquarter in Dearborn, Michigan, a suburb of Detroit. It was founded by Henry _____ and incorporated on June 16, 1903. The company sells automobiles and commercial vehicles under the _____ brand and most luxury cars under the Lincoln brand. _____ also owns Brazilian SUV manufacturer Troller, an 8% stake in Aston Martin of the United Kingdom and a 32% stake in Jiangling Motors. It also has joint-ventures in China , Taiwan , Thailand , Turkey , and Russia . The company is listed on the New York Stock Exchange and is controlled by the _____ family; they have minority ownership but the majority of the voting power.

Exam Probability: **Medium**

14. *Answer choices:*

(see index for correct answer)

- a. Ford
- b. hierarchical perspective
- c. corporate values
- d. open system

Guidance: level 1

:: Summary statistics ::

_____ is the number of occurrences of a repeating event per unit of time. It is also referred to as temporal _____, which emphasizes the contrast to spatial _____ and angular _____. The period is the duration of time of one cycle in a repeating event, so the period is the reciprocal of the _____. For example: if a newborn baby's heart beats at a _____ of 120 times a minute, its period—the time interval between beats—is half a second. _____ is an important parameter used in science and engineering to specify the rate of oscillatory and vibratory phenomena, such as mechanical vibrations, audio signals, radio waves, and light.

Exam Probability: **Low**

15. *Answer choices:*

(see index for correct answer)

- a. Quartile
- b. Location parameter
- c. Five-number summary
- d. Frequency

Guidance: level 1

:: Advertising ::

A _____ is a document used by creative professionals and agencies to develop creative deliverables: visual design, copy, advertising, web sites, etc. The document is usually developed by the requestor and approved by the creative team of designers, writers, and project managers. In some cases, the project's _____ may need creative director approval before work will commence.

Exam Probability: **Medium**

16. *Answer choices:*

(see index for correct answer)

- a. Ad serving
- b. Creative brief
- c. Privilege sign
- d. Sponsor

Guidance: level 1

:: Product management ::

A _____, trade mark, or trade-mark is a recognizable sign, design, or expression which identifies products or services of a particular source from those of others, although _____ s used to identify services are usually called service marks. The _____ owner can be an individual, business organization, or any legal entity. A _____ may be located on a package, a label, a voucher, or on the product itself. For the sake of corporate identity, _____ s are often displayed on company buildings. It is legally recognized as a type of intellectual property.

Exam Probability: **Low**

17. *Answer choices:*

(see index for correct answer)

- a. Service product management
- b. Product information
- c. Whole product
- d. Trademark

Guidance: level 1

:: Management ::

A _____ is a promise of value to be delivered, communicated, and acknowledged. It is also a belief from the customer about how value will be delivered, experienced and acquired.

Exam Probability: **High**

18. *Answer choices:*

(see index for correct answer)

- a. Business relationship management
- b. Voice of the customer
- c. Business plan
- d. Tata Management Training Centre

Guidance: level 1

:: Marketing ::

_____s are structured marketing strategies designed by merchants to encourage customers to continue to shop at or use the services of businesses associated with each program. These programs exist covering most types of commerce, each one having varying features and rewards-schemes.

Exam Probability: **High**

19. *Answer choices:*

(see index for correct answer)

- a. Premium pricing
- b. Customer franchise
- c. Loyalty program
- d. Price skimming

Guidance: level 1

:: Packaging ::

In work place, _____ or job _____ means good ranking with the hypothesized conception of requirements of a role. There are two types of job _____ s: contextual and task. Task _____ is related to cognitive ability while contextual _____ is dependent upon personality. Task _____ are behavioral roles that are recognized in job descriptions and by remuneration systems, they are directly related to organizational _____, whereas, contextual _____ are value based and additional behavioral roles that are not recognized in job descriptions and covered by compensation; they are extra roles that are indirectly related to organizational _____. Citizenship _____ like contextual _____ means a set of individual activity/contribution that supports the organizational culture.

Exam Probability: **High**

20. *Answer choices:*

(see index for correct answer)

- a. Thermal bag
- b. Wrap rage
- c. Performance
- d. Skin pack

Guidance: level 1

:: Business models ::

A _____, _____ company or daughter company is a company that is owned or controlled by another company, which is called the parent company, parent, or holding company. The _____ can be a company, corporation, or limited liability company. In some cases it is a government or state-owned enterprise. In some cases, particularly in the music and book publishing industries, subsidiaries are referred to as imprints.

Exam Probability: **Medium**

21. *Answer choices:*

(see index for correct answer)

- a. Subsidiary
- b. Lawyers on Demand
- c. Revenue model
- d. Blended value

Guidance: level 1

:: ::

An _____, often referred to as a creative agency or an ad agency, is a business dedicated to creating, planning, and handling advertising and sometimes other forms of promotion and marketing for its clients. An ad agency is generally independent from the client; it may be an internal department or agency that provides an outside point of view to the effort of selling the client's products or services, or an outside firm. An agency can also handle overall marketing and branding strategies promotions for its clients, which may include sales as well.

Exam Probability: **Low**

22. *Answer choices:*

(see index for correct answer)

- a. hierarchical perspective
- b. open system
- c. Advertising agency
- d. personal values

Guidance: level 1

:: Marketing ::

_____ is multi-channel online marketing technique focused at reaching a specific audience on their smartphones, tablets, or any other related devices through websites, E-mail, SMS and MMS, social media, or mobile applications. _____ can provide customers with time and location sensitive, personalized information that promotes goods, services and ideas. In a more theoretical manner, academic Andreas Kaplan defines _____ as "any marketing activity conducted through a ubiquitous network to which consumers are constantly connected using a personal mobile device".

Exam Probability: **Medium**

23. *Answer choices:*

(see index for correct answer)

- a. Democratized transactional giving
- b. Mobile marketing
- c. Processing fluency theory of aesthetic pleasure
- d. Jobbing house

Guidance: level 1

:: Health promotion ::

_____ is a form of advertising, it has been a large industry for some time now. Originally with newspapers and billboards, but now we have advanced to huge LCD screens and online advertisement on social medias and websites. The most common use of _____ in today's society is through social media.. It has the primary goal of achieving "social good". Traditional commercial marketing aims are primarily financial, though they can have positive social affects as well. In the context of public health, _____ would promote general health, raise awareness and induce changes in behaviour. To see _____ as only the use of standard commercial marketing practices to achieve non-commercial goals is an oversimplified view.

Exam Probability: **Low**

24. *Answer choices:*

(see index for correct answer)

- a. Care Continuum Alliance
- b. Health promotion
- c. Eberhard Wenzel
- d. Health impact assessment

Guidance: level 1

:: Internet privacy ::

An _____ is a private network accessible only to an organization's staff. Often, a wide range of information and services are available on an organization's internal _____ that are unavailable to the public, unlike the Internet. A company-wide _____ can constitute an important focal point of internal communication and collaboration, and provide a single starting point to access internal and external resources. In its simplest form, an _____ is established with the technologies for local area networks and wide area networks . Many modern _____ s have search engines, user profiles, blogs, mobile apps with notifications, and events planning within their infrastructure.

Exam Probability: **Medium**

25. *Answer choices:*

(see index for correct answer)

- a. Internet censorship circumvention
- b. Split tunneling
- c. Intranet
- d. Cypherpunk

Guidance: level 1

:: Contract law ::

In contract law, a _____ is a promise which is not a condition of the contract or an innominate term: it is a term "not going to the root of the contract", and which only entitles the innocent party to damages if it is breached: i.e. the _____ is not true or the defaulting party does not perform the contract in accordance with the terms of the _____ . A _____ is not guarantee. It is a mere promise. It may be enforced if it is breached by an award for the legal remedy of damages.

Exam Probability: **Low**

26. *Answer choices:*

(see index for correct answer)

- a. Pre-existing duty rule
- b. Flexible contracts
- c. Warranty
- d. Unconscionability

Guidance: level 1

:: Auctioneering ::

An _____ is a process of buying and selling goods or services by offering them up for bid, taking bids, and then selling the item to the highest bidder. The open ascending price _____ is arguably the most common form of _____ in use today. Participants bid openly against one another, with each subsequent bid required to be higher than the previous bid. An _____ eer may announce prices, bidders may call out their bids themselves, or bids may be submitted electronically with the highest current bid publicly displayed. In a Dutch _____, the _____ eer begins with a high asking price for some quantity of like items; the price is lowered until a participant is willing to accept the _____ eer's price for some quantity of the goods in the lot or until the seller's reserve price is met. While _____ s are most associated in the public imagination with the sale of antiques, paintings, rare collectibles and expensive wines, _____ s are also used for commodities, livestock, radio spectrum and used cars. In economic theory, an _____ may refer to any mechanism or set of trading rules for exchange.

Exam Probability: **Medium**

27. *Answer choices:*

(see index for correct answer)

- a. Public auction
- b. How Much Wood Would a Woodchuck Chuck
- c. Call for bids
- d. Auctionata

Guidance: level 1

:: Monopoly (economics) ::

A _____ exists when a specific person or enterprise is the only supplier of a particular commodity. This contrasts with a monopsony which relates to a single entity's control of a market to purchase a good or service, and with oligopoly which consists of a few sellers dominating a market. Monopolies are thus characterized by a lack of economic competition to produce the good or service, a lack of viable substitute goods, and the possibility of a high _____ price well above the seller's marginal cost that leads to a high _____ profit. The verb monopolise or monopolize refers to the process by which a company gains the ability to raise prices or exclude competitors. In economics, a _____ is a single seller. In law, a _____ is a business entity that has significant market power, that is, the power to charge overly high prices. Although monopolies may be big businesses, size is not a characteristic of a _____. A small business may still have the power to raise prices in a small industry.

Exam Probability: **High**

28. *Answer choices:*

(see index for correct answer)

- a. Herfindahl index
- b. Network effect
- c. Wartime Law on Industrial Property
- d. Monopoly

Guidance: level 1

:: Sales ::

_____ is a business discipline which is focused on the practical application of sales techniques and the management of a firm's sales operations. It is an important business function as net sales through the sale of products and services and resulting profit drive most commercial business. These are also typically the goals and performance indicators of _____.

Exam Probability: **Low**

29. *Answer choices:*

(see index for correct answer)

- a. Worshipful Company of Loriners
- b. Sales management
- c. Hit rate
- d. Contract of sale

Guidance: level 1

:: Costs ::

In economics, _____ is the total economic cost of production and is made up of variable cost, which varies according to the quantity of a good produced and includes inputs such as labour and raw materials, plus fixed cost, which is independent of the quantity of a good produced and includes inputs that cannot be varied in the short term: fixed costs such as buildings and machinery, including sunk costs if any. Since cost is measured per unit of time, it is a flow variable.

Exam Probability: **Low**

30. *Answer choices:*

(see index for correct answer)

- a. Average cost
- b. Cost per paper
- c. Flyaway cost
- d. Opportunity cost of capital

Guidance: level 1

:: Direct selling ::

_____ consists of two main business models: single-level marketing, in which a direct seller makes money by buying products from a parent organization and selling them directly to customers, and multi-level marketing, in which the direct seller may earn money from both direct sales to customers and by sponsoring new direct sellers and potentially earning a commission from their efforts.

Exam Probability: **High**

31. *Answer choices:*

(see index for correct answer)

- a. Direct Selling Association
- b. CVSL

- c. Direct Selling News
- d. Direct selling

Guidance: level 1

:: Business law ::

A _____ is an arrangement where parties, known as partners, agree to cooperate to advance their mutual interests. The partners in a _____ may be individuals, businesses, interest-based organizations, schools, governments or combinations. Organizations may partner to increase the likelihood of each achieving their mission and to amplify their reach. A _____ may result in issuing and holding equity or may be only governed by a contract.

Exam Probability: **Low**

32. *Answer choices:*

(see index for correct answer)

- a. Enhanced use lease
- b. Partnership
- c. Unfair competition
- d. Statutory authority

Guidance: level 1

:: Direct marketing ::

_____ is a form of advertising where organizations communicate directly to customers through a variety of media including cell phone text messaging, email, websites, online adverts, database marketing, fliers, catalog distribution, promotional letters, targeted television, newspapers, magazine advertisements, and outdoor advertising. Among practitioners, it is also known as direct response marketing.

Exam Probability: **Medium**

33. *Answer choices:*

(see index for correct answer)

- a. Direct marketing
- b. Scentura
- c. Solo Ads
- d. Tupperware Brands

Guidance: level 1

:: Marketing ::

_____ uses different marketing channels and tools in combination: Marketing communication channels focus on any way a business communicates a message to its desired market, or the market in general. A marketing communication tool can be anything from: advertising, personal selling, direct marketing, sponsorship, communication, and promotion to public relations.

Exam Probability: **Low**

34. *Answer choices:*

(see index for correct answer)

- a. Marketing communications
- b. Customer value proposition
- c. Product churning
- d. Online lead generation

Guidance: level 1

:: Income ::

_____ is a ratio between the net profit and cost of investment resulting from an investment of some resources. A high ROI means the investment's gains favorably to its cost. As a performance measure, ROI is used to evaluate the efficiency of an investment or to compare the efficiencies of several different investments. In purely economic terms, it is one way of relating profits to capital invested. _____ is a performance measure used by businesses to identify the efficiency of an investment or number of different investments.

Exam Probability: **High**

35. *Answer choices:*

(see index for correct answer)

- a. Return of investment
- b. bottom line

- c. Implied level of government service
- d. Gratuity

Guidance: level 1

:: Graphic design ::

An _____ is an artifact that depicts visual perception, such as a photograph or other two-dimensional picture, that resembles a subject—usually a physical object—and thus provides a depiction of it. In the context of signal processing, an _____ is a distributed amplitude of color.

Exam Probability: **Low**

36. *Answer choices:*

(see index for correct answer)

- a. Mecenato
- b. Communicate knowledge manifesto
- c. Jade Magnet
- d. First Things First 2000 manifesto

Guidance: level 1

:: Business models ::

_____ es are privately owned corporations, partnerships, or sole proprietorships that have fewer employees and/or less annual revenue than a regular-sized business or corporation. Businesses are defined as "small" in terms of being able to apply for government support and qualify for preferential tax policy varies depending on the country and industry. _____ es range from fifteen employees under the Australian Fair Work Act 2009, fifty employees according to the definition used by the European Union, and fewer than five hundred employees to qualify for many U.S. _____ Administration programs. While _____ es can also be classified according to other methods, such as annual revenues, shipments, sales, assets, or by annual gross or net revenue or net profits, the number of employees is one of the most widely used measures.

Exam Probability: **Medium**

37. *Answer choices:*

(see index for correct answer)

- a. Small business
- b. Praenumeration
- c. Data as a service
- d. IASME

Guidance: level 1

:: ::

_____ is the collection of techniques, skills, methods, and processes used in the production of goods or services or in the accomplishment of objectives, such as scientific investigation. _____ can be the knowledge of techniques, processes, and the like, or it can be embedded in machines to allow for operation without detailed knowledge of their workings. Systems applying _____ by taking an input, changing it according to the system's use, and then producing an outcome are referred to as _____ systems or technological systems.

Exam Probability: **High**

38. *Answer choices:*
(see index for correct answer)

- a. surface-level diversity
- b. imperative
- c. personal values
- d. information systems assessment

Guidance: level 1

:: Marketing terminology ::

_____ is used in marketing to describe the inability to assess the value gained from engaging in an activity using any tangible evidence. It is often used to describe services where there is no tangible product that the customer can purchase, that can be seen or touched.

Exam Probability: **Medium**

39. *Answer choices:*

(see index for correct answer)

- a. Intangibility
- b. Low-end market
- c. Aspirational age
- d. Dump months

Guidance: level 1

:: ::

In international relations, _____ is – from the perspective of governments – a voluntary transfer of resources from one country to another.

Exam Probability: **Low**

40. *Answer choices:*

(see index for correct answer)

- a. corporate values
- b. cultural
- c. Aid
- d. similarity-attraction theory

Guidance: level 1

:: ::

The _____ is an agreement signed by Canada, Mexico, and the United States, creating a trilateral trade bloc in North America. The agreement came into force on January 1, 1994, and superseded the 1988 Canada–United States Free Trade Agreement between the United States and Canada. The NAFTA trade bloc is one of the largest trade blocs in the world by gross domestic product.

Exam Probability: **Low**

41. *Answer choices:*

(see index for correct answer)

- a. North American Free Trade Agreement
- b. personal values
- c. surface-level diversity
- d. hierarchical

Guidance: level 1

:: ::

In logic and philosophy, an _____ is a series of statements, called the premises or premisses, intended to determine the degree of truth of another statement, the conclusion. The logical form of an _____ in a natural language can be represented in a symbolic formal language, and independently of natural language formally defined "_____ s" can be made in math and computer science.

Exam Probability: **Low**

42. *Answer choices:*

(see index for correct answer)

- a. Argument
- b. cultural
- c. process perspective
- d. hierarchical

Guidance: level 1

:: Monopoly (economics) ::

_____ is a category of property that includes intangible creations of the human intellect. _____ encompasses two types of rights: industrial property rights and copyright. It was not until the 19th century that the term "_____" began to be used, and not until the late 20th century that it became commonplace in the majority of the world.

Exam Probability: **Medium**

43. *Answer choices:*

(see index for correct answer)

- a. Intellectual property
- b. Special 301 Report
- c. Rate-of-return regulation
- d. Trust

Guidance: level 1

:: Marketing ::

_____, in marketing, manufacturing, call centres and management, is the use of flexible computer-aided manufacturing systems to produce custom output. Such systems combine the low unit costs of mass production processes with the flexibility of individual customization.

Exam Probability: **Low**

44. *Answer choices:*

(see index for correct answer)

- a. Electronic money
- b. Matomy Media
- c. Mass customization
- d. Product proliferation

Guidance: level 1

:: ::

_____ involves decision making. It can include judging the merits of multiple options and selecting one or more of them. One can make a _____ between imagined options or between real options followed by the corresponding action. For example, a traveler might choose a route for a journey based on the preference of arriving at a given destination as soon as possible. The preferred route can then follow from information such as the length of each of the possible routes, traffic conditions, etc. The arrival at a _____ can include more complex motivators such as cognition, instinct, and feeling.

Exam Probability: **Medium**

45. *Answer choices:*
(see index for correct answer)

- a. co-culture
- b. deep-level diversity
- c. hierarchical perspective
- d. imperative

Guidance: level 1

:: ::

_____ is an abstract concept of management of complex systems according to a set of rules and trends. In systems theory, these types of rules exist in various fields of biology and society, but the term has slightly different meanings according to context. For example.

Exam Probability: **Low**

46. *Answer choices:*

(see index for correct answer)

- a. Regulation
- b. similarity-attraction theory
- c. process perspective
- d. deep-level diversity

Guidance: level 1

:: ::

_____ is a process whereby a person assumes the parenting of another, usually a child, from that person's biological or legal parent or parents. Legal _____ s permanently transfers all rights and responsibilities, along with filiation, from the biological parent or parents.

Exam Probability: **Low**

47. *Answer choices:*

(see index for correct answer)

- a. personal values
- b. Adoption
- c. levels of analysis
- d. deep-level diversity

Guidance: level 1

:: Direct marketing ::

_____ is a form of direct marketing using databases of customers or potential customers to generate personalized communications in order to promote a product or service for marketing purposes. The method of communication can be any addressable medium, as in direct marketing.

Exam Probability: **Low**

48. *Answer choices:*

(see index for correct answer)

- a. Database marketing
- b. Scentura
- c. Ed Valenti
- d. Mailshot

Guidance: level 1

:: Market research ::

An _____ or lighthouse customer is an early customer of a given company, product, or technology. The term originates from Everett M. Rogers' Diffusion of Innovations.

Exam Probability: **Medium**

49. *Answer choices:*

(see index for correct answer)

- a. Indian Readership Survey
- b. Early adopter
- c. Advertising Research Foundation
- d. TNS NIPO

Guidance: level 1

:: Social psychology ::

_____s is a qualitative methodology used to describe consumers on psychological attributes. _____s have been applied to the study of personality, values, opinions, attitudes, interests, and lifestyles. While _____s are often equated with lifestyle research, it has been argued that _____s should apply to the study of cognitive attributes such as attitudes, interests, opinions, and beliefs while lifestyle should apply to the study of overt behavior. Because this area of research focuses on activities, interests, and opinions, _____ factors are sometimes abbreviated to 'AIO variables'.

Exam Probability: **Medium**

50. *Answer choices:*

(see index for correct answer)

- a. Mind control
- b. Psychographic
- c. thought control
- d. post-feminism

Guidance: level 1

:: Production and manufacturing ::

_____ consists of organization-wide efforts to "install and make permanent climate where employees continuously improve their ability to provide on demand products and services that customers will find of particular value." "Total" emphasizes that departments in addition to production are obligated to improve their operations; "management" emphasizes that executives are obligated to actively manage quality through funding, training, staffing, and goal setting. While there is no widely agreed-upon approach, TQM efforts typically draw heavily on the previously developed tools and techniques of quality control. TQM enjoyed widespread attention during the late 1980s and early 1990s before being overshadowed by ISO 9000, Lean manufacturing, and Six Sigma.

Exam Probability: **High**

51. *Answer choices:*

(see index for correct answer)

- a. Resource Breakdown
- b. Total Quality Management
- c. Earned value
- d. Job shop

Guidance: level 1

:: Marketing ::

_____ is a marketing practice of individuals or organizations . It allows them to sell products or services to other companies or organizations that resell them, use them in their products or services or use them to support their works.

Exam Probability: **Medium**

52. *Answer choices:*

(see index for correct answer)

- a. Discounts and allowances
- b. Positioning
- c. Price skimming
- d. Place branding

Guidance: level 1

:: ::

_____ or commercialisation is the process of introducing a new product or production method into commerce—making it available on the market. The term often connotes especially entry into the mass market , but it also includes a move from the laboratory into commerce. Many technologies begin in a research and development laboratory or in an inventor`s workshop and may not be practical for commercial use in their infancy . The "development" segment of the "research and development" spectrum requires time and money as systems are engineered with a view to making the product or method a paying commercial proposition. The product launch of a new product is the final stage of new product development - at this point advertising, sales promotion, and other marketing efforts encourage commercial adoption of the product or method. Beyond _____ can lie consumerization .

Exam Probability: **Low**

53. Answer choices:

(see index for correct answer)

- a. hierarchical perspective
- b. information systems assessment
- c. cultural
- d. Commercialization

Guidance: level 1

:: ::

In production, research, retail, and accounting, a _____ is the value of money that has been used up to produce something or deliver a service, and hence is not available for use anymore. In business, the _____ may be one of acquisition, in which case the amount of money expended to acquire it is counted as _____ . In this case, money is the input that is gone in order to acquire the thing. This acquisition _____ may be the sum of the _____ of production as incurred by the original producer, and further _____ s of transaction as incurred by the acquirer over and above the price paid to the producer. Usually, the price also includes a mark-up for profit over the _____ of production.

Exam Probability: **Medium**

54. Answer choices:

(see index for correct answer)

- a. Cost

- b. deep-level diversity
- c. information systems assessment
- d. interpersonal communication

Guidance: level 1

:: ::

A _____ is any person who contracts to acquire an asset in return for some form of consideration.

Exam Probability: **Medium**

55. *Answer choices:*

(see index for correct answer)

- a. Buyer
- b. information systems assessment
- c. similarity-attraction theory
- d. process perspective

Guidance: level 1

:: Information technology management ::

B2B is often contrasted with business-to-consumer. In B2B commerce, it is often the case that the parties to the relationship have comparable negotiating power, and even when they do not, each party typically involves professional staff and legal counsel in the negotiation of terms, whereas B2C is shaped to a far greater degree by economic implications of information asymmetry. However, within a B2B context, large companies may have many commercial, resource and information advantages over smaller businesses. The United Kingdom government, for example, created the post of Small Business Commissioner under the Enterprise Act 2016 to "enable small businesses to resolve disputes" and "consider complaints by small business suppliers about payment issues with larger businesses that they supply."

Exam Probability: **High**

56. *Answer choices:*

(see index for correct answer)

- a. Operational-level agreement
- b. Business-to-business
- c. ISO/IEC 27000-series
- d. National Biological Information Infrastructure

Guidance: level 1

:: Marketing ::

A _____ is an overall experience of a customer that distinguishes an organization or product from its rivals in the eyes of the customer. _____ s are used in business, marketing, and advertising. Name _____ s are sometimes distinguished from generic or store _____ s.

Exam Probability: **Medium**

57. *Answer choices:*

(see index for correct answer)

- a. HyTrust
- b. Movement marketing
- c. Market share
- d. Market environment

Guidance: level 1

:: ::

In regulatory jurisdictions that provide for it , _____ is a group of laws and organizations designed to ensure the rights of consumers as well as fair trade, competition and accurate information in the marketplace. The laws are designed to prevent the businesses that engage in fraud or specified unfair practices from gaining an advantage over competitors. They may also provides additional protection for those most vulnerable in society. _____ laws are a form of government regulation that aim to protect the rights of consumers. For example, a government may require businesses to disclose detailed information about products—particularly in areas where safety or public health is an issue, such as food.

Exam Probability: **Low**

58. *Answer choices:*

(see index for correct answer)

- a. Character
- b. process perspective
- c. hierarchical perspective
- d. Consumer Protection

Guidance: level 1

:: Promotion and marketing communications ::

> _____ is one of the elements of the promotional mix. . _____ uses both media and non-media marketing communications for a pre-determined, limited time to increase consumer demand, stimulate market demand or improve product availability. Examples include contests, coupons, freebies, loss leaders, point of purchase displays, premiums, prizes, product samples, and rebates.

Exam Probability: **Medium**

59. *Answer choices:*

(see index for correct answer)

- a. Dumb Ways to Die
- b. Reach

- c. Slasher Sale
- d. Youth marketing

Guidance: level 1

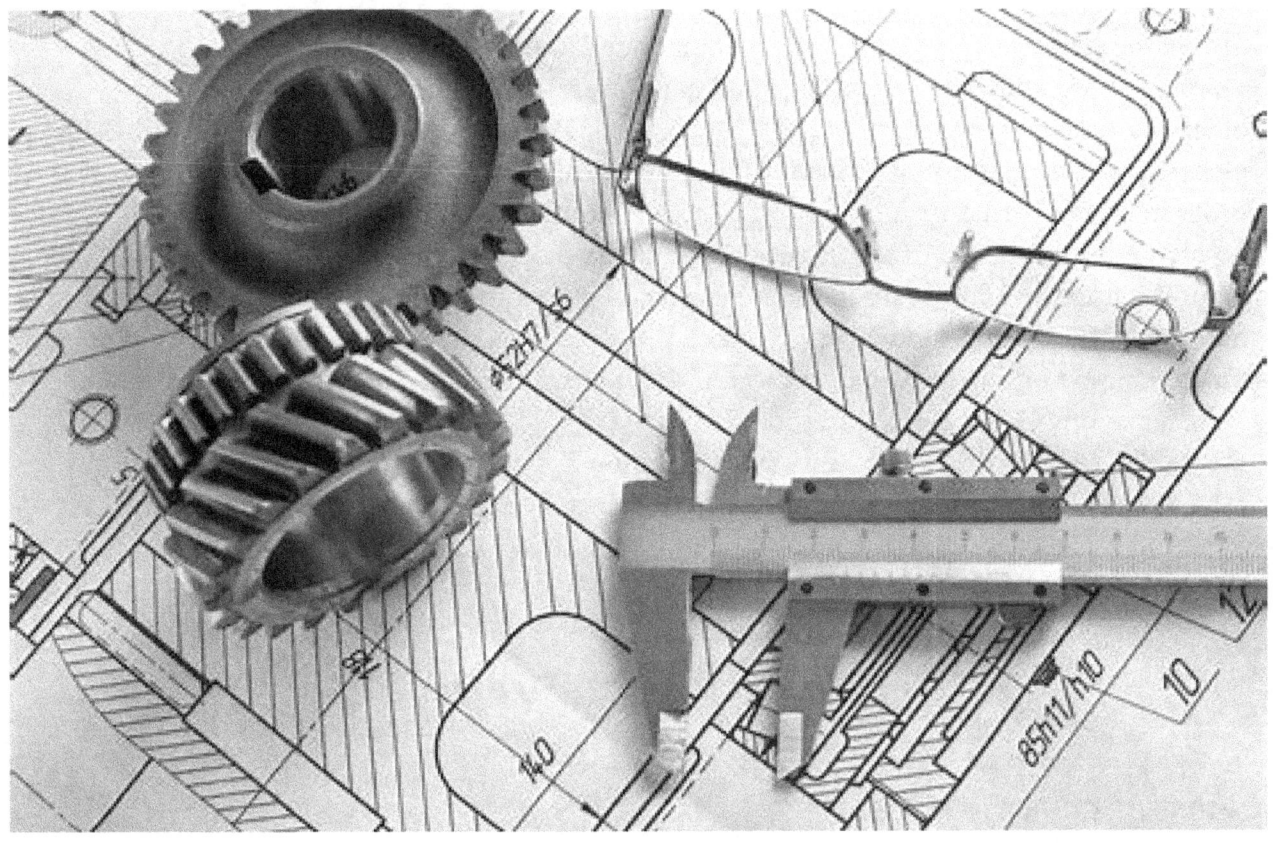

Manufacturing

Manufacturing is the production of merchandise for use or sale using labor and machines, tools, chemical and biological processing, or formulation. The term may refer to a range of human activity, from handicraft to high tech, but is most commonly applied to industrial design , in which raw materials are transformed into finished goods on a large scale. Such finished goods may be sold to other manufacturers for the production of other, more complex products, such as aircraft, household appliances, furniture, sports equipment or automobiles, or sold to wholesalers, who in turn sell them to retailers, who then sell them to end users and consumers.

:: Elementary mathematics ::

In mathematics, a _____ is an enumerated collection of objects in which repetitions are allowed. Like a set, it contains members. The number of elements is called the length of the _____ . Unlike a set, the same elements can appear multiple times at different positions in a _____ , and order matters. Formally, a _____ can be defined as a function whose domain is either the set of the natural numbers or the set of the first n natural numbers. The position of an element in a _____ is its rank or index; it is the natural number from which the element is the image. It depends on the context or a specific convention, if the first element has index 0 or 1. When a symbol has been chosen for denoting a _____ , the nth element of the _____ is denoted by this symbol with n as subscript; for example, the nth element of the Fibonacci _____ is generally denoted Fn.

Exam Probability: **Medium**

1. *Answer choices:*

(see index for correct answer)

- a. Sequence
- b. Periodic function
- c. Elementary mathematics
- d. Function

Guidance: level 1

:: Goods ::

In most contexts, the concept of _____ denotes the conduct that should be preferred when posed with a choice between possible actions. _____ is generally considered to be the opposite of evil, and is of interest in the study of morality, ethics, religion and philosophy. The specific meaning and etymology of the term and its associated translations among ancient and contemporary languages show substantial variation in its inflection and meaning depending on circumstances of place, history, religious, or philosophical context.

Exam Probability: **Medium**

2. *Answer choices:*

(see index for correct answer)

- a. Neutral good
- b. Inferior good
- c. Public good
- d. Speciality goods

Guidance: level 1

:: Information technology management ::

_____ concerns a cycle of organizational activity: the acquisition of information from one or more sources, the custodianship and the distribution of that information to those who need it, and its ultimate disposition through archiving or deletion.

Exam Probability: **High**

3. *Answer choices:*

(see index for correct answer)

- a. Incident management
- b. Runbook
- c. ISO/IEC 27000-series
- d. Enterprise information management

Guidance: level 1

:: Marketing techniques ::

A _____ is an award to be given to a person, a group of people like a sports team, or organization to recognise and reward actions or achievements. Official _____ s often involve monetary rewards as well as the fame that comes with them. Some _____ s are also associated with extravagant awarding ceremonies, such as the Academy Awards.

Exam Probability: **High**

4. *Answer choices:*

(see index for correct answer)

- a. Prize
- b. Product displacement

- c. Stunt casting
- d. Geodemographic segmentation

Guidance: level 1

:: Materials ::

A _____, also known as a feedstock, unprocessed material, or primary commodity, is a basic material that is used to produce goods, finished products, energy, or intermediate materials which are feedstock for future finished products. As feedstock, the term connotes these materials are bottleneck assets and are highly important with regard to producing other products. An example of this is crude oil, which is a _____ and a feedstock used in the production of industrial chemicals, fuels, plastics, and pharmaceutical goods; lumber is a _____ used to produce a variety of products including all types of furniture. The term "_____" denotes materials in minimally processed or unprocessed in states; e.g., raw latex, crude oil, cotton, coal, raw biomass, iron ore, air, logs, or water i.e. "...any product of agriculture, forestry, fishing and any other mineral that is in its natural form or which has undergone the transformation required to prepare it for internationally marketing in substantial volumes."

Exam Probability: **Low**

5. *Answer choices:*

(see index for correct answer)

- a. Latex
- b. Glass microsphere
- c. Raw material

- d. Agamassan

Guidance: level 1

:: Procurement ::

Purchasing is the formal process of buying goods and services. The _____ can vary from one organization to another, but there are some common key elements.

Exam Probability: **High**

6. *Answer choices:*

(see index for correct answer)

- a. Building Schools for the Future
- b. Purchasing process
- c. Procurement outsourcing
- d. Proposal theme statement

Guidance: level 1

:: Metal forming ::

_____ is a type of motion that combines rotation and translation of that object with respect to a surface, such that, if ideal conditions exist, the two are in contact with each other without sliding.

Exam Probability: **Low**

7. *Answer choices:*

(see index for correct answer)

- a. Impact extrusion
- b. Pancake die
- c. Rolling
- d. Goldbeating

Guidance: level 1

:: Project management ::

A _____ is the approximation of the cost of a program, project, or operation. The _____ is the product of the cost estimating process. The _____ has a single total value and may have identifiable component values. A problem with a cost overrun can be avoided with a credible, reliable, and accurate _____. A cost estimator is the professional who prepares _____ s. There are different types of cost estimators, whose title may be preceded by a modifier, such as building estimator, or electrical estimator, or chief estimator. Other professionals such as quantity surveyors and cost engineers may also prepare _____ s or contribute to _____ s. In the US, according to the Bureau of Labor Statistics, there were 185,400 cost estimators in 2010. There are around 75,000 professional quantity surveyors working in the UK.

Exam Probability: **Medium**

8. *Answer choices:*

(see index for correct answer)

- a. Pre-mortem
- b. Bottleneck
- c. Work package
- d. Project sponsorship

Guidance: level 1

:: ::

_____ is the production of products for use or sale using labour and machines, tools, chemical and biological processing, or formulation. The term may refer to a range of human activity, from handicraft to high tech, but is most commonly applied to industrial design, in which raw materials are transformed into finished goods on a large scale. Such finished goods may be sold to other manufacturers for the production of other, more complex products, such as aircraft, household appliances, furniture, sports equipment or automobiles, or sold to wholesalers, who in turn sell them to retailers, who then sell them to end users and consumers.

Exam Probability: **Medium**

9. *Answer choices:*

(see index for correct answer)

- a. Manufacturing
- b. open system
- c. process perspective
- d. Character

Guidance: level 1

:: Asset ::

In financial accounting, an _____ is any resource owned by the business. Anything tangible or intangible that can be owned or controlled to produce value and that is held by a company to produce positive economic value is an _____. Simply stated, _____ s represent value of ownership that can be converted into cash. The balance sheet of a firm records the monetary value of the _____ s owned by that firm. It covers money and other valuables belonging to an individual or to a business.

Exam Probability: **Low**

10. *Answer choices:*

(see index for correct answer)

- a. Fixed asset
- b. Current asset

Guidance: level 1

:: ::

A _____ or till is a mechanical or electronic device for registering and calculating transactions at a point of sale. It is usually attached to a drawer for storing cash and other valuables. A modern _____ is usually attached to a printer that can print out receipts for record-keeping purposes.

Exam Probability: **Medium**

11. *Answer choices:*

(see index for correct answer)

- a. levels of analysis
- b. Sarbanes-Oxley act of 2002
- c. cultural
- d. Cash register

Guidance: level 1

:: Distribution, retailing, and wholesaling ::

The _____ is a distribution channel phenomenon in which forecasts yield supply chain inefficiencies. It refers to increasing swings in inventory in response to shifts in customer demand as one moves further up the supply chain. The concept first appeared in Jay Forrester's Industrial Dynamics and thus it is also known as the Forrester effect. The _____ was named for the way the amplitude of a whip increases down its length. The further from the originating signal, the greater the distortion of the wave pattern. In a similar manner, forecast accuracy decreases as one moves upstream along the supply chain. For example, many consumer goods have fairly consistent consumption at retail but this signal becomes more chaotic and unpredictable as the focus moves away from consumer purchasing behavior.

Exam Probability: **High**

12. *Answer choices:*

(see index for correct answer)

- a. Pallet racking

- b. Bullwhip effect
- c. Stock management
- d. Cash and carry

Guidance: level 1

:: Management ::

_____ is a category of business activity made possible by software tools that aim to provide customers with both independence from vendors and better means for engaging with vendors. These same tools can also apply to individuals' relations with other institutions and organizations.

Exam Probability: **Medium**

13. *Answer choices:*
(see index for correct answer)

- a. Business rule
- b. Participative decision-making
- c. Business workflow analysis
- d. Vendor relationship management

Guidance: level 1

:: Project management ::

In economics and business decision-making, a sunk cost is a cost that has already been incurred and cannot be recovered.

Exam Probability: **Medium**

14. *Answer choices:*

(see index for correct answer)

- a. Sunk costs
- b. Critical path drag
- c. Pmhub
- d. Time to completion

Guidance: level 1

:: Fault-tolerant computer systems ::

_____ decision-making is a group decision-making process in which group members develop, and agree to support a decision in the best interest of the whole group or common goal. _____ may be defined professionally as an acceptable resolution, one that can be supported, even if not the "favourite" of each individual. It has its origin in the Latin word consensus, which is from consentio meaning literally feel together. It is used to describe both the decision and the process of reaching a decision. _____ decision-making is thus concerned with the process of deliberating and finalizing a decision, and the social, economic, legal, environmental and political effects of applying this process.

Exam Probability: **Low**

15. *Answer choices:*

(see index for correct answer)

- a. Raft
- b. Paxos
- c. Consensus
- d. Uptime

Guidance: level 1

:: Costs ::

In microeconomic theory, the _____ , or alternative cost, of making a particular choice is the value of the most valuable choice out of those that were not taken. In other words, opportunity that will require sacrifices.

Exam Probability: **Low**

16. *Answer choices:*

(see index for correct answer)

- a. Economic cost
- b. Cost of products sold
- c. Travel and subsistence
- d. Incremental cost-effectiveness ratio

Guidance: level 1

:: Commerce ::

A _____ is an employee within a company, business or other organization who is responsible at some level for buying or approving the acquisition of goods and services needed by the company. Responsible for buying the best quality products, goods and services for their company at the most competitive prices. _____ s work in a wide range of sectors for many different organizations. The position responsibilities may be the same as that of a buyer or purchasing agent, or may include wider supervisory or managerial responsibilities. A _____ may oversee the acquisition of materials needed for production, general supplies for offices and facilities, equipment, or construction contracts. A _____ often supervises purchasing agents and buyers, but in small companies the _____ may also be the purchasing agent or buyer. The _____ position may also carry the title "Procurement Manager" or in the public sector, "Procurement Officer". He or she can come from both an Engineering or Economics background.

Exam Probability: **High**

17. *Answer choices:*

(see index for correct answer)

- a. Return merchandise authorization
- b. Deal transaction
- c. Purchasing manager
- d. Third-party source

Guidance: level 1

:: Management ::

_____ is the discipline of strategically planning for, and managing, all interactions with third party organizations that supply goods and/or services to an organization in order to maximize the value of those interactions. In practice, SRM entails creating closer, more collaborative relationships with key suppliers in order to uncover and realize new value and reduce risk of failure.

Exam Probability: **High**

18. *Answer choices:*

(see index for correct answer)

- a. Relevance paradox
- b. Dominant design
- c. Supplier relationship management
- d. Discovery-driven planning

Guidance: level 1

:: Outsourcing ::

_____ is the practice of sourcing from the global market for goods and services across geopolitical boundaries. _____ often aims to exploit global efficiencies in the delivery of a product or service. These efficiencies include low cost skilled labor, low cost raw material and other economic factors like tax breaks and low trade tariffs. A large number of Information Technology projects and Services, including IS Applications and Mobile Apps and database services are outsourced globally to countries like Pakistan and India for more economical pricing.

Exam Probability: **Medium**

19. *Answer choices:*

(see index for correct answer)

- a. Global sourcing
- b. MITIE Group
- c. IQor
- d. Strategic sourcing

Guidance: level 1

:: Data management ::

_____ is an object-oriented program and library developed by CERN. It was originally designed for particle physics data analysis and contains several features specific to this field, but it is also used in other applications such as astronomy and data mining. The latest release is 6.16.00, as of 2018-11-14.

Exam Probability: **High**

20. *Answer choices:*

(see index for correct answer)

- a. Semantic warehousing
- b. Database engine
- c. ROOT
- d. SIGMOD Edgar F. Codd Innovations Award

Guidance: level 1

:: Promotion and marketing communications ::

The _____ of American Manufacturers, now ThomasNet, is an online platform for supplier discovery and product sourcing in the US and Canada. It was once known as the "big green books" and "Thomas Registry", and was a multi-volume directory of industrial product information covering 650,000 distributors, manufacturers and service companies within 67,000-plus industrial categories that is now published on ThomasNet.

Exam Probability: **Medium**

21. *Answer choices:*

(see index for correct answer)

- a. Press kit
- b. Thomas Register

- c. ACNielsen
- d. Promotional merchandise

Guidance: level 1

:: Marketing ::

_____ or stock is the goods and materials that a business holds for the ultimate goal of resale .

Exam Probability: **High**

22. *Answer choices:*
(see index for correct answer)

- a. Inventory
- b. Jobbing house
- c. Electronic money
- d. Albuquerque Craft Beer Market

Guidance: level 1

:: Distribution, retailing, and wholesaling ::

_____ measures the performance of a system. Certain goals are defined and the _____ gives the percentage to which those goals should be achieved. Fill rate is different from _____ .

Exam Probability: **Low**

23. *Answer choices:*

(see index for correct answer)

- a. Free box
- b. Service level
- c. Slab-O-Concrete
- d. Adjustable shelving

Guidance: level 1

:: Gas technologies ::

A _____ is a device used to transfer heat between two or more fluids. _____ s are used in both cooling and heating processes. The fluids may be separated by a solid wall to prevent mixing or they may be in direct contact. They are widely used in space heating, refrigeration, air conditioning, power stations, chemical plants, petrochemical plants, petroleum refineries, natural-gas processing, and sewage treatment. The classic example of a _____ is found in an internal combustion engine in which a circulating fluid known as engine coolant flows through radiator coils and air flows past the coils, which cools the coolant and heats the incoming air. Another example is the heat sink, which is a passive _____ that transfers the heat generated by an electronic or a mechanical device to a fluid medium, often air or a liquid coolant.

Exam Probability: **Low**

24. *Answer choices:*

(see index for correct answer)

- a. Heat exchanger
- b. Air filter
- c. Liquid ring pump
- d. Oxygen tank

Guidance: level 1

:: Project management ::

_____ s can take many forms depending on the type of project being implemented and the nature of the organization. The _____ details the project deliverables and describes the major objectives. The objectives should include measurable success criteria for the project.

Exam Probability: **High**

25. *Answer choices:*

(see index for correct answer)

- a. Project management office
- b. Scope statement
- c. Value of work done
- d. NetPoint

Guidance: level 1

:: Supply chain management ::

A _____ is a type of auction in which the traditional roles of buyer and seller are reversed. Thus, there is one buyer and many potential sellers. In an ordinary auction, buyers compete to obtain goods or services by offering increasingly higher prices. In contrast, in a _____ , the sellers compete to obtain business from the buyer and prices will typically decrease as the sellers underbid each other.

Exam Probability: **Medium**

26. Answer choices:

(see index for correct answer)

- a. Strategic material
- b. Reverse auction
- c. Capconn
- d. Supply chain management software

Guidance: level 1

:: Evaluation ::

_____ is a way of preventing mistakes and defects in manufactured products and avoiding problems when delivering products or services to customers; which ISO 9000 defines as "part of quality management focused on providing confidence that quality requirements will be fulfilled". This defect prevention in _____ differs subtly from defect detection and rejection in quality control and has been referred to as a shift left since it focuses on quality earlier in the process .

Exam Probability: **Low**

27. Answer choices:

(see index for correct answer)

- a. Quality assurance
- b. Knowledge survey
- c. Formative assessment

- d. XTS-400

Guidance: level 1

:: ::

Some scenarios associate "this kind of planning" with learning "life skills". Schedules are necessary, or at least useful, in situations where individuals need to know what time they must be at a specific location to receive a specific service, and where people need to accomplish a set of goals within a set time period.

Exam Probability: **Medium**

28. *Answer choices:*

(see index for correct answer)

- a. Scheduling
- b. corporate values
- c. Sarbanes-Oxley act of 2002
- d. similarity-attraction theory

Guidance: level 1

:: Project management ::

A _____ is a source or supply from which a benefit is produced and it has some utility. _____ s can broadly be classified upon their availability—they are classified into renewable and non-renewable _____ s. Examples of non renewable _____ s are coal, crude oil natural gas nuclear energy etc. Examples of renewable _____ s are air, water, wind, solar energy etc. They can also be classified as actual and potential on the basis of level of development and use, on the basis of origin they can be classified as biotic and abiotic, and on the basis of their distribution, as ubiquitous and localized. An item becomes a _____ with time and developing technology. Typically, _____ s are materials, energy, services, staff, knowledge, or other assets that are transformed to produce benefit and in the process may be consumed or made unavailable. Benefits of _____ utilization may include increased wealth, proper functioning of a system, or enhanced well-being. From a human perspective a natural _____ is anything obtained from the environment to satisfy human needs and wants. From a broader biological or ecological perspective a _____ satisfies the needs of a living organism.

Exam Probability: **Medium**

29. *Answer choices:*

(see index for correct answer)

- a. Gold plating
- b. Project initiation document
- c. Resource
- d. Pre-mortem

Guidance: level 1

:: Finance ::

_____ is a financial estimate intended to help buyers and owners determine the direct and indirect costs of a product or system. It is a management accounting concept that can be used in full cost accounting or even ecological economics where it includes social costs.

Exam Probability: **High**

30. *Answer choices:*

(see index for correct answer)

- a. Total cost of ownership
- b. Strict foreclosure
- c. Shoe leather cost
- d. Present value of revenues auction

Guidance: level 1

:: Quality ::

_____ is a concept first outlined by quality expert Joseph M. Juran in publications, most notably Juran on _____ . Designing for quality and innovation is one of the three universal processes of the Juran Trilogy, in which Juran describes what is required to achieve breakthroughs in new products, services, and processes. Juran believed that quality could be planned, and that most quality crises and problems relate to the way in which quality was planned.

Exam Probability: **High**

31. *Answer choices:*

(see index for correct answer)

- a. Quality by Design
- b. Dualistic Petri nets
- c. Ringtest
- d. Process architecture

Guidance: level 1

:: Unit operations ::

_____ is the process of separating the components or substances from a liquid mixture by using selective boiling and condensation. _____ may result in essentially complete separation, or it may be a partial separation that increases the concentration of selected components in the mixture. In either case, the process exploits differences in the volatility of the mixture's components. In industrial chemistry, _____ is a unit operation of practically universal importance, but it is a physical separation process, not a chemical reaction.

Exam Probability: **Low**

32. *Answer choices:*

(see index for correct answer)

- a. Separation process
- b. Sedimentation coefficient

- c. Distillation
- d. Settling

Guidance: level 1

:: Industrial engineering ::

The _____ is the design of any task that aims to describe or explain the variation of information under conditions that are hypothesized to reflect the variation. The term is generally associated with experiments in which the design introduces conditions that directly affect the variation, but may also refer to the design of quasi-experiments, in which natural conditions that influence the variation are selected for observation.

Exam Probability: **Low**

33. *Answer choices:*

(see index for correct answer)

- a. Pilot plant
- b. Institute of Industrial Engineers
- c. Richard Muther
- d. Design of experiments

Guidance: level 1

:: Teams ::

A _____ usually refers to a group of individuals who work together from different geographic locations and rely on communication technology such as email, FAX, and video or voice conferencing services in order to collaborate. The term can also refer to groups or teams that work together asynchronously or across organizational levels. Powell, Piccoli and Ives define _____ s as "groups of geographically, organizationally and/or time dispersed workers brought together by information and telecommunication technologies to accomplish one or more organizational tasks." According to Ale Ebrahim et. al., _____ s can also be defined as "small temporary groups of geographically, organizationally and/or time dispersed knowledge workers who coordinate their work predominantly with electronic information and communication technologies in order to accomplish one or more organization tasks."

Exam Probability: **Medium**

34. *Answer choices:*

(see index for correct answer)

- a. Virtual team
- b. Team-building

Guidance: level 1

:: Supply chain management terms ::

In business and finance, _____ is a system of organizations, people, activities, information, and resources involved in moving a product or service from supplier to customer. _____ activities involve the transformation of natural resources, raw materials, and components into a finished product that is delivered to the end customer. In sophisticated _____ systems, used products may re-enter the _____ at any point where residual value is recyclable. _____ s link value chains.

Exam Probability: **Low**

35. *Answer choices:*

(see index for correct answer)

- a. Direct shipment
- b. Supply chain
- c. Stockout
- d. Price look-up code

Guidance: level 1

:: Industrial processes ::

A _____ is a device used for high-temperature heating. The name derives from Latin word fornax, which means oven. The heat energy to fuel a _____ may be supplied directly by fuel combustion, by electricity such as the electric arc _____ , or through induction heating in induction _____ s.

Exam Probability: **Medium**

36. *Answer choices:*

(see index for correct answer)

- a. Calo tester
- b. Betterton-Kroll process
- c. Vapor-compression refrigeration
- d. Furnace

Guidance: level 1

:: Production and manufacturing ::

_____ was a management-led program to eliminate defects in industrial production that enjoyed brief popularity in American industry from 1964 to the early 1970s. Quality expert Philip Crosby later incorporated it into his "Absolutes of Quality Management" and it enjoyed a renaissance in the American automobile industry—as a performance goal more than as a program—in the 1990s. Although applicable to any type of enterprise, it has been primarily adopted within supply chains wherever large volumes of components are being purchased .

Exam Probability: **High**

37. *Answer choices:*

(see index for correct answer)

- a. Performance supervision system

- b. EFQM Excellence Model
- c. PROFIsafe
- d. Zero Defects

Guidance: level 1

:: Management ::

A _____ is an idea of the future or desired result that a person or a group of people envisions, plans and commits to achieve. People endeavor to reach _____ s within a finite time by setting deadlines.

Exam Probability: **High**

38. *Answer choices:*
(see index for correct answer)

- a. Matrix management
- b. Marketing plan
- c. Supply chain optimization
- d. Local management board

Guidance: level 1

:: Gas technologies ::

A _____ is a rotary mechanical device that extracts energy from a fluid flow and converts it into useful work. The work produced by a _____ can be used for generating electrical power when combined with a generator. A _____ is a turbomachine with at least one moving part called a rotor assembly, which is a shaft or drum with blades attached. Moving fluid acts on the blades so that they move and impart rotational energy to the rotor. Early _____ examples are windmills and waterwheels.

Exam Probability: **High**

39. *Answer choices:*

(see index for correct answer)

- a. Odorizer
- b. Loading arm
- c. Turbine
- d. Liquid ring pump

Guidance: level 1

:: Lean manufacturing ::

_____ is the Sino-Japanese word for "improvement". In business, _____ refers to activities that continuously improve all functions and involve all employees from the CEO to the assembly line workers. It also applies to processes, such as purchasing and logistics, that cross organizational boundaries into the supply chain. It has been applied in healthcare, psychotherapy, life-coaching, government, and banking.

Exam Probability: **High**

40. *Answer choices:*

(see index for correct answer)

- a. 5S
- b. Oobeya
- c. Kaizen
- d. Kanban

Guidance: level 1

:: Alchemical processes ::

In chemistry, a _____ is a special type of homogeneous mixture composed of two or more substances. In such a mixture, a solute is a substance dissolved in another substance, known as a solvent. The mixing process of a _____ happens at a scale where the effects of chemical polarity are involved, resulting in interactions that are specific to solvation. The _____ assumes the phase of the solvent when the solvent is the larger fraction of the mixture, as is commonly the case. The concentration of a solute in a _____ is the mass of that solute expressed as a percentage of the mass of the whole _____ . The term aqueous _____ is when one of the solvents is water.

Exam Probability: **High**

41. *Answer choices:*

(see index for correct answer)

- a. Solution
- b. Putrefaction
- c. Fixation
- d. Digestion

Guidance: level 1

:: Inventory ::

The _____ is the level of inventory which triggers an action to replenish that particular inventory stock. It is a minimum amount of an item which a firm holds in stock, such that, when stock falls to this amount, the item must be reordered. It is normally calculated as the forecast usage during the replenishment lead time plus safety stock. In the EOQ model, it was assumed that there is no time lag between ordering and procuring of materials. Therefore the _____ for replenishing the stocks occurs at that level when the inventory level drops to zero and because instant delivery by suppliers, the stock level bounce back.

Exam Probability: **High**

42. *Answer choices:*
(see index for correct answer)

- a. just-in-time manufacturing
- b. Spare part
- c. Safety stock
- d. Decomposition

Guidance: level 1

:: Consortia ::

A _____ is an association of two or more individuals, companies, organizations or governments with the objective of participating in a common activity or pooling their resources for achieving a common goal.

Exam Probability: **Low**

43. *Answer choices:*

(see index for correct answer)

- a. Consortium
- b. Lex Mundi
- c. Kamco
- d. Open Mobile Terminal Platform

Guidance: level 1

:: Quality assurance ::

Organizations that issue credentials or certify third parties against official standards are themselves formally accredited by _____ bodies ; hence they are sometimes known as "accredited certification bodies". The _____ process ensures that their certification practices are acceptable, typically meaning that they are competent to test and certify third parties, behave ethically and employ suitable quality assurance.

Exam Probability: **Medium**

44. *Answer choices:*

(see index for correct answer)

- a. Arab Network for Quality Assurance in Higher Education
- b. European Association for Quality Assurance in Higher Education
- c. Certified Quality Engineer
- d. The Compliance Team

Guidance: level 1

:: Production and manufacturing ::

_____ is a production planning, scheduling, and inventory control system used to manage manufacturing processes. Most MRP systems are software-based, but it is possible to conduct MRP by hand as well.

Exam Probability: **Medium**

45. Answer choices:

(see index for correct answer)

- a. Capacity planning
- b. WorkPLAN
- c. Job shop
- d. Material requirements planning

Guidance: level 1

:: ::

In a supply chain, a _____, or a seller, is an enterprise that contributes goods or services. Generally, a supply chain _____ manufactures inventory/stock items and sells them to the next link in the chain. Today, these terms refer to a supplier of any good or service.

Exam Probability: **Medium**

46. Answer choices:

(see index for correct answer)

- a. hierarchical
- b. Sarbanes-Oxley act of 2002
- c. Vendor
- d. imperative

Guidance: level 1

:: Data management ::

_____ refers to a data-driven improvement cycle used for improving, optimizing and stabilizing business processes and designs. The _____ improvement cycle is the core tool used to drive Six Sigma projects. However, _____ is not exclusive to Six Sigma and can be used as the framework for other improvement applications.

Exam Probability: **Medium**

47. *Answer choices:*

(see index for correct answer)

- a. Three-phase commit protocol
- b. Conference on Innovative Data Systems Research
- c. DMAIC
- d. Customer data management

Guidance: level 1

:: Management accounting ::

"_____s are the structural determinants of the cost of an activity, reflecting any linkages or interrelationships that affect it". Therefore we could assume that the _____s determine the cost behavior within the activities, reflecting the links that these have with other activities and relationships that affect them.

Exam Probability: **High**

48. *Answer choices:*

(see index for correct answer)

- a. Cost driver
- b. Financial statement analysis
- c. Dual overhead rate
- d. Chartered Cost Accountant

Guidance: level 1

:: Software testing ::

_____ 1 was the first artificial Earth satellite. The Soviet Union launched it into an elliptical low Earth orbit on 4 October 1957, orbiting for three weeks before its batteries died, then silently for two more months before falling back into the atmosphere. It was a 58 cm diameter polished metal sphere, with four external radio antennas to broadcast radio pulses. Its radio signal was easily detectable even by radio amateurs, and the 65° inclination and duration of its orbit made its flight path cover virtually the entire inhabited Earth. This surprise success precipitated the American _____ crisis and triggered the Space Race, a part of the Cold War. The launch was the beginning of a new era of political, military, technological, and scientific developments.

Exam Probability: **Low**

49. *Answer choices:*

(see index for correct answer)

- a. Fuzz testing
- b. Sputnik
- c. Keyword-driven testing
- d. Test plan

Guidance: level 1

:: Project management ::

Some scenarios associate "this kind of planning" with learning "life skills". _____ s are necessary, or at least useful, in situations where individuals need to know what time they must be at a specific location to receive a specific service, and where people need to accomplish a set of goals within a set time period.

Exam Probability: **High**

50. *Answer choices:*

(see index for correct answer)

- a. Deployment Plan
- b. Pre-mortem
- c. Product flow diagram
- d. Elemental cost planning

Guidance: level 1

:: Production and manufacturing ::

_____ consists of organization-wide efforts to "install and make permanent climate where employees continuously improve their ability to provide on demand products and services that customers will find of particular value." "Total" emphasizes that departments in addition to production are obligated to improve their operations; "management" emphasizes that executives are obligated to actively manage quality through funding, training, staffing, and goal setting. While there is no widely agreed-upon approach, TQM efforts typically draw heavily on the previously developed tools and techniques of quality control. TQM enjoyed widespread attention during the late 1980s and early 1990s before being overshadowed by ISO 9000, Lean manufacturing, and Six Sigma.

Exam Probability: **Low**

51. *Answer choices:*

(see index for correct answer)

- a. Multi-Point Interface
- b. Manufacturing process management
- c. Total quality management
- d. Highly accelerated life test

Guidance: level 1

:: Project management ::

A _____ is a team whose members usually belong to different groups, functions and are assigned to activities for the same project. A team can be divided into sub-teams according to need. Usually _____s are only used for a defined period of time. They are disbanded after the project is deemed complete. Due to the nature of the specific formation and disbandment, _____s are usually in organizations.

Exam Probability: **High**

52. *Answer choices:*
(see index for correct answer)

- a. Project team
- b. Constructability
- c. Changes clause
- d. LibrePlan

Guidance: level 1

:: Production and manufacturing ::

A BOM can define products as they are designed, as they are ordered, as they are built, or as they are maintained. The different types of BOMs depend on the business need and use for which they are intended. In process industries, the BOM is also known as the formula, recipe, or ingredients list. The phrase "bill of material" is frequently used by engineers as an adjective to refer not to the literal bill, but to the current production configuration of a product, to distinguish it from modified or improved versions under study or in test.

Exam Probability: **Medium**

53. *Answer choices:*

(see index for correct answer)

- a. Food processing
- b. Bill of materials
- c. Traditional engineering
- d. Pre-shipment inspection

Guidance: level 1

:: ::

A _____ consists of an orchestrated and repeatable pattern of business activity enabled by the systematic organization of resources into processes that transform materials, provide services, or process information. It can be depicted as a sequence of operations, the work of a person or group, the work of an organization of staff, or one or more simple or complex mechanisms.

Exam Probability: **High**

54. *Answer choices:*

(see index for correct answer)

- a. personal values
- b. open system

- c. Workflow
- d. deep-level diversity

Guidance: level 1

:: Quality ::

The _____ , formerly the _____ Control , is a knowledge-based global community of quality professionals, with nearly 80,000 members dedicated to promoting and advancing quality tools, principles, and practices in their workplaces and communities.

Exam Probability: **Low**

55. *Answer choices:*

(see index for correct answer)

- a. Root cause
- b. Japanese quality
- c. American Society for Quality
- d. Software Engineering Process Group

Guidance: level 1

:: ::

The _____ is a project plan of how the production budget will be spent over a given timescale, for every phase of a business project.

Exam Probability: **Medium**

56. *Answer choices:*

(see index for correct answer)

- a. Production schedule
- b. personal values
- c. levels of analysis
- d. empathy

Guidance: level 1

:: Direct marketing ::

_____ Inc. is an American privately owned multi-level marketing company. According to Direct Selling News, _____ was the sixth largest network marketing company in the world in 2018, with a wholesale volume of US$3.25 billion. _____ is based in Addison, Texas, outside Dallas. The company was founded by _____ Ash in 1963. Richard Rogers, _____'s son, is the chairman, and David Holl is president and was named CEO in 2006.

Exam Probability: **Medium**

57. *Answer choices:*

(see index for correct answer)

- a. Direct marketing educational foundation
- b. Direct Marketing Association
- c. Flyer
- d. Mailing list

Guidance: level 1

:: Business process ::

A _____ or business method is a collection of related, structured activities or tasks by people or equipment which in a specific sequence produce a service or product for a particular customer or customers. _____ es occur at all organizational levels and may or may not be visible to the customers. A _____ may often be visualized as a flowchart of a sequence of activities with interleaving decision points or as a process matrix of a sequence of activities with relevance rules based on data in the process. The benefits of using _____ es include improved customer satisfaction and improved agility for reacting to rapid market change. Process-oriented organizations break down the barriers of structural departments and try to avoid functional silos.

Exam Probability: **High**

58. *Answer choices:*

(see index for correct answer)

- a. Process mapping

- b. Business process
- c. Signavio
- d. Business process reengineering

Guidance: level 1

:: Business ::

The seller, or the provider of the goods or services, completes a sale in response to an acquisition, appropriation, requisition or a direct interaction with the buyer at the point of sale. There is a passing of title of the item, and the settlement of a price, in which agreement is reached on a price for which transfer of ownership of the item will occur. The seller, not the purchaser typically executes the sale and it may be completed prior to the obligation of payment. In the case of indirect interaction, a person who sells goods or service on behalf of the owner is known as a _____ man or _____ woman or _____ person, but this often refers to someone selling goods in a store/shop, in which case other terms are also common, including _____ clerk, shop assistant, and retail clerk.

Exam Probability: **Low**

59. *Answer choices:*

(see index for correct answer)

- a. Westnile Distilling Company Limited
- b. Service recovery
- c. Sales
- d. Legal governance, risk management, and compliance

Guidance: level 1

Commerce

Commerce relates to "the exchange of goods and services, especially on a large scale." It includes legal, economic, political, social, cultural and technological systems that operate in any country or internationally.

The _____ is a political and economic union of 28 member states that are located primarily in Europe. It has an area of 4,475,757 km2 and an estimated population of about 513 million. The EU has developed an internal single market through a standardised system of laws that apply in all member states in those matters, and only those matters, where members have agreed to act as one. EU policies aim to ensure the free movement of people, goods, services and capital within the internal market, enact legislation in justice and home affairs and maintain common policies on trade, agriculture, fisheries and regional development. For travel within the Schengen Area, passport controls have been abolished. A monetary union was established in 1999 and came into full force in 2002 and is composed of 19 EU member states which use the euro currency.

Exam Probability: **High**

1. *Answer choices:*

(see index for correct answer)

- a. open system
- b. European Union
- c. interpersonal communication
- d. hierarchical perspective

Guidance: level 1

:: Debt ::

_____ is the trust which allows one party to provide money or resources to another party wherein the second party does not reimburse the first party immediately , but promises either to repay or return those resources at a later date. In other words, _____ is a method of making reciprocity formal, legally enforceable, and extensible to a large group of unrelated people.

Exam Probability: **Low**

2. *Answer choices:*

(see index for correct answer)

- a. Sum certain
- b. Credit
- c. Creditor
- d. Compulsive buying disorder

Guidance: level 1

:: Debt ::

_____ , in finance and economics, is payment from a borrower or deposit-taking financial institution to a lender or depositor of an amount above repayment of the principal sum , at a particular rate. It is distinct from a fee which the borrower may pay the lender or some third party. It is also distinct from dividend which is paid by a company to its shareholders from its profit or reserve, but not at a particular rate decided beforehand, rather on a pro rata basis as a share in the reward gained by risk taking entrepreneurs when the revenue earned exceeds the total costs.

Exam Probability: **High**

3. *Answer choices:*

(see index for correct answer)

- a. Internal debt
- b. Debt-lag
- c. Sum certain
- d. Interest

Guidance: level 1

:: Commerce ::

An _____ is a bank that offers card association branded payment cards directly to consumers. The name is derived from the practice of issuing payment to the acquiring bank on behalf of its customer.

Exam Probability: **Medium**

4. *Answer choices:*

(see index for correct answer)

- a. Requisition
- b. Issuing bank
- c. Netflix
- d. Statutory holdback

Guidance: level 1

:: ::

A _____ consists of one people who live in the same dwelling and share meals. It may also consist of a single family or another group of people. A dwelling is considered to contain multiple _____ s if meals or living spaces are not shared. The _____ is the basic unit of analysis in many social, microeconomic and government models, and is important to economics and inheritance.

Exam Probability: **Medium**

5. *Answer choices:*

(see index for correct answer)

- a. information systems assessment
- b. Household
- c. similarity-attraction theory
- d. interpersonal communication

Guidance: level 1

:: Marketing ::

_____ is a concept introduced in a book of the same name in 1999 by marketing expert Seth Godin. _____ is a non-traditional marketing technique that advertises goods and services when advance consent is given.

Exam Probability: **Low**

6. *Answer choices:*

(see index for correct answer)

- a. Content partnership
- b. Permission marketing
- c. Product planning
- d. Point of difference

Guidance: level 1

:: Stock market ::

The _____ of a corporation is all of the shares into which ownership of the corporation is divided. In American English, the shares are commonly known as "_____ s". A single share of the _____ represents fractional ownership of the corporation in proportion to the total number of shares. This typically entitles the _____ holder to that fraction of the company's earnings, proceeds from liquidation of assets, or voting power, often dividing these up in proportion to the amount of money each _____ holder has invested. Not all _____ is necessarily equal, as certain classes of _____ may be issued for example without voting rights, with enhanced voting rights, or with a certain priority to receive profits or liquidation proceeds before or after other classes of shareholders.

Exam Probability: **High**

7. *Answer choices:*

(see index for correct answer)

- a. Lock-up period
- b. Stock
- c. Prime Standard
- d. Matchbook FX

Guidance: level 1

:: Consortia ::

A _____ is an association of two or more individuals, companies, organizations or governments with the objective of participating in a common activity or pooling their resources for achieving a common goal.

Exam Probability: **Low**

8. *Answer choices:*

(see index for correct answer)

- a. EDAPS
- b. Consortium
- c. Builder homesite
- d. Open Grid Forum

Guidance: level 1

:: ::

_____ is the principled guide to action taken by the administrative executive branches of the state with regard to a class of issues, in a manner consistent with law and institutional customs.

Exam Probability: **High**

9. *Answer choices:*

(see index for correct answer)

- a. levels of analysis
- b. Sarbanes-Oxley act of 2002
- c. Character
- d. Public policy

Guidance: level 1

:: ::

In marketing jargon, product lining is offering several related products for sale individually. Unlike product bundling, where several products are combined into one group, which is then offered for sale as a units, product lining involves offering the products for sale separately. A line can comprise related products of various sizes, types, colors, qualities, or prices. Line depth refers to the number of subcategories a category has. Line consistency refers to how closely related the products that make up the line are. Line vulnerability refers to the percentage of sales or profits that are derived from only a few products in the line.

Exam Probability: **Low**

10. *Answer choices:*

(see index for correct answer)

- a. Sarbanes-Oxley act of 2002
- b. empathy
- c. Product mix
- d. interpersonal communication

Guidance: level 1

:: Business models ::

A _____, _____ company or daughter company is a company that is owned or controlled by another company, which is called the parent company, parent, or holding company. The _____ can be a company, corporation, or limited liability company. In some cases it is a government or state-owned enterprise. In some cases, particularly in the music and book publishing industries, subsidiaries are referred to as imprints.

Exam Probability: **Medium**

11. *Answer choices:*

(see index for correct answer)

- a. Premium business model
- b. Parent company
- c. Gratis
- d. Subsidiary

Guidance: level 1

:: Cryptography ::

In cryptography, _____ is the process of encoding a message or information in such a way that only authorized parties can access it and those who are not authorized cannot. _____ does not itself prevent interference, but denies the intelligible content to a would-be interceptor. In an _____ scheme, the intended information or message, referred to as plaintext, is encrypted using an _____ algorithm – a cipher – generating ciphertext that can be read only if decrypted. For technical reasons, an _____ scheme usually uses a pseudo-random _____ key generated by an algorithm. It is in principle possible to decrypt the message without possessing the key, but, for a well-designed _____ scheme, considerable computational resources and skills are required. An authorized recipient can easily decrypt the message with the key provided by the originator to recipients but not to unauthorized users.

Exam Probability: **Low**

12. *Answer choices:*

(see index for correct answer)

- a. Encryption
- b. plaintext
- c. ciphertext
- d. backdoor

Guidance: level 1

:: ::

Advertising is a marketing communication that employs an openly sponsored, non-personal message to promote or sell a product, service or idea. Sponsors of advertising are typically businesses wishing to promote their products or services. Advertising is differentiated from public relations in that an advertiser pays for and has control over the message. It differs from personal selling in that the message is non-personal, i.e., not directed to a particular individual.Advertising is communicated through various mass media, including traditional media such as newspapers, magazines, television, radio, outdoor advertising or direct mail; and new media such as search results, blogs, social media, websites or text messages. The actual presentation of the message in a medium is referred to as an _____ , or "ad" or advert for short.

Exam Probability: **Low**

13. *Answer choices:*

(see index for correct answer)

- a. surface-level diversity
- b. Advertisement
- c. process perspective
- d. imperative

Guidance: level 1

_____ is both a research area and a practical skill encompassing the ability of an individual or organization to "lead" or guide other individuals, teams, or entire organizations. Specialist literature debates various viewpoints, contrasting Eastern and Western approaches to _____, and also United States versus European approaches. U.S. academic environments define _____ as "a process of social influence in which a person can enlist the aid and support of others in the accomplishment of a common task".

Exam Probability: **High**

14. *Answer choices:*

(see index for correct answer)

- a. hierarchical
- b. surface-level diversity
- c. open system
- d. corporate values

Guidance: level 1

:: Organizational structure ::

An _____ defines how activities such as task allocation, coordination, and supervision are directed toward the achievement of organizational aims.

Exam Probability: **Medium**

15. *Answer choices:*

(see index for correct answer)

- a. Automated Bureaucracy
- b. Organization of the New York City Police Department
- c. Followership
- d. Organizational structure

Guidance: level 1

:: E-commerce ::

Customer to customer markets provide an innovative way to allow customers to interact with each other. Traditional markets require business to customer relationships, in which a customer goes to the business in order to purchase a product or service. In customer to customer markets, the business facilitates an environment where customers can sell goods or services to each other. Other types of markets include business to business and business to customer.

Exam Probability: **Medium**

16. *Answer choices:*

(see index for correct answer)

- a. Consumer-to-consumer
- b. Conversion as a service
- c. Friend-to-friend
- d. Micropayment

Guidance: level 1

:: ::

Business is the activity of making one's living or making money by producing or buying and selling products. Simply put, it is "any activity or enterprise entered into for profit. It does not mean it is a company, a corporation, partnership, or have any such formal organization, but it can range from a street peddler to General Motors."

Exam Probability: **Low**

17. *Answer choices:*

(see index for correct answer)

- a. cultural
- b. Firm
- c. similarity-attraction theory
- d. corporate values

Guidance: level 1

:: International trade ::

A _____ is a document issued by a carrier to acknowledge receipt of cargo for shipment. Although the term historically related only to carriage by sea, a _____ may today be used for any type of carriage of goods.

Exam Probability: **Medium**

18. *Answer choices:*

(see index for correct answer)

- a. Bill of lading
- b. East forum Berlin
- c. Team Canada Mission
- d. Bound tariff rate

Guidance: level 1

:: Commerce ::

A _____ is an employee within a company, business or other organization who is responsible at some level for buying or approving the acquisition of goods and services needed by the company. Responsible for buying the best quality products, goods and services for their company at the most competitive prices, _____ s work in a wide range of sectors for many different organizations. The position responsibilities may be the same as that of a buyer or purchasing agent, or may include wider supervisory or managerial responsibilities. A _____ may oversee the acquisition of materials needed for production, general supplies for offices and facilities, equipment, or construction contracts. A _____ often supervises purchasing agents and buyers, but in small companies the _____ may also be the purchasing agent or buyer. The _____ position may also carry the title "Procurement Manager" or in the public sector, "Procurement Officer". He or she can come from both an Engineering or Economics background.

Exam Probability: **High**

19. *Answer choices:*

(see index for correct answer)

- a. DataCash
- b. Purchasing manager
- c. Contingent payment sales
- d. V-commerce

Guidance: level 1

:: ::

A _____ is a fund into which a sum of money is added during an employee's employment years, and from which payments are drawn to support the person's retirement from work in the form of periodic payments. A _____ may be a "defined benefit plan" where a fixed sum is paid regularly to a person, or a "defined contribution plan" under which a fixed sum is invested and then becomes available at retirement age. _____ s should not be confused with severance pay; the former is usually paid in regular installments for life after retirement, while the latter is typically paid as a fixed amount after involuntary termination of employment prior to retirement.

Exam Probability: **Low**

20. *Answer choices:*

(see index for correct answer)

- a. Pension
- b. corporate values
- c. levels of analysis
- d. hierarchical perspective

Guidance: level 1

:: E-commerce ::

_____ is a type of performance-based marketing in which a business rewards one or more affiliates for each visitor or customer brought by the affiliate's own marketing efforts.

Exam Probability: **Low**

21. *Answer choices:*

(see index for correct answer)

- a. APazari Desktop
- b. Switchwise
- c. TRADACOMS
- d. Discovery shopping

Guidance: level 1

:: Basic financial concepts ::

_____ is a sustained increase in the general price level of goods and services in an economy over a period of time. When the general price level rises, each unit of currency buys fewer goods and services; consequently, _____ reflects a reduction in the purchasing power per unit of money a loss of real value in the medium of exchange and unit of account within the economy. The measure of _____ is the _____ rate, the annualized percentage change in a general price index, usually the consumer price index, over time. The opposite of _____ is deflation.

Exam Probability: **High**

22. *Answer choices:*

(see index for correct answer)

- a. Base effect
- b. Leverage cycle
- c. Financial transaction
- d. Inflation

Guidance: level 1

:: ::

A _____ is a person who trades in commodities produced by other people. Historically, a _____ is anyone who is involved in business or trade. _____ s have operated for as long as industry, commerce, and trade have existed. During the 16th-century, in Europe, two different terms for _____ s emerged: One term, meerseniers, described local traders such as bakers, grocers, etc.; while a new term, koopman (Dutch: koopman, described _____ s who operated on a global stage, importing and exporting goods over vast distances, and offering added-value services such as credit and finance.

Exam Probability: **High**

23. *Answer choices:*

(see index for correct answer)

- a. Merchant
- b. co-culture
- c. functional perspective
- d. hierarchical perspective

Guidance: level 1

:: Meetings ::

A _____ is a body of one or more persons that is subordinate to a deliberative assembly. Usually, the assembly sends matters into a _____ as a way to explore them more fully than would be possible if the assembly itself were considering them. _____ s may have different functions and their type of work differ depending on the type of the organization and its needs.

Exam Probability: **High**

24. *Answer choices:*

(see index for correct answer)

- a. Prayer meeting
- b. Committee
- c. Audience
- d. Skeptics in the Pub

Guidance: level 1

:: ::

In Christian denominations that practice infant baptism, confirmation is seen as the sealing of Christianity created in baptism. Those being _____ are known as confirmands. In some denominations, such as the Anglican Communion and Methodist Churches, confirmation bestows full membership in a local congregation upon the recipient. In others, such as the Roman Catholic Church, Confirmation "renders the bond with the Church more perfect", because, while a baptized person is already a member, "reception of the sacrament of Confirmation is necessary for the completion of baptismal grace".

Exam Probability: **Medium**

25. *Answer choices:*

(see index for correct answer)

- a. cultural
- b. imperative
- c. surface-level diversity
- d. Confirmed

Guidance: level 1

:: Banking ::

A _____ is a financial institution that accepts deposits from the public and creates credit. Lending activities can be performed either directly or indirectly through capital markets. Due to their importance in the financial stability of a country, _____ s are highly regulated in most countries. Most nations have institutionalized a system known as fractional reserve _____ ing under which _____ s hold liquid assets equal to only a portion of their current liabilities. In addition to other regulations intended to ensure liquidity, _____ s are generally subject to minimum capital requirements based on an international set of capital standards, known as the Basel Accords.

Exam Probability: **High**

26. *Answer choices:*

(see index for correct answer)

- a. Coin roll hunting
- b. Variance swap
- c. International Bank of Azerbaijan-Georgia
- d. Asset-based lending

Guidance: level 1

:: ::

A _____ or GM is an executive who has overall responsibility for managing both the revenue and cost elements of a company's income statement, known as profit & loss responsibility. A _____ usually oversees most or all of the firm's marketing and sales functions as well as the day-to-day operations of the business. Frequently, the _____ is responsible for effective planning, delegating, coordinating, staffing, organizing, and decision making to attain desirable profit making results for an organization.

Exam Probability: **Medium**

27. *Answer choices:*

(see index for correct answer)

- a. deep-level diversity
- b. open system
- c. General manager
- d. co-culture

Guidance: level 1

:: Project management ::

A _____ is a source or supply from which a benefit is produced and it has some utility. _____ s can broadly be classified upon their availability—they are classified into renewable and non-renewable _____ s. Examples of non renewable _____ s are coal, crude oil natural gas nuclear energy etc. Examples of renewable _____ s are air, water, wind, solar energy etc. They can also be classified as actual and potential on the basis of level of development and use, on the basis of origin they can be classified as biotic and abiotic, and on the basis of their distribution, as ubiquitous and localized. An item becomes a _____ with time and developing technology. Typically, _____ s are materials, energy, services, staff, knowledge, or other assets that are transformed to produce benefit and in the process may be consumed or made unavailable. Benefits of _____ utilization may include increased wealth, proper functioning of a system, or enhanced well-being. From a human perspective a natural _____ is anything obtained from the environment to satisfy human needs and wants. From a broader biological or ecological perspective a _____ satisfies the needs of a living organism.

Exam Probability: **Low**

28. *Answer choices:*

(see index for correct answer)

- a. Grandfather principle
- b. Defense Acquisition Workforce Improvement Act
- c. Resource
- d. Deliverable

Guidance: level 1

:: Management accounting ::

_____ s are costs that change as the quantity of the good or service that a business produces changes. _____ s are the sum of marginal costs over all units produced. They can also be considered normal costs. Fixed costs and _____ s make up the two components of total cost. Direct costs are costs that can easily be associated with a particular cost object. However, not all _____ s are direct costs. For example, variable manufacturing overhead costs are _____ s that are indirect costs, not direct costs. _____ s are sometimes called unit-level costs as they vary with the number of units produced.

Exam Probability: **Medium**

29. *Answer choices:*

(see index for correct answer)

- a. Target costing
- b. Cost accounting
- c. Fixed assets management
- d. Variable cost

Guidance: level 1

:: ::

In logic and philosophy, an _____ is a series of statements, called the premises or premisses, intended to determine the degree of truth of another statement, the conclusion. The logical form of an _____ in a natural language can be represented in a symbolic formal language, and independently of natural language formally defined "_____ s" can be made in math and computer science.

Exam Probability: **High**

30. *Answer choices:*

(see index for correct answer)

- a. open system
- b. co-culture
- c. levels of analysis
- d. similarity-attraction theory

Guidance: level 1

:: Business law ::

A _____ is a group of people who jointly supervise the activities of an organization, which can be either a for-profit business, nonprofit organization, or a government agency. Such a board's powers, duties, and responsibilities are determined by government regulations and the organization's own constitution and bylaws. These authorities may specify the number of members of the board, how they are to be chosen, and how often they are to meet.

Exam Probability: **Medium**

31. *Answer choices:*

(see index for correct answer)

- a. Starting a Business Index
- b. Single business enterprise
- c. Board of directors
- d. Secret rebate

Guidance: level 1

:: Management ::

In business, a _____ is the attribute that allows an organization to outperform its competitors. A _____ may include access to natural resources, such as high-grade ores or a low-cost power source, highly skilled labor, geographic location, high entry barriers, and access to new technology.

Exam Probability: **High**

32. *Answer choices:*

(see index for correct answer)

- a. Purchasing management
- b. Event management
- c. Mushroom management

- d. Omnex

Guidance: level 1

:: ::

In law, an _____ is the process in which cases are reviewed, where parties request a formal change to an official decision. _____ s function both as a process for error correction as well as a process of clarifying and interpreting law. Although appellate courts have existed for thousands of years, common law countries did not incorporate an affirmative right to _____ into their jurisprudence until the 19th century.

Exam Probability: **Medium**

33. *Answer choices:*

(see index for correct answer)

- a. cultural
- b. similarity-attraction theory
- c. imperative
- d. Appeal

Guidance: level 1

:: Management ::

The term _____ refers to measures designed to increase the degree of autonomy and self-determination in people and in communities in order to enable them to represent their interests in a responsible and self-determined way, acting on their own authority. It is the process of becoming stronger and more confident, especially in controlling one's life and claiming one's rights. _____ as action refers both to the process of self-_____ and to professional support of people, which enables them to overcome their sense of powerlessness and lack of influence, and to recognize and use their resources. To do work with power.

Exam Probability: **High**

34. *Answer choices:*

(see index for correct answer)

- a. Continuous monitoring
- b. Project stakeholder
- c. Information excellence
- d. Empowerment

Guidance: level 1

:: ::

_____ is a concept of English common law and is a necessity for simple contracts but not for special contracts. The concept has been adopted by other common law jurisdictions, including the US.

Exam Probability: **Medium**

35. *Answer choices:*

(see index for correct answer)

- a. Character
- b. process perspective
- c. hierarchical perspective
- d. Sarbanes-Oxley act of 2002

Guidance: level 1

:: Commerce ::

_____, Inc. is an American media-services provider headquartered in Los Gatos, California, founded in 1997 by Reed Hastings and Marc Randolph in Scotts Valley, California. The company's primary business is its subscription-based streaming OTT service which offers online streaming of a library of films and television programs, including those produced in-house. As of April 2019, _____ had over 148 million paid subscriptions worldwide, including 60 million in the United States, and over 154 million subscriptions total including free trials. It is available almost worldwide except in mainland China as well as Syria, North Korea, and Crimea. The company also has offices in the Netherlands, Brazil, India, Japan, and South Korea. _____ is a member of the Motion Picture Association of America.

Exam Probability: **Low**

36. *Answer choices:*

(see index for correct answer)

- a. Economic entity
- b. Netflix
- c. TradeCard
- d. Statutory holdback

Guidance: level 1

:: E-commerce ::

_____ is the business-to-business or business-to-consumer or business-to-government purchase and sale of supplies, work, and services through the Internet as well as other information and networking systems, such as electronic data interchange and enterprise resource planning.

Exam Probability: **High**

37. *Answer choices:*

(see index for correct answer)

- a. E-procurement
- b. POLi Payments
- c. Presumed security
- d. Confinity

Guidance: level 1

:: Payments ::

A _____ or government incentive is a form of financial aid or support extended to an economic sector generally with the aim of promoting economic and social policy. Although commonly extended from government, the term _____ can relate to any type of support – for example from NGOs or as implicit subsidies. Subsidies come in various forms including: direct and indirect .

Exam Probability: **Medium**

38. *Answer choices:*

(see index for correct answer)

- a. Tuition payments
- b. County payments
- c. Subsidy
- d. Direct Payments

Guidance: level 1

:: Commercial item transport and distribution ::

In commerce, supply-chain management, the management of the flow of goods and services, involves the movement and storage of raw materials, of work-in-process inventory, and of finished goods from point of origin to point of consumption. Interconnected or interlinked networks, channels and node businesses combine in the provision of products and services required by end customers in a supply chain. Supply-chain management has been defined as the "design, planning, execution, control, and monitoring of supply-chain activities with the objective of creating net value, building a competitive infrastructure, leveraging worldwide logistics, synchronizing supply with demand and measuring performance globally."SCM practice draws heavily from the areas of industrial engineering, systems engineering, operations management, logistics, procurement, information technology, and marketing and strives for an integrated approach. Marketing channels play an important role in supply-chain management. Current research in supply-chain management is concerned with topics related to sustainability and risk management, among others. Some suggest that the "people dimension" of SCM, ethical issues, internal integration, transparency/visibility, and human capital/talent management are topics that have, so far, been underrepresented on the research agenda.

Exam Probability: **Low**

39. *Answer choices:*

(see index for correct answer)

- a. Humanitarian Logistics
- b. Steam wagon
- c. Semi-trailer
- d. Supply chain management

Guidance: level 1

:: Materials ::

A _____, also known as a feedstock, unprocessed material, or primary commodity, is a basic material that is used to produce goods, finished products, energy, or intermediate materials which are feedstock for future finished products. As feedstock, the term connotes these materials are bottleneck assets and are highly important with regard to producing other products. An example of this is crude oil, which is a _____ and a feedstock used in the production of industrial chemicals, fuels, plastics, and pharmaceutical goods; lumber is a _____ used to produce a variety of products including all types of furniture. The term "_____" denotes materials in minimally processed or unprocessed in states; e.g., raw latex, crude oil, cotton, coal, raw biomass, iron ore, air, logs, or water i.e. "...any product of agriculture, forestry, fishing and any other mineral that is in its natural form or which has undergone the transformation required to prepare it for internationally marketing in substantial volumes."

Exam Probability: **Medium**

40. *Answer choices:*

(see index for correct answer)

- a. Aerospace materials
- b. Mineral wool
- c. Space blanket
- d. Raw material

Guidance: level 1

:: Supply chain management ::

_____ is the process of finding and agreeing to terms, and acquiring goods, services, or works from an external source, often via a tendering or competitive bidding process. _____ is used to ensure the buyer receives goods, services, or works at the best possible price when aspects such as quality, quantity, time, and location are compared. Corporations and public bodies often define processes intended to promote fair and open competition for their business while minimizing risks such as exposure to fraud and collusion.

Exam Probability: **Medium**

41. *Answer choices:*

(see index for correct answer)

- a. Security risk
- b. Supply chain cyber security
- c. Procurement
- d. Blinco Systems Inc.

Guidance: level 1

:: Investment ::

In finance, the benefit from an _____ is called a return. The return may consist of a gain realised from the sale of property or an _____ , unrealised capital appreciation , or _____ income such as dividends, interest, rental income etc., or a combination of capital gain and income. The return may also include currency gains or losses due to changes in foreign currency exchange rates.

Exam Probability: **Low**

42. *Answer choices:*

(see index for correct answer)

- a. Dispersion
- b. Special settlement
- c. Investment
- d. Self-invested personal pension

Guidance: level 1

:: Production economics ::

In microeconomics, _____ are the cost advantages that enterprises obtain due to their scale of operation, with cost per unit of output decreasing with increasing scale.

Exam Probability: **High**

43. *Answer choices:*

(see index for correct answer)

- a. Isocost
- b. Product pipeline
- c. Industrial production index
- d. Diminishing returns

Guidance: level 1

:: Marketing analytics ::

_____ is a long-term, forward-looking approach to planning with the fundamental goal of achieving a sustainable competitive advantage. Strategic planning involves an analysis of the company's strategic initial situation prior to the formulation, evaluation and selection of market-oriented competitive position that contributes to the company's goals and marketing objectives.

Exam Probability: **Medium**

44. *Answer choices:*

(see index for correct answer)

- a. Mission-driven marketing
- b. Sumall
- c. Marketing strategy
- d. Perceptual map

Guidance: level 1

:: ::

A _____ is any person who contracts to acquire an asset in return for some form of consideration.

Exam Probability: **Low**

45. *Answer choices:*

(see index for correct answer)

- a. empathy
- b. surface-level diversity
- c. hierarchical
- d. Buyer

Guidance: level 1

:: ::

_____ is the production of products for use or sale using labour and machines, tools, chemical and biological processing, or formulation. The term may refer to a range of human activity, from handicraft to high tech, but is most commonly applied to industrial design, in which raw materials are transformed into finished goods on a large scale. Such finished goods may be sold to other manufacturers for the production of other, more complex products, such as aircraft, household appliances, furniture, sports equipment or automobiles, or sold to wholesalers, who in turn sell them to retailers, who then sell them to end users and consumers.

Exam Probability: **Low**

46. *Answer choices:*

(see index for correct answer)

- a. open system
- b. surface-level diversity
- c. Sarbanes-Oxley act of 2002
- d. Manufacturing

Guidance: level 1

:: Industry ::

_____ , also known as flow production or continuous production, is the production of large amounts of standardized products, including and especially on assembly lines. Together with job production and batch production, it is one of the three main production methods.

Exam Probability: **High**

47. *Answer choices:*

(see index for correct answer)

- a. United Nations Industrial Development Organization
- b. Reindustrialization
- c. Productivity
- d. Heavy industry

Guidance: level 1

:: ::

In legal terminology, a _____ is any formal legal document that sets out the facts and legal reasons that the filing party or parties believes are sufficient to support a claim against the party or parties against whom the claim is brought that entitles the plaintiff to a remedy. For example, the Federal Rules of Civil Procedure that govern civil litigation in United States courts provide that a civil action is commenced with the filing or service of a pleading called a _____. Civil court rules in states that have incorporated the Federal Rules of Civil Procedure use the same term for the same pleading.

Exam Probability: **Medium**

48. *Answer choices:*

(see index for correct answer)

- a. surface-level diversity
- b. functional perspective
- c. Complaint
- d. personal values

Guidance: level 1

:: Credit cards ::

A _____ is a payment card issued to users to enable the cardholder to pay a merchant for goods and services based on the cardholder's promise to the card issuer to pay them for the amounts plus the other agreed charges. The card issuer creates a revolving account and grants a line of credit to the cardholder, from which the cardholder can borrow money for payment to a merchant or as a cash advance.

Exam Probability: **Low**

49. *Answer choices:*

(see index for correct answer)

- a. BC Card
- b. Barclaycard
- c. Centurion Card
- d. Credit card

Guidance: level 1

:: Generally Accepted Accounting Principles ::

Expenditure is an outflow of money to another person or group to pay for an item or service, or for a category of costs. For a tenant, rent is an _____. For students or parents, tuition is an _____. Buying food, clothing, furniture or an automobile is often referred to as an _____. An _____ is a cost that is "paid" or "remitted", usually in exchange for something of value. Something that seems to cost a great deal is "expensive". Something that seems to cost little is "inexpensive". "_____ s of the table" are _____ s of dining, refreshments, a feast, etc.

Exam Probability: **High**

50. *Answer choices:*

(see index for correct answer)

- a. Expense
- b. Financial position of the United States
- c. Operating income before depreciation and amortization
- d. Cash method of accounting

Guidance: level 1

:: Industry ::

A _____ is a set of sequential operations established in a factory where materials are put through a refining process to produce an end-product that is suitable for onward consumption; or components are assembled to make a finished article.

Exam Probability: **Low**

51. *Answer choices:*

(see index for correct answer)

- a. Cleaner
- b. Permissible exposure limit
- c. Production line

- d. Economic importance of bacteria

Guidance: level 1

:: Supply chain management ::

_____ is the removal of intermediaries in economics from a supply chain, or cutting out the middlemen in connection with a transaction or a series of transactions. Instead of going through traditional distribution channels, which had some type of intermediary, companies may now deal with customers directly, for example via the Internet. Hence, the use of factory direct and direct from the factory to mean the same thing.

Exam Probability: **Medium**

52. *Answer choices:*
(see index for correct answer)

- a. Application service provider
- b. Design for logistics
- c. Dealer Business System
- d. Disintermediation

Guidance: level 1

:: ::

Regulatory economics is the economics of regulation. It is the application of law by government or independent administrative agencies for various purposes, including remedying market failure, protecting the environment, centrally-planning an economy, enriching well-connected firms, or benefiting politicians.

Exam Probability: **Low**

53. *Answer choices:*

(see index for correct answer)

- a. Economic regulation
- b. functional perspective
- c. surface-level diversity
- d. interpersonal communication

Guidance: level 1

:: Economic globalization ::

_____ is an agreement in which one company hires another company to be responsible for a planned or existing activity that is or could be done internally, and sometimes involves transferring employees and assets from one firm to another.

Exam Probability: **High**

54. Answer choices:

(see index for correct answer)

- a. global financial
- b. reshoring

Guidance: level 1

:: Information retrieval ::

_____ is a technique used by recommender systems. _____ has two senses, a narrow one and a more general one.

Exam Probability: **High**

55. Answer choices:

(see index for correct answer)

- a. Document retrieval
- b. Collaborative filtering
- c. Learning to rank
- d. Gain

Guidance: level 1

:: Business terms ::

_____ ning is an organization's process of defining its strategy, or direction, and making decisions on allocating its resources to pursue this strategy. It may also extend to control mechanisms for guiding the implementation of the strategy. _____ ning became prominent in corporations during the 1960s and remains an important aspect of strategic management. It is executed by _____ ners or strategists, who involve many parties and research sources in their analysis of the organization and its relationship to the environment in which it competes.

Exam Probability: **Low**

56. *Answer choices:*

(see index for correct answer)

- a. organizational capital
- b. Strategic plan
- c. Strategic partner
- d. year-to-date

Guidance: level 1

:: Marketing ::

A _____ is an overall experience of a customer that distinguishes an organization or product from its rivals in the eyes of the customer. _____ s are used in business, marketing, and advertising. Name _____ s are sometimes distinguished from generic or store _____ s.

Exam Probability: **Medium**

57. Answer choices:

(see index for correct answer)

- a. Marketing warfare strategies
- b. Corporate anniversary
- c. Blind taste test
- d. Brand

Guidance: level 1

:: Theories ::

A _____ union is a type of multinational political union where negotiated power is delegated to an authority by governments of member states.

Exam Probability: **Low**

58. Answer choices:

(see index for correct answer)

- a. Taylorism
- b. Supranational

Guidance: level 1

:: Income ::

_____ is the application of disciplined analytics that predict consumer behaviour at the micro-market levels and optimize product availability and price to maximize revenue growth. The primary aim of _____ is selling the right product to the right customer at the right time for the right price and with the right pack. The essence of this discipline is in understanding customers' perception of product value and accurately aligning product prices, placement and availability with each customer segment.

Exam Probability: **Low**

59. *Answer choices:*

(see index for correct answer)

- a. Aggregate income
- b. Income Per User
- c. Imputed income
- d. Revenue management

Guidance: level 1

Business ethics

Business ethics (also known as corporate ethics) is a form of applied ethics or professional ethics, that examines ethical principles and moral or ethical problems that can arise in a business environment. It applies to all aspects of business conduct and is relevant to the conduct of individuals and entire organizations. These ethics originate from individuals, organizational statements or from the legal system. These norms, values, ethical, and unethical practices are what is used to guide business. They help those businesses maintain a better connection with their stakeholders.

:: Monopoly (economics) ::

A _____ is a form of intellectual property that gives its owner the legal right to exclude others from making, using, selling, and importing an invention for a limited period of years, in exchange for publishing an enabling public disclosure of the invention. In most countries _____ rights fall under civil law and the _____ holder needs to sue someone infringing the _____ in order to enforce his or her rights. In some industries _____ s are an essential form of competitive advantage; in others they are irrelevant.

Exam Probability: **High**

1. *Answer choices:*

(see index for correct answer)

- a. Competition Commission
- b. Coercive monopoly
- c. Patent
- d. Ownership unbundling

Guidance: level 1

:: Electronic waste ::

_____ or e-waste describes discarded electrical or electronic devices. Used electronics which are destined for refurbishment, reuse, resale, salvage, recycling through material recovery, or disposal are also considered e-waste. Informal processing of e-waste in developing countries can lead to adverse human health effects and environmental pollution.

Exam Probability: **Medium**

2. *Answer choices:*

(see index for correct answer)

- a. World Reuse, Repair and Recycling Association
- b. Global waste trade
- c. Electronic waste
- d. Computer liquidator

Guidance: level 1

:: Business ethics ::

_____ is a persistent pattern of mistreatment from others in the workplace that causes either physical or emotional harm. It can include such tactics as verbal, nonverbal, psychological, physical abuse and humiliation. This type of workplace aggression is particularly difficult because, unlike the typical school bully, workplace bullies often operate within the established rules and policies of their organization and their society. In the majority of cases, bullying in the workplace is reported as having been by someone who has authority over their victim. However, bullies can also be peers, and occasionally subordinates. Research has also investigated the impact of the larger organizational context on bullying as well as the group-level processes that impact on the incidence and maintenance of bullying behaviour. Bullying can be covert or overt. It may be missed by superiors; it may be known by many throughout the organization. Negative effects are not limited to the targeted individuals, and may lead to a decline in employee morale and a change in organizational culture. It can also take place as overbearing supervision, constant criticism, and blocking promotions.

Exam Probability: **Medium**

3. *Answer choices:*

(see index for correct answer)

- a. Hostile work environment
- b. Workplace bullying
- c. Destructionism
- d. Minecode

Guidance: level 1

:: Carbon finance ::

The _____ is an international treaty which extends the 1992 United Nations Framework Convention on Climate Change that commits state parties to reduce greenhouse gas emissions, based on the scientific consensus that global warming is occurring and it is extremely likely that human-made CO_2 emissions have predominantly caused it. The _____ was adopted in Kyoto, Japan on 11 December 1997 and entered into force on 16 February 2005. There are currently 192 parties to the Protocol.

Exam Probability: **High**

4. *Answer choices:*

(see index for correct answer)

- a. Emissions Trading Registry

- b. Plant A Tree Today Foundation
- c. Kyoto Protocol
- d. Carbon finance

Guidance: level 1

:: Advertising techniques ::

> The _____ is a story from the Trojan War about the subterfuge that the Greeks used to enter the independent city of Troy and win the war. In the canonical version, after a fruitless 10-year siege, the Greeks constructed a huge wooden horse, and hid a select force of men inside including Odysseus. The Greeks pretended to sail away, and the Trojans pulled the horse into their city as a victory trophy. That night the Greek force crept out of the horse and opened the gates for the rest of the Greek army, which had sailed back under cover of night. The Greeks entered and destroyed the city of Troy, ending the war.

Exam Probability: **Low**

5. *Answer choices:*

(see index for correct answer)

- a. Trojan horse
- b. Repetition variation
- c. FAST marketing
- d. Roll-in

Guidance: level 1

_____ is a cognitive process that elicits emotion and rational associations based on an individual's moral philosophy or value system. _____ stands in contrast to elicited emotion or thought due to associations based on immediate sensory perceptions and reflexive responses, as in sympathetic central nervous system responses. In common terms, _____ is often described as leading to feelings of remorse when a person commits an act that conflicts with their moral values. An individual's moral values and their dissonance with familial, social, cultural and historical interpretations of moral philosophy are considered in the examination of cultural relativity in both the practice and study of psychology. The extent to which _____ informs moral judgment before an action and whether such moral judgments are or should be based on reason has occasioned debate through much of modern history between theories of modern western philosophy in juxtaposition to the theories of romanticism and other reactionary movements after the end of the Middle Ages.

Exam Probability: **High**

6. *Answer choices:*

(see index for correct answer)

- a. personal values
- b. co-culture
- c. surface-level diversity
- d. Conscience

Guidance: level 1

:: White-collar criminals ::

_____ refers to financially motivated, nonviolent crime committed by businesses and government professionals. It was first defined by the sociologist Edwin Sutherland in 1939 as "a crime committed by a person of respectability and high social status in the course of their occupation". Typical _____ s could include wage theft, fraud, bribery, Ponzi schemes, insider trading, labor racketeering, embezzlement, cybercrime, copyright infringement, money laundering, identity theft, and forgery. Lawyers can specialize in _____ .

Exam Probability: **Low**

7. *Answer choices:*

(see index for correct answer)

- a. Tongsun Park
- b. Du Jun

Guidance: level 1

:: ::

A _____ is the ability to carry out a task with determined results often within a given amount of time, energy, or both. _____ s can often be divided into domain-general and domain-specific _____ s. For example, in the domain of work, some general _____ s would include time management, teamwork and leadership, self-motivation and others, whereas domain-specific _____ s would be used only for a certain job. _____ usually requires certain environmental stimuli and situations to assess the level of _____ being shown and used.

Exam Probability: **Medium**

8. *Answer choices:*

(see index for correct answer)

- a. Skill
- b. information systems assessment
- c. Character
- d. cultural

Guidance: level 1

:: ::

Sustainability is the process of people maintaining change in a balanced environment, in which the exploitation of resources, the direction of investments, the orientation of technological development and institutional change are all in harmony and enhance both current and future potential to meet human needs and aspirations. For many in the field, sustainability is defined through the following interconnected domains or pillars: environment, economic and social, which according to Fritjof Capra is based on the principles of Systems Thinking. Sub-domains of _____ development have been considered also: cultural, technological and political. While _____ development may be the organizing principle for sustainability for some, for others, the two terms are paradoxical. _____ development is the development that meets the needs of the present without compromising the ability of future generations to meet their own needs. Brundtland Report for the World Commission on Environment and Development introduced the term of _____ development.

Exam Probability: **High**

9. *Answer choices:*

(see index for correct answer)

- a. imperative
- b. hierarchical
- c. Sustainable
- d. cultural

Guidance: level 1

A _____ is a set of rules, often written, with regards to clothing. _____s are created out of social perceptions and norms, and vary based on purpose, circumstances and occasions. Different societies and cultures are likely to have different _____s.

Exam Probability: **Medium**

10. *Answer choices:*

(see index for correct answer)

- a. information systems assessment
- b. functional perspective
- c. cultural
- d. Dress code

Guidance: level 1

:: Social philosophy ::

The _____ describes the unintended social benefits of an individual's self-interested actions. Adam Smith first introduced the concept in The Theory of Moral Sentiments, written in 1759, invoking it in reference to income distribution. In this work, however, the idea of the market is not discussed, and the word "capitalism" is never used.

Exam Probability: **High**

11. *Answer choices:*
(see index for correct answer)

- a. Societal attitudes towards abortion
- b. Veil of Ignorance
- c. Freedom to contract
- d. Invisible hand

Guidance: level 1

:: Business law ::

A _____ is an arrangement where parties, known as partners, agree to cooperate to advance their mutual interests. The partners in a _____ may be individuals, businesses, interest-based organizations, schools, governments or combinations. Organizations may partner to increase the likelihood of each achieving their mission and to amplify their reach. A _____ may result in issuing and holding equity or may be only governed by a contract.

Exam Probability: **Low**

12. *Answer choices:*
(see index for correct answer)

- a. Finance lease
- b. Partnership
- c. Statutory authority
- d. Limited partnership

Guidance: level 1

:: Price fixing convictions ::

_____ AG is a German multinational conglomerate company headquartered in Berlin and Munich and the largest industrial manufacturing company in Europe with branch offices abroad.

Exam Probability: **Low**

13. *Answer choices:*

(see index for correct answer)

- a. British Airways
- b. Grolsch Brewery
- c. Siemens
- d. SK Foods

Guidance: level 1

:: Occupational safety and health ::

_____ is a chemical element with symbol Pb and atomic number 82. It is a heavy metal that is denser than most common materials. _____ is soft and malleable, and also has a relatively low melting point. When freshly cut, _____ is silvery with a hint of blue; it tarnishes to a dull gray color when exposed to air. _____ has the highest atomic number of any stable element and three of its isotopes are endpoints of major nuclear decay chains of heavier elements.

Exam Probability: **Medium**

14. *Answer choices:*

(see index for correct answer)

- a. Lead
- b. Mercury
- c. Industrial noise
- d. Cadmium

Guidance: level 1

:: ::

The Federal National Mortgage Association, commonly known as _____, is a United States government-sponsored enterprise and, since 1968, a publicly traded company. Founded in 1938 during the Great Depression as part of the New Deal, the corporation's purpose is to expand the secondary mortgage market by securitizing mortgage loans in the form of mortgage-backed securities, allowing lenders to reinvest their assets into more lending and in effect increasing the number of lenders in the mortgage market by reducing the reliance on locally based savings and loan associations. Its brother organization is the Federal Home Loan Mortgage Corporation, better known as Freddie Mac. As of 2018, _____ is ranked #21 on the Fortune 500 rankings of the largest United States corporations by total revenue.

Exam Probability: **Medium**

15. *Answer choices:*

(see index for correct answer)

- a. similarity-attraction theory
- b. Character
- c. hierarchical
- d. Fannie Mae

Guidance: level 1

_____ is the introduction of contaminants into the natural environment that cause adverse change. _____ can take the form of chemical substances or energy, such as noise, heat or light. Pollutants, the components of _____ , can be either foreign substances/energies or naturally occurring contaminants. _____ is often classed as point source or nonpoint source _____ .In 2015, _____ killed 9 million people in the world.

Exam Probability: **Medium**

16. *Answer choices:*

(see index for correct answer)

- a. Pollution
- b. surface-level diversity
- c. hierarchical perspective
- d. Character

Guidance: level 1

:: Criminal law ::

_____ is the body of law that relates to crime. It proscribes conduct perceived as threatening, harmful, or otherwise endangering to the property, health, safety, and moral welfare of people inclusive of one's self. Most _____ is established by statute, which is to say that the laws are enacted by a legislature. _____ includes the punishment and rehabilitation of people who violate such laws. _____ varies according to jurisdiction, and differs from civil law, where emphasis is more on dispute resolution and victim compensation, rather than on punishment or rehabilitation. Criminal procedure is a formalized official activity that authenticates the fact of commission of a crime and authorizes punitive or rehabilitative treatment of the offender.

Exam Probability: **High**

17. *Answer choices:*

(see index for correct answer)

- a. Mala prohibita
- b. mitigating factor
- c. Criminal law
- d. Self-incrimination

Guidance: level 1

_____ in the United States is a federal and state program that helps with medical costs for some people with limited income and resources. _____ also offers benefits not normally covered by Medicare, including nursing home care and personal care services. The Health Insurance Association of America describes _____ as "a government insurance program for persons of all ages whose income and resources are insufficient to pay for health care." _____ is the largest source of funding for medical and health-related services for people with low income in the United States, providing free health insurance to 74 million low-income and disabled people as of 2017. It is a means-tested program that is jointly funded by the state and federal governments and managed by the states, with each state currently having broad leeway to determine who is eligible for its implementation of the program. States are not required to participate in the program, although all have since 1982. _____ recipients must be U.S. citizens or qualified non-citizens, and may include low-income adults, their children, and people with certain disabilities. Poverty alone does not necessarily qualify someone for _____ .

Exam Probability: **High**

18. *Answer choices:*

(see index for correct answer)

- a. surface-level diversity
- b. personal values
- c. Character
- d. co-culture

Guidance: level 1

:: Corporate scandals ::

The _____ was a privately held international group of financial services companies controlled by Allen Stanford, until it was seized by United States authorities in early 2009. Headquartered in the Galleria Tower II in Uptown Houston, Texas, it had 50 offices in several countries, mainly in the Americas, included the Stanford International Bank, and said it managed US$8.5 billion of assets for more than 30,000 clients in 136 countries on six continents. On February 17, 2009, U.S. Federal agents placed the company into receivership due to charges of fraud. Ten days later, the U.S. Securities and Exchange Commission amended its complaint to accuse Stanford of turning the company into a "massive Ponzi scheme".

Exam Probability: **High**

19. *Answer choices:*

(see index for correct answer)

- a. ExtenZe
- b. Aluminium price-fixing conspiracy
- c. Stanford Financial Group
- d. Cash for comment affair

Guidance: level 1

:: ::

The Ethics & Compliance Initiative was formed in 2015 and consists of three nonprofit organizations: the Ethics Research Center, the Ethics & Compliance Association, and the Ethics & Compliance Certification Institute. Based in Arlington, Virginia, United States, ECI is devoted to the advancement of high ethical standards and practices in public and private institutions, and provides research about ethical standards, workplace integrity, and compliance practices and processes.

Exam Probability: **High**

20. *Answer choices:*

(see index for correct answer)

- a. open system
- b. Ethics Resource Center
- c. hierarchical perspective
- d. Character

Guidance: level 1

:: Ethical banking ::

A _____ or community development finance institution - abbreviated in both cases to CDFI - is a financial institution that provides credit and financial services to underserved markets and populations, primarily in the USA but also in the UK. A CDFI may be a community development bank, a community development credit union , a community development loan fund , a community development venture capital fund , a microenterprise development loan fund, or a community development corporation.

Exam Probability: **High**

21. *Answer choices:*

(see index for correct answer)

- a. The Co-operative Bank
- b. Reliance Bank
- c. GLS Bank
- d. ShoreBank

Guidance: level 1

:: Coal ::

_____ is a combustible black or brownish-black sedimentary rock, formed as rock strata called _____ seams. _____ is mostly carbon with variable amounts of other elements; chiefly hydrogen, sulfur, oxygen, and nitrogen. _____ is formed if dead plant matter decays into peat and over millions of years the heat and pressure of deep burial converts the peat into _____. Vast deposits of _____ originates in former wetlands—called _____ forests—that covered much of the Earth's tropical land areas during the late Carboniferous and Permian times.

Exam Probability: **Medium**

22. *Answer choices:*

(see index for correct answer)

- a. Coal
- b. Pulverized coal-fired boiler
- c. World Coal Association
- d. Carbolineum

Guidance: level 1

:: Corporate scandals ::

_____ was a bank based in the Caribbean, which operated from 1986 to 2009 when it went into receivership. It was an affiliate of the Stanford Financial Group and failed when the its parent was seized by United States authorities in early 2009 as part of the investigation into Allen Stanford.

Exam Probability: **Low**

23. *Answer choices:*

(see index for correct answer)

- a. Stanford International Bank
- b. Alexander Yakovlev
- c. Product recall
- d. YoungStartup Ventures

Guidance: level 1

:: Progressive Era in the United States ::

The Clayton Antitrust Act of 1914, was a part of United States antitrust law with the goal of adding further substance to the U.S. antitrust law regime; the _____ sought to prevent anticompetitive practices in their incipiency. That regime started with the Sherman Antitrust Act of 1890, the first Federal law outlawing practices considered harmful to consumers. The _____ specified particular prohibited conduct, the three-level enforcement scheme, the exemptions, and the remedial measures.

Exam Probability: **High**

24. *Answer choices:*

(see index for correct answer)

- a. Mann Act
- b. Clayton Antitrust Act
- c. pragmatism

Guidance: level 1

:: Renewable energy ::

_____ is the conversion of energy from sunlight into electricity, either directly using photovoltaics, indirectly using concentrated _____, or a combination. Concentrated _____ systems use lenses or mirrors and tracking systems to focus a large area of sunlight into a small beam. Photovoltaic cells convert light into an electric current using the photovoltaic effect.

Exam Probability: **Low**

25. *Answer choices:*

(see index for correct answer)

- a. Energy hierarchy
- b. Biomass Energy Centre
- c. Crosswind kite power
- d. Solar power

Guidance: level 1

:: International trade ::

_____ involves the transfer of goods or services from one person or entity to another, often in exchange for money. A system or network that allows _____ is called a market.

Exam Probability: **High**

26. *Answer choices:*

(see index for correct answer)

- a. International Standards of Accounting and Reporting
- b. Spice trade
- c. Rybczynski theorem
- d. European Union Customs Union

Guidance: level 1

:: ::

_____ is a bundle of characteristics, including ways of thinking, feeling, and acting, which humans are said to have naturally. The term is often regarded as capturing what it is to be human, or the essence of humanity. The term is controversial because it is disputed whether or not such an essence exists. Arguments about _____ have been a mainstay of philosophy for centuries and the concept continues to provoke lively philosophical debate. The concept also continues to play a role in science, with neuroscientists, psychologists and social scientists sometimes claiming that their results have yielded insight into _____. _____ is traditionally contrasted with characteristics that vary among humans, such as characteristics associated with specific cultures. Debates about _____ are related to, although not the same as, debates about the comparative importance of genes and environment in development.

Exam Probability: **High**

27. *Answer choices:*

(see index for correct answer)

- a. surface-level diversity
- b. corporate values
- c. empathy
- d. Human nature

Guidance: level 1

:: Cognitive biases ::

In personality psychology, _____ is the degree to which people believe that they have control over the outcome of events in their lives, as opposed to external forces beyond their control. Understanding of the concept was developed by Julian B. Rotter in 1954, and has since become an aspect of personality studies. A person's "locus" is conceptualized as internal or external.

Exam Probability: **High**

28. *Answer choices:*

(see index for correct answer)

- a. Forer effect
- b. Picture superiority effect
- c. Empathy gap
- d. Locus of control

Guidance: level 1

:: ::

_____ is a product prepared from the leaves of the _____ plant by curing them. The plant is part of the genus Nicotiana and of the Solanaceae family. While more than 70 species of _____ are known, the chief commercial crop is N. tabacum. The more potent variant N. rustica is also used around the world.

Exam Probability: **Medium**

29. *Answer choices:*

(see index for correct answer)

- a. surface-level diversity
- b. Sarbanes-Oxley act of 2002
- c. functional perspective
- d. Tobacco

Guidance: level 1

:: Workplace ::

In business management, _____ is a management style whereby a manager closely observes and/or controls the work of his/her subordinates or employees.

Exam Probability: **Low**

30. *Answer choices:*

(see index for correct answer)

- a. Workplace conflict
- b. Work etiquette
- c. Workplace spirituality
- d. Control freak

Guidance: level 1

:: Auditing ::

_____ refers to the independence of the internal auditor or of the external auditor from parties that may have a financial interest in the business being audited. Independence requires integrity and an objective approach to the audit process. The concept requires the auditor to carry out his or her work freely and in an objective manner.

Exam Probability: **Medium**

31. *Answer choices:*

(see index for correct answer)

- a. Auditor independence
- b. Mitigating control
- c. SOFT audit
- d. Performance audit

Guidance: level 1

:: Office work ::

_____ is the process and behavior in human interactions involving power and authority. It is also a tool to assess the operational capacity and to balance diverse views of interested parties. It is also known as office politics and organizational politics.It is the use of power and social networking within an organization to achieve changes that benefit the organization or individuals within it. Influence by individuals may serve personal interests without regard to their effect on the organization itself. Some of the personal advantages may include access to tangible assets, or intangible benefits such as status or pseudo-authority that influences the behavior of others. On the other hand, organizational politics can increase efficiency, form interpersonal relationships, expedite change, and profit the organization and its members simultaneously.Both individuals and groups may engage in office politics which can be highly destructive, as people focus on personal gains at the expense of the organization. "Self-serving political actions can negatively influence our social groupings, cooperation, information sharing, and many other organizational functions." Thus, it is vital to pay attention to organizational politics and create the right political landscape. "Politics is the lubricant that oils your organization`s internal gears."
Office politics has also been described as "simply how power gets worked out on a practical, day-to-day basis."

Exam Probability: **Medium**

32. *Answer choices:*

(see index for correct answer)

- a. Clerk
- b. Copier service

- c. Workplace politics
- d. Paperless office

Guidance: level 1

:: Anti-competitive behaviour ::

_____ is a secret cooperation or deceitful agreement in order to deceive others, although not necessarily illegal, as a conspiracy. A secret agreement between two or more parties to limit open competition by deceiving, misleading, or defrauding others of their legal rights, or to obtain an objective forbidden by law typically by defrauding or gaining an unfair market advantage is an example of _____ . It is an agreement among firms or individuals to divide a market, set prices, limit production or limit opportunities.It can involve "unions, wage fixing, kickbacks, or misrepresenting the independence of the relationship between the colluding parties". In legal terms, all acts effected by _____ are considered void.

Exam Probability: **Medium**

33. *Answer choices:*

(see index for correct answer)

- a. Restraint of trade
- b. Collusion
- c. Bid rigging
- d. SK Hynix

Guidance: level 1

:: Electronic feedback ::

_____ occurs when outputs of a system are routed back as inputs as part of a chain of cause-and-effect that forms a circuit or loop. The system can then be said to feed back into itself. The notion of cause-and-effect has to be handled carefully when applied to _____ systems.

Exam Probability: **Low**

34. *Answer choices:*
(see index for correct answer)

- a. feedback loop
- b. Feedback

Guidance: level 1

:: Social enterprise ::

Corporate social responsibility is a type of international private business self-regulation. While once it was possible to describe CSR as an internal organisational policy or a corporate ethic strategy, that time has passed as various international laws have been developed and various organisations have used their authority to push it beyond individual or even industry-wide initiatives. While it has been considered a form of corporate self-regulation for some time, over the last decade or so it has moved considerably from voluntary decisions at the level of individual organisations, to mandatory schemes at regional, national and even transnational levels.

Exam Probability: **Low**

35. *Answer choices:*

(see index for correct answer)

- a. Social venture
- b. Corporate citizenship

Guidance: level 1

:: Social responsibility ::

The United Nations Global Compact is a non-binding United Nations pact to encourage businesses worldwide to adopt sustainable and socially responsible policies, and to report on their implementation. The _____ is a principle-based framework for businesses, stating ten principles in the areas of human rights, labor, the environment and anti-corruption. Under the Global Compact, companies are brought together with UN agencies, labor groups and civil society. Cities can join the Global Compact through the Cities Programme.

Exam Probability: **High**

36. *Answer choices:*

(see index for correct answer)

- a. Footprints network
- b. Clann Credo
- c. Creating shared value
- d. UN Global Compact

Guidance: level 1

:: ::

_____ refers to a business initiative to increase the access between a company and their current and potential customers through the use of the Internet. The Internet allows the company to market themselves and attract new customers to their website where they can provide product information and better customer service. Customers can place orders electronically, therefore reducing expensive long distant phone calls and postage costs of placing orders, while saving time on behalf of the customer and company.

Exam Probability: **Low**

37. *Answer choices:*

(see index for correct answer)

- a. Global reach

- b. functional perspective
- c. deep-level diversity
- d. imperative

Guidance: level 1

:: Types of marketing ::

_____ is an advertisement strategy in which a company uses surprise and/or unconventional interactions in order to promote a product or service. It is a type of publicity. The term was popularized by Jay Conrad Levinson's 1984 book _____ .

Exam Probability: **High**

38. *Answer choices:*

(see index for correct answer)

- a. Menu engineering
- b. Affinity marketing
- c. Shopper marketing
- d. Alliance marketing

Guidance: level 1

:: Ethically disputed business practices ::

_____ is the trading of a public company's stock or other securities by individuals with access to nonpublic information about the company. In various countries, some kinds of trading based on insider information is illegal. This is because it is seen as unfair to other investors who do not have access to the information, as the investor with insider information could potentially make larger profits than a typical investor could make. The rules governing _____ are complex and vary significantly from country to country. The extent of enforcement also varies from one country to another. The definition of insider in one jurisdiction can be broad, and may cover not only insiders themselves but also any persons related to them, such as brokers, associates and even family members. A person who becomes aware of non-public information and trades on that basis may be guilty of a crime.

Exam Probability: **Medium**

39. *Answer choices:*

(see index for correct answer)

- a. Conflict of interest
- b. Coffin ship
- c. Error account
- d. Suicide bidding

Guidance: level 1

_____ Corporation was an American energy, commodities, and services company based in Houston, Texas. It was founded in 1985 as a merger between Houston Natural Gas and InterNorth, both relatively small regional companies. Before its bankruptcy on December 3, 2001, _____ employed approximately 29,000 staff and was a major electricity, natural gas, communications and pulp and paper company, with claimed revenues of nearly $101 billion during 2000. Fortune named _____ "America's Most Innovative Company" for six consecutive years.

Exam Probability: **Medium**

40. *Answer choices:*

(see index for correct answer)

- a. interpersonal communication
- b. hierarchical perspective
- c. information systems assessment
- d. Enron

Guidance: level 1

:: Auditing ::

_____ , as defined by accounting and auditing, is a process for assuring of an organization's objectives in operational effectiveness and efficiency, reliable financial reporting, and compliance with laws, regulations and policies. A broad concept, _____ involves everything that controls risks to an organization.

Exam Probability: **Medium**

41. *Answer choices:*

(see index for correct answer)

- a. International Federation of Audit Bureaux of Circulations
- b. Risk based internal audit
- c. Continuous auditing
- d. Internal control

Guidance: level 1

:: ::

The _____ of 1977 is a United States federal law known primarily for two of its main provisions: one that addresses accounting transparency requirements under the Securities Exchange Act of 1934 and another concerning bribery of foreign officials. The Act was amended in 1988 and in 1998, and has been subject to continued congressional concerns, namely whether its enforcement discourages U.S. companies from investing abroad.

Exam Probability: **High**

42. *Answer choices:*

(see index for correct answer)

- a. imperative
- b. information systems assessment

- c. hierarchical perspective
- d. open system

Guidance: level 1

:: ::

In regulatory jurisdictions that provide for it, _____ is a group of laws and organizations designed to ensure the rights of consumers as well as fair trade, competition and accurate information in the marketplace. The laws are designed to prevent the businesses that engage in fraud or specified unfair practices from gaining an advantage over competitors. They may also provides additional protection for those most vulnerable in society. _____ laws are a form of government regulation that aim to protect the rights of consumers. For example, a government may require businesses to disclose detailed information about products—particularly in areas where safety or public health is an issue, such as food.

Exam Probability: **Medium**

43. *Answer choices:*
(see index for correct answer)

- a. Consumer Protection
- b. imperative
- c. functional perspective
- d. hierarchical

Guidance: level 1

:: Law ::

_____ is a body of law which defines the role, powers, and structure of different entities within a state, namely, the executive, the parliament or legislature, and the judiciary; as well as the basic rights of citizens and, in federal countries such as the United States and Canada, the relationship between the central government and state, provincial, or territorial governments.

Exam Probability: **Low**

44. *Answer choices:*

(see index for correct answer)

- a. Legal case
- b. Constitutional law

Guidance: level 1

:: Leadership ::

_____ is leadership that is directed by respect for ethical beliefs and values and for the dignity and rights of others. It is thus related to concepts such as trust, honesty, consideration, charisma, and fairness.

Exam Probability: **High**

45. *Answer choices:*

(see index for correct answer)

- a. Three levels of leadership model
- b. Ethical leadership
- c. Servant leadership
- d. Spirit of Enniskillen Trust

Guidance: level 1

:: Fraud ::

In the United States, _____ is the claiming of Medicare health care reimbursement to which the claimant is not entitled. There are many different types of _____ , all of which have the same goal: to collect money from the Medicare program illegitimately.

Exam Probability: **Medium**

46. *Answer choices:*

(see index for correct answer)

- a. Corporate scandal
- b. World Luxury Association
- c. Shell corporation
- d. Medicare fraud

Guidance: level 1

:: Decentralization ::

_____ or sub _____ mainly refers to the unrestricted growth in many urban areas of housing, commercial development, and roads over large expanses of land, with little concern for urban planning. In addition to describing a particular form of urbanization, the term also relates to the social and environmental consequences associated with this development. In Continental Europe the term "peri-urbanisation" is often used to denote similar dynamics and phenomena, although the term _____ is currently being used by the European Environment Agency. There is widespread disagreement about what constitutes sprawl and how to quantify it. For example, some commentators measure sprawl only with the average number of residential units per acre in a given area. But others associate it with decentralization, discontinuity, segregation of uses, and so forth.

Exam Probability: **Low**

47. *Answer choices:*

(see index for correct answer)

- a. Urban sprawl
- b. Ralph Borsodi
- c. Home rule
- d. National Question

Guidance: level 1

:: ::

The _____ Group is a global financial investment management and insurance company headquartered in Des Moines, Iowa.

Exam Probability: **High**

48. *Answer choices:*
(see index for correct answer)

- a. surface-level diversity
- b. Sarbanes-Oxley act of 2002
- c. similarity-attraction theory
- d. cultural

Guidance: level 1

:: Professional ethics ::

In the mental health field, a _____ is a situation where multiple roles exist between a therapist, or other mental health practitioner, and a client. _____ s are also referred to as multiple relationships, and these two terms are used interchangeably in the research literature. The American Psychological Association Ethical Principles of Psychologists and Code of Conduct is a resource that outlines ethical standards and principles to which practitioners are expected to adhere. Standard 3.05 of the APA ethics code outlines the definition of multiple relationships. Dual or multiple relationships occur when.

Exam Probability: **Low**

49. *Answer choices:*

(see index for correct answer)

- a. Dual relationship
- b. Continuous professional development
- c. ethical code

Guidance: level 1

:: Supply chain management terms ::

In business and finance, _____ is a system of organizations, people, activities, information, and resources involved in moving a product or service from supplier to customer. _____ activities involve the transformation of natural resources, raw materials, and components into a finished product that is delivered to the end customer. In sophisticated _____ systems, used products may re-enter the _____ at any point where residual value is recyclable. _____ s link value chains.

Exam Probability: **Low**

50. *Answer choices:*

(see index for correct answer)

- a. Supply Chain
- b. Supply-chain management

- c. Work in process
- d. Price look-up code

Guidance: level 1

:: United States federal trade legislation ::

The _____ of 1914 established the Federal Trade Commission. The Act, signed into law by Woodrow Wilson in 1914, outlaws unfair methods of competition and outlaws unfair acts or practices that affect commerce.

Exam Probability: **High**

51. *Answer choices:*

(see index for correct answer)

- a. Carriage of Goods by Sea Act
- b. Gould Amendment
- c. Tariff of 1832
- d. Federal Trade Commission Act

Guidance: level 1

:: Cultural appropriation ::

_____ is a social and economic order that encourages the acquisition of goods and services in ever-increasing amounts. With the industrial revolution, but particularly in the 20th century, mass production led to an economic crisis: there was overproduction—the supply of goods would grow beyond consumer demand, and so manufacturers turned to planned obsolescence and advertising to manipulate consumer spending. In 1899, a book on _____ published by Thorstein Veblen, called The Theory of the Leisure Class, examined the widespread values and economic institutions emerging along with the widespread "leisure time" in the beginning of the 20th century. In it Veblen "views the activities and spending habits of this leisure class in terms of conspicuous and vicarious consumption and waste. Both are related to the display of status and not to functionality or usefulness."

Exam Probability: **Medium**

52. *Answer choices:*

(see index for correct answer)

- a. Washington Redskins
- b. Consumerism
- c. Customization
- d. Portrayal of Native Americans in film

Guidance: level 1

:: Socialism ::

_____ is a label used to define the first currents of modern socialist thought as exemplified by the work of Henri de Saint-Simon, Charles Fourier, Étienne Cabet and Robert Owen.

Exam Probability: **Low**

53. *Answer choices:*

(see index for correct answer)

- a. Social imperialism
- b. Orthodox Marxism
- c. Utopian socialism
- d. Edinburgh University Socialist Society

Guidance: level 1

:: Corporations law ::

A normal _____ consists of various departments that contribute to the company's overall mission and goals. Common departments include Marketing, [Finance, [[Operations managementOperations, Human Resource, and IT. These five divisions represent the major departments within a publicly traded company, though there are often smaller departments within autonomous firms. There is typically a CEO, and Board of Directors composed of the directors of each department. There are also company presidents, vice presidents, and CFOs.There is a great diversity in corporate forms as enterprises may range from single company to multi-corporate conglomerate. The four main _____ s are Functional, Divisional, Geographic, and the Matrix.Realistically, most corporations tend to have a "hybrid" structure, which is a combination of different models with one dominant strategy.

Exam Probability: **Medium**

54. *Answer choices:*

(see index for correct answer)

- a. Corporate lawyer
- b. Company seal
- c. Business judgment rule
- d. Corporate structure

Guidance: level 1

:: Renewable energy ::

A _____ is a fuel that is produced through contemporary biological processes, such as agriculture and anaerobic digestion, rather than a fuel produced by geological processes such as those involved in the formation of fossil fuels, such as coal and petroleum, from prehistoric biological matter. If the source biomatter can regrow quickly, the resulting fuel is said to be a form of renewable energy.

Exam Probability: **Low**

55. *Answer choices:*

(see index for correct answer)

- a. Algaculture
- b. Solar thermal energy
- c. Yield co
- d. Biofuel

Guidance: level 1

A _____ is a proceeding by a party or parties against another in the civil court of law. The archaic term "suit in law" is found in only a small number of laws still in effect today. The term " _____ " is used in reference to a civil action brought in a court of law in which a plaintiff, a party who claims to have incurred loss as a result of a defendant's actions, demands a legal or equitable remedy. The defendant is required to respond to the plaintiff's complaint. If the plaintiff is successful, judgment is in the plaintiff's favor, and a variety of court orders may be issued to enforce a right, award damages, or impose a temporary or permanent injunction to prevent an act or compel an act. A declaratory judgment may be issued to prevent future legal disputes.

Exam Probability: **High**

56. *Answer choices:*

(see index for correct answer)

- a. levels of analysis
- b. co-culture
- c. Lawsuit
- d. deep-level diversity

Guidance: level 1

:: False advertising law ::

The Lanham Act is the primary federal trademark statute of law in the United States. The Act prohibits a number of activities, including trademark infringement, trademark dilution, and false advertising.

Exam Probability: **Low**

57. *Answer choices:*

(see index for correct answer)

- a. Lanham Act
- b. POM Wonderful LLC v. Coca-Cola Co.

Guidance: level 1

:: Culture ::

_____ is a society which is characterized by individualism, which is the prioritization or emphasis, of the individual over the entire group. _____ s are oriented around the self, being independent instead of identifying with a group mentality. They see each other as only loosely linked, and value personal goals over group interests. _____ s tend to have a more diverse population and are characterized with emphasis on personal achievements, and a rational assessment of both the beneficial and detrimental aspects of relationships with others. _____ s have such unique aspects of communication as being a low power-distance culture and having a low-context communication style. The United States, Australia, Great Britain, Canada, the Netherlands, and New Zealand have been identified as highly _____ s.

Exam Probability: **Medium**

58. *Answer choices:*

(see index for correct answer)

- a. High-context
- b. Intracultural
- c. cultural framework
- d. Individualistic culture

Guidance: level 1

:: Statutory law ::

_____ or statute law is written law set down by a body of legislature or by a singular legislator. This is as opposed to oral or customary law; or regulatory law promulgated by the executive or common law of the judiciary. Statutes may originate with national, state legislatures or local municipalities.

Exam Probability: **Medium**

59. *Answer choices:*

(see index for correct answer)

- a. incorporation by reference
- b. Statute of repose
- c. ratification
- d. statute law

Guidance: level 1

Accounting

Accounting or accountancy is the measurement, processing, and communication of financial information about economic entities such as businesses and corporations. The modern field was established by the Italian mathematician Luca Pacioli in 1494. Accounting, which has been called the "language of business", measures the results of an organization's economic activities and conveys this information to a variety of users, including investors, creditors, management, and regulators.

:: Management accounting ::

_____ is a professional business study of Accounts and management in which we learn importance of accounts in our management system.

Exam Probability: **High**

1. *Answer choices:*

(see index for correct answer)

- a. Environmental full-cost accounting
- b. Revenue center
- c. Hedge accounting
- d. Indirect costs

Guidance: level 1

:: ::

A _____ is a fund into which a sum of money is added during an employee's employment years, and from which payments are drawn to support the person's retirement from work in the form of periodic payments. A _____ may be a "defined benefit plan" where a fixed sum is paid regularly to a person, or a "defined contribution plan" under which a fixed sum is invested and then becomes available at retirement age. _____ s should not be confused with severance pay; the former is usually paid in regular installments for life after retirement, while the latter is typically paid as a fixed amount after involuntary termination of employment prior to retirement.

Exam Probability: **Low**

2. Answer choices:

(see index for correct answer)

- a. hierarchical perspective
- b. cultural
- c. Pension
- d. imperative

Guidance: level 1

:: Project management ::

_____ is the widespread practice of collecting information and attempting to spot a pattern. In some fields of study, the term " _____ " has more formally defined meanings.

Exam Probability: **Low**

3. Answer choices:

(see index for correct answer)

- a. Scope
- b. Theory Z of Ouchi
- c. Project management process
- d. Trend analysis

Guidance: level 1

:: Financial statements ::

A Statement of changes in equity and similarly the statement of changes in owner's equity for a sole trader, statement of changes in partners' equity for a partnership, statement of changes in Shareholders' equity for a Company or statement of changes in Taxpayers' equity for Government financial statements is one of the four basic financial statements.

Exam Probability: **Medium**

4. *Answer choices:*

(see index for correct answer)

- a. Statement of retained earnings
- b. Quarterly finance report
- c. Government financial statements
- d. Emphasis of matter

Guidance: level 1

:: ::

Generally speaking, a _____ begins on the New Year's Day of the given calendar system and ends on the day before the following New Year's Day, and thus consists of a whole number of days. A year can also be measured by starting on any other named day of the calendar, and ending on the day before this named day in the following year. This may be termed a "year's time", but not a "_____". To reconcile the _____ with the astronomical cycle certain years contain extra days.

Exam Probability: **Low**

5. *Answer choices:*

(see index for correct answer)

- a. imperative
- b. interpersonal communication
- c. Calendar year
- d. Sarbanes-Oxley act of 2002

Guidance: level 1

:: Competition (economics) ::

In taxation and accounting, _____ refers to the rules and methods for pricing transactions within and between enterprises under common ownership or control. Because of the potential for cross-border controlled transactions to distort taxable income, tax authorities in many countries can adjust intragroup transfer prices that differ from what would have been charged by unrelated enterprises dealing at arm's length . The OECD and World Bank recommend intragroup pricing rules based on the arm's-length principle, and 19 of the 20 members of the G20 have adopted similar measures through bilateral treaties and domestic legislation, regulations, or administrative practice. Countries with _____ legislation generally follow the OECD _____ Guidelines for Multinational Enterprises and Tax Administrations in most respects, although their rules can differ on some important details.

Exam Probability: **Medium**

6. *Answer choices:*

(see index for correct answer)

- a. Competition
- b. Transfer pricing
- c. Tax competition
- d. Regulatory competition

Guidance: level 1

:: Organizational behavior ::

_____ is the state or fact of exclusive rights and control over property, which may be an object, land/real estate or intellectual property. _____ involves multiple rights, collectively referred to as title, which may be separated and held by different parties.

Exam Probability: **High**

7. *Answer choices:*

(see index for correct answer)

- a. Informal organization
- b. Organizational commitment
- c. Organizational storytelling
- d. Ownership

Guidance: level 1

:: Stock market ::

A _____ , equity market or share market is the aggregation of buyers and sellers of stocks , which represent ownership claims on businesses; these may include securities listed on a public stock exchange, as well as stock that is only traded privately. Examples of the latter include shares of private companies which are sold to investors through equity crowdfunding platforms. Stock exchanges list shares of common equity as well as other security types, e.g. corporate bonds and convertible bonds.

Exam Probability: **Low**

8. *Answer choices:*

(see index for correct answer)

- a. Red chip
- b. Trader
- c. Volume-weighted average price
- d. Shareholders

Guidance: level 1

:: Management ::

_____ is a style of business management that focuses on identifying and handling cases that deviate from the norm, recommended as best practice by the project management method PRINCE2.

Exam Probability: **High**

9. *Answer choices:*

(see index for correct answer)

- a. Industrial market segmentation
- b. Court of Assistants
- c. Modes of leadership
- d. Management by exception

Guidance: level 1

:: ::

_____ is capital that is contributed to a corporation by investors by purchase of stock from the corporation, the primary market, not by purchase of stock in the open market from other stockholders. It includes share capital as well as additional _____ .

Exam Probability: **Low**

10. *Answer choices:*

(see index for correct answer)

- a. Sarbanes-Oxley act of 2002
- b. co-culture
- c. similarity-attraction theory
- d. information systems assessment

Guidance: level 1

:: Insolvency ::

_____ is the process in accounting by which a company is brought to an end in the United Kingdom, Republic of Ireland and United States. The assets and property of the company are redistributed. _____ is also sometimes referred to as winding-up or dissolution, although dissolution technically refers to the last stage of _____. The process of _____ also arises when customs, an authority or agency in a country responsible for collecting and safeguarding customs duties, determines the final computation or ascertainment of the duties or drawback accruing on an entry.

Exam Probability: **Medium**

11. *Answer choices:*

(see index for correct answer)

- a. Conservatorship
- b. Insolvency law of Russia
- c. Bankruptcy
- d. Liquidation

Guidance: level 1

:: Income taxes ::

An _____ is a tax imposed on individuals or entities that varies with respective income or profits. _____ generally is computed as the product of a tax rate times taxable income. Taxation rates may vary by type or characteristics of the taxpayer.

Exam Probability: **Medium**

12. *Answer choices:*

(see index for correct answer)

- a. Shome Panel
- b. Depreciation recapture
- c. Income splitting
- d. Income tax

Guidance: level 1

:: Manufacturing ::

_____ s are goods that have completed the manufacturing process but have not yet been sold or distributed to the end user.

Exam Probability: **High**

13. *Answer choices:*

(see index for correct answer)

- a. Blowmolding machine
- b. Finished good
- c. Lean production
- d. International Manufacturing Technology Show

Guidance: level 1

:: Financial ratios ::

_____ is a financial ratio that indicates the percentage of a company's assets that are provided via debt. It is the ratio of total debt and total assets.

Exam Probability: **Medium**

14. *Answer choices:*

(see index for correct answer)

- a. Current ratio
- b. Bid-to-cover ratio
- c. Debt ratio
- d. Debt service coverage ratio

Guidance: level 1

:: Generally Accepted Accounting Principles ::

In accounting, _____ is the income that a business have from its normal business activities, usually from the sale of goods and services to customers. _____ is also referred to as sales or turnover. Some companies receive _____ from interest, royalties, or other fees. _____ may refer to business income in general, or it may refer to the amount, in a monetary unit, earned during a period of time, as in "Last year, Company X had _____ of $42 million". Profits or net income generally imply total _____ minus total expenses in a given period. In accounting, in the balance statement it is a subsection of the Equity section and _____ increases equity, it is often referred to as the "top line" due to its position on the income statement at the very top. This is to be contrasted with the "bottom line" which denotes net income.

Exam Probability: **High**

15. *Answer choices:*

(see index for correct answer)

- a. Normal balance
- b. Access to finance
- c. Historical cost
- d. Insurance asset management

Guidance: level 1

:: Taxation in the United States ::

Basis, as used in United States tax law, is the original cost of property, adjusted for factors such as depreciation. When property is sold, the taxpayer pays/ taxes on a capital gain/ that equals the amount realized on the sale minus the sold property's basis.

Exam Probability: **Low**

16. *Answer choices:*

(see index for correct answer)

- a. Cost basis
- b. Adjusted gross income
- c. Endowment tax
- d. Two-Percent Haircut

Guidance: level 1

:: ::

An _____ is a contingent motivator. Traditional _____ s are extrinsic motivators which reward actions to yield a desired outcome. The effectiveness of traditional _____ s has changed as the needs of Western society have evolved. While the traditional _____ model is effective when there is a defined procedure and goal for a task, Western society started to require a higher volume of critical thinkers, so the traditional model became less effective. Institutions are now following a trend in implementing strategies that rely on intrinsic motivations rather than the extrinsic motivations that the traditional _____ s foster.

Exam Probability: **Low**

17. *Answer choices:*

(see index for correct answer)

- a. Character
- b. Sarbanes-Oxley act of 2002
- c. hierarchical perspective
- d. personal values

Guidance: level 1

:: United States Generally Accepted Accounting Principles ::

In the United States, the _____ , Subpart F of the OMB Uniform Guidance, is a rigorous, organization-wide audit or examination of an entity that expends $750,000 or more of federal assistance received for its operations. Usually performed annually, the _____ 's objective is to provide assurance to the US federal government as to the management and use of such funds by recipients such as states, cities, universities, non-profit organizations, and Indian Tribes. The audit is typically performed by an independent certified public accountant and encompasses both financial and compliance components. The _____ s must be submitted to the Federal Audit Clearinghouse along with a data collection form, Form SF-SAC.

Exam Probability: **High**

18. *Answer choices:*

(see index for correct answer)

- a. GASB 45
- b. Working Group on Financial Markets
- c. Asset retirement obligation
- d. Impaired asset

Guidance: level 1

:: Financial regulatory authorities of the United States ::

The _____ is the revenue service of the United States federal government. The government agency is a bureau of the Department of the Treasury, and is under the immediate direction of the Commissioner of Internal Revenue, who is appointed to a five-year term by the President of the United States. The IRS is responsible for collecting taxes and administering the Internal Revenue Code, the main body of federal statutory tax law of the United States. The duties of the IRS include providing tax assistance to taxpayers and pursuing and resolving instances of erroneous or fraudulent tax filings. The IRS has also overseen various benefits programs, and enforces portions of the Affordable Care Act.

Exam Probability: **Medium**

19. *Answer choices:*

(see index for correct answer)

- a. Farm Credit Administration
- b. Internal Revenue Service
- c. National Futures Association
- d. U.S. Securities and Exchange Commission

Guidance: level 1

:: Classification systems ::

_____ is the practice of comparing business processes and performance metrics to industry bests and best practices from other companies. Dimensions typically measured are quality, time and cost.

Exam Probability: **Low**

20. *Answer choices:*
(see index for correct answer)

- a. Fanaroff-Riley classification
- b. Benchmarking
- c. Physiographic regions of the world
- d. Classification of Types of Construction

Guidance: level 1

:: Actuarial science ::

The _____ is the greater benefit of receiving money now rather than an identical sum later. It is founded on time preference.

Exam Probability: **High**

21. *Answer choices:*

(see index for correct answer)

- a. Actuarial reserves
- b. Late-life mortality deceleration
- c. Lexis diagram
- d. Time value of money

Guidance: level 1

:: Accounting terminology ::

_____ or capital expense is the money a company spends to buy, maintain, or improve its fixed assets, such as buildings, vehicles, equipment, or land. It is considered a _____ when the asset is newly purchased or when money is used towards extending the useful life of an existing asset, such as repairing the roof.

Exam Probability: **Medium**

22. *Answer choices:*

(see index for correct answer)

- a. Total absorption costing
- b. revenue recognition principle

- c. Accrual
- d. outstanding balance

Guidance: level 1

:: Accounting terminology ::

_____ is a legally enforceable claim for payment held by a business for goods supplied and/or services rendered that customers/clients have ordered but not paid for. These are generally in the form of invoices raised by a business and delivered to the customer for payment within an agreed time frame. _____ is shown in a balance sheet as an asset. It is one of a series of accounting transactions dealing with the billing of a customer for goods and services that the customer has ordered. These may be distinguished from notes receivable, which are debts created through formal legal instruments called promissory notes.

Exam Probability: **Low**

23. *Answer choices:*

(see index for correct answer)

- a. Accounts receivable
- b. Total absorption costing
- c. Share premium
- d. Basis of accounting

Guidance: level 1

In accounting, the _____ is a measure of the number of times inventory is sold or used in a time period such as a year. It is calculated to see if a business has an excessive inventory in comparison to its sales level. The equation for _____ equals the cost of goods sold divided by the average inventory. _____ is also known as inventory turns, merchandise turnover, stockturn, stock turns, turns, and stock turnover.

Exam Probability: **Low**

24. *Answer choices:*

(see index for correct answer)

- a. Inventory turnover
- b. corporate values
- c. empathy
- d. hierarchical perspective

Guidance: level 1

_____ is a process whereby a person assumes the parenting of another, usually a child, from that person's biological or legal parent or parents. Legal _____s permanently transfers all rights and responsibilities, along with filiation, from the biological parent or parents.

Exam Probability: **Medium**

25. *Answer choices:*

(see index for correct answer)

- a. surface-level diversity
- b. Adoption
- c. functional perspective
- d. empathy

Guidance: level 1

:: Data security ::

_____ is the concept of having more than one person required to complete a task. In business the separation by sharing of more than one individual in one single task is an internal control intended to prevent fraud and error. The concept is alternatively called segregation of duties or, in the political realm, separation of powers. In democracies, the separation of legislation from administration serves a similar purpose. The concept is addressed in technical systems and in information technology equivalently and generally addressed as redundancy.

Exam Probability: **Low**

26. *Answer choices:*

(see index for correct answer)

- a. Actiance
- b. Separation of duties
- c. Context-based access control
- d. First Department

Guidance: level 1

:: Financial ratios ::

_____ is a measure of how revenue growth translates into growth in operating income. It is a measure of leverage, and of how risky, or volatile, a company's operating income is.

Exam Probability: **High**

27. *Answer choices:*

(see index for correct answer)

- a. Infection ratio
- b. Market-to-book
- c. CASA ratio
- d. Diluted earnings per share

Guidance: level 1

:: Generally Accepted Accounting Principles ::

In business and accounting, _____ is an entity's income minus cost of goods sold, expenses and taxes for an accounting period. It is computed as the residual of all revenues and gains over all expenses and losses for the period, and has also been defined as the net increase in shareholders' equity that results from a company's operations. In the context of the presentation of financial statements, the IFRS Foundation defines _____ as synonymous with profit and loss. The difference between revenue and the cost of making a product or providing a service, before deducting overheads, payroll, taxation, and interest payments. This is different from operating income .

Exam Probability: **Medium**

28. *Answer choices:*

(see index for correct answer)

- a. Cash method of accounting
- b. Expense
- c. Write-off
- d. Net income

Guidance: level 1

:: Real estate ::

Amortisation is paying off an amount owed over time by making planned, incremental payments of principal and interest. To amortise a loan means "to kill it off". In accounting, amortisation refers to charging or writing off an intangible asset's cost as an operational expense over its estimated useful life to reduce a company's taxable income.

Exam Probability: **Low**

29. *Answer choices:*

(see index for correct answer)

- a. Amortization
- b. Property investment club
- c. Earnest payment
- d. Boundary

Guidance: level 1

:: Free accounting software ::

A _____ is the principal book or computer file for recording and totaling economic transactions measured in terms of a monetary unit of account by account type, with debits and credits in separate columns and a beginning monetary balance and ending monetary balance for each account.

Exam Probability: **Low**

30. *Answer choices:*

(see index for correct answer)

- a. SQL-Ledger
- b. Ofuz
- c. HomeBank
- d. GnuCash

Guidance: level 1

:: Financial accounting ::

_____ refers to any one of several methods by which a company, for `financial accounting` or tax purposes, depreciates a fixed asset in such a way that the amount of depreciation taken each year is higher during the earlier years of an asset's life. For financial accounting purposes, _____ is expected to be much more productive during its early years, so that depreciation expense will more accurately represent how much of an asset's usefulness is being used up each year. For tax purposes, _____ provides a way of deferring corporate income taxes by reducing taxable income in current years, in exchange for increased taxable income in future years. This is a valuable tax incentive that encourages businesses to purchase new assets.

Exam Probability: **High**

31. *Answer choices:*

(see index for correct answer)

- a. Money measurement concept

- b. Accelerated depreciation
- c. Hidden asset
- d. Tax amortization benefit

Guidance: level 1

:: Budgets ::

_____ is a method of budgeting in which all expenses must be justified and approved for each new period. Developed by Peter Pyhrr in the 1970s, _____ starts from a "zero base" at the beginning of every budget period, analyzing needs and costs of every function within an organization and allocating funds accordingly, regardless of how much money has previously been budgeted to any given line item.

Exam Probability: **Low**

32. *Answer choices:*

(see index for correct answer)

- a. Zero-based budgeting
- b. Budget constraint
- c. Film budgeting
- d. Zero budget

Guidance: level 1

:: Accounting software ::

_____ is a freely available and global framework for exchanging business information. _____ allows the expression of semantic meaning commonly required in business reporting. The language is XML-based and uses the XML syntax and related XML technologies such as XML Schema, XLink, XPath, and Namespaces. One use of _____ is to define and exchange financial information, such as a financial statement. The _____ Specification is developed and published by _____ International, Inc. .

Exam Probability: **Medium**

33. *Answer choices:*

(see index for correct answer)

- a. XBRL
- b. Amortization calculator
- c. Gem Accounts
- d. FinanceWorks

Guidance: level 1

:: Banking terms ::

An _____ occurs when money is withdrawn from a bank account and the available balance goes below zero. In this situation the account is said to be "overdrawn". If there is a prior agreement with the account provider for an _____, and the amount overdrawn is within the authorized _____ limit, then interest is normally charged at the agreed rate. If the negative balance exceeds the agreed terms, then additional fees may be charged and higher interest rates may apply.

Exam Probability: **Medium**

34. *Answer choices:*

(see index for correct answer)

- a. GRG Banking
- b. 3-6-3 Rule
- c. Unbanked
- d. Overdraft

Guidance: level 1

:: Pricing ::

_____ is the difference between a lower selling price and a higher purchase price, resulting in a financial loss for the seller.

Exam Probability: **High**

35. *Answer choices:*

(see index for correct answer)

- a. Price of petroleum
- b. Arbitrage pricing theory
- c. Ecopass
- d. Capital loss

Guidance: level 1

:: Legal terms ::

An _____ is an action which is inaccurate or incorrect. In some usages, an _____ is synonymous with a mistake. In statistics, "_____" refers to the difference between the value which has been computed and the correct value. An _____ could result in failure or in a deviation from the intended performance or behaviour.

Exam Probability: **High**

36. *Answer choices:*

(see index for correct answer)

- a. European Authorized Representative
- b. Grievous bodily harm
- c. Felony
- d. Error

Guidance: level 1

:: Cash flow ::

In corporate finance, _____ or _____ to firm is a way of looking at a business's cash flow to see what is available for distribution among all the securities holders of a corporate entity. This may be useful to parties such as equity holders, debt holders, preferred stock holders, and convertible security holders when they want to see how much cash can be extracted from a company without causing issues to its operations.

Exam Probability: **High**

37. *Answer choices:*

(see index for correct answer)

- a. Cash flow loan
- b. Free cash flow
- c. Cash carrier
- d. First Chicago Method

Guidance: level 1

:: Business ethics ::

In accounting and in most Schools of economic thought, _____ is a rational and unbiased estimate of the potential market price of a good, service, or asset. It takes into account such objectivity factors as.

Exam Probability: **Medium**

38. *Answer choices:*

(see index for correct answer)

- a. Fair value
- b. Product stewardship
- c. Corporate social responsibility
- d. Contingent work

Guidance: level 1

:: ::

The U.S. _____ is an independent agency of the United States federal government. The SEC holds primary responsibility for enforcing the federal securities laws, proposing securities rules, and regulating the securities industry, the nation`s stock and options exchanges, and other activities and organizations, including the electronic securities markets in the United States.

Exam Probability: **Low**

39. Answer choices:

(see index for correct answer)

- a. levels of analysis
- b. cultural
- c. similarity-attraction theory
- d. Securities and Exchange Commission

Guidance: level 1

:: Business law ::

An _____ is a natural person, business, or corporation that provides goods or services to another entity under terms specified in a contract or within a verbal agreement. Unlike an employee, an _____ does not work regularly for an employer but works as and when required, during which time they may be subject to law of agency. _____ s are usually paid on a freelance basis. Contractors often work through a limited company or franchise, which they themselves own, or may work through an umbrella company.

Exam Probability: **Medium**

40. Answer choices:

(see index for correct answer)

- a. Independent contractor
- b. Partnership
- c. United States labor law

- d. Vehicle leasing

Guidance: level 1

:: Commercial crimes ::

_____ is the act of withholding assets for the purpose of conversion of such assets, by one or more persons to whom the assets were entrusted, either to be held or to be used for specific purposes. _____ is a type of financial fraud. For example, a lawyer might embezzle funds from the trust accounts of their clients; a financial advisor might embezzle the funds of investors; and a husband or a wife might embezzle funds from a bank account jointly held with the spouse.

Exam Probability: **Medium**

41. *Answer choices:*

(see index for correct answer)

- a. FATF blacklist
- b. Warehouse bank
- c. Shill
- d. Embezzlement

Guidance: level 1

:: Financial ratios ::

_____ is the difference between revenue and cost of goods sold divided by revenue. _____ is expressed as a percentage. Generally, it is calculated as the selling price of an item, less the cost of goods sold . _____ is often used interchangeably with Gross Profit, but the terms are different. When speaking about a monetary amount, it is technically correct to use the term Gross Profit; when referring to a percentage or ratio, it is correct to use _____ . In other words, _____ is a percentage value, while Gross Profit is a monetary value.

Exam Probability: **Medium**

42. *Answer choices:*

(see index for correct answer)

- a. Cash flow return on investment
- b. Sortino ratio
- c. Gross margin
- d. Days payable outstanding

Guidance: level 1

:: Accounting ::

_____ is the recording of financial transactions, and is part of the process of accounting in business. Transactions include purchases, sales, receipts, and payments by an individual person or an organization/corporation. There are several standard methods of _____, including the single-entry and double-entry _____ systems. While these may be viewed as "real" _____, any process for recording financial transactions is a _____ process.

Exam Probability: **High**

43. *Answer choices:*

(see index for correct answer)

- a. Bookkeeping
- b. CPA Site Solutions
- c. Profit model
- d. Tour accountant

Guidance: level 1

:: Fundamental analysis ::

_____ is the monetary value of earnings per outstanding share of common stock for a company.

Exam Probability: **Low**

44. Answer choices:

(see index for correct answer)

- a. economic Value Added
- b. Market value added
- c. Equity value
- d. Growth stock

Guidance: level 1

:: Business models ::

A _____, _____ company or daughter company is a company that is owned or controlled by another company, which is called the parent company, parent, or holding company. The _____ can be a company, corporation, or limited liability company. In some cases it is a government or state-owned enterprise. In some cases, particularly in the music and book publishing industries, subsidiaries are referred to as imprints.

Exam Probability: **Low**

45. Answer choices:

(see index for correct answer)

- a. Dependent growth business model
- b. Volatility, uncertainty, complexity and ambiguity
- c. Subsidiary
- d. Brainsworking

Guidance: level 1

:: Legal terms ::

_____ or _____ interest, in law, is anything that functions contrary to a party's interest. This word should not be confused with averse.

Exam Probability: **Medium**

46. *Answer choices:*
(see index for correct answer)

- a. Advisory jury
- b. Promiscuous Judge
- c. Adverse
- d. Legal age

Guidance: level 1

:: Asset ::

In accounting, a _____ is any asset which can reasonably be expected to be sold, consumed, or exhausted through the normal operations of a business within the current fiscal year or operating cycle. Typical _____ s include cash, cash equivalents, short-term investments, accounts receivable, stock inventory, supplies, and the portion of prepaid liabilities which will be paid within a year. In simple words, assets which are held for a short period are known as _____ s. Such assets are expected to be realised in cash or consumed during the normal operating cycle of the business.

Exam Probability: **High**

47. *Answer choices:*

(see index for correct answer)

- a. Fixed asset
- b. Current asset

Guidance: level 1

:: Inventory ::

_____ is a system of inventory in which updates are made on a periodic basis. This differs from perpetual inventory systems, where updates are made as seen fit.

Exam Probability: **High**

48. *Answer choices:*

(see index for correct answer)

- a. Inventory control problem
- b. Periodic inventory
- c. Reorder point
- d. Perpetual inventory

Guidance: level 1

:: Accounting terminology ::

_____ are liabilities that reflect expenses that have not yet been paid or logged under accounts payable during an accounting period; in other words, a company's obligation to pay for goods and services that have been provided for which invoices have not yet been received. Examples would include accrued wages payable, accrued sales tax payable, and accrued rent payable.

Exam Probability: **Low**

49. *Answer choices:*

(see index for correct answer)

- a. Fund accounting
- b. General ledger
- c. Record to report
- d. Accrual

Guidance: level 1

:: Loans ::

In finance, a _____ is the lending of money by one or more individuals, organizations, or other entities to other individuals, organizations etc. The recipient incurs a debt, and is usually liable to pay interest on that debt until it is repaid, and also to repay the principal amount borrowed.

Exam Probability: **Medium**

50. *Answer choices:*

(see index for correct answer)

- a. Loan
- b. BankBazaar
- c. Predatory lending
- d. Gross loan

Guidance: level 1

:: Real property law ::

A _____ or millage rate is an ad valorem tax on the value of a property, usually levied on real estate. The tax is levied by the governing authority of the jurisdiction in which the property is located. This can be a national government, a federated state, a county or geographical region or a municipality. Multiple jurisdictions may tax the same property. This tax can be contrasted to a rent tax which is based on rental income or imputed rent, and a land value tax, which is a levy on the value of land, excluding the value of buildings and other improvements.

Exam Probability: **Medium**

51. *Answer choices:*

(see index for correct answer)

- a. Short Assured Tenancy
- b. Right of entry
- c. Commissioner of deeds
- d. Property tax

Guidance: level 1

:: Management accounting ::

_____ is an accountancy practice, the aim of which is to provide an offset to the mark-to-market movement of the derivative in the profit and loss account. There are two types of hedge recognized. For a fair value hedge the offset is achieved either by marking-to-market an asset or a liability which offsets the P&L movement of the derivative. For a cash flow hedge some of the derivative volatility into a separate component of the entity's equity called the cash flow hedge reserve. Where a hedge relationship is effective, most of the mark-to-market derivative volatility will be offset in the profit and loss account. _____ entails much compliance - involving documenting the hedge relationship and both prospectively and retrospectively proving that the hedge relationship is effective.

Exam Probability: **High**

52. *Answer choices:*

(see index for correct answer)

- a. Hedge accounting
- b. Certified Management Accountants of Canada
- c. Relevant cost
- d. Cost driver

Guidance: level 1

:: Management accounting ::

A _____ is a cost that differs between alternatives being considered. In order for a cost to be a _____ it must be.

Exam Probability: **High**

53. *Answer choices:*

(see index for correct answer)

- a. Management control system
- b. Holding cost
- c. Activity-based management
- d. Relevant cost

Guidance: level 1

:: ::

_____ is the income that is gained by governments through taxation. Taxation is the primary source of income for a state. Revenue may be extracted from sources such as individuals, public enterprises, trade, royalties on natural resources and/or foreign aid. An inefficient collection of taxes is greater in countries characterized by poverty, a large agricultural sector and large amounts of foreign aid.

Exam Probability: **High**

54. *Answer choices:*

(see index for correct answer)

- a. hierarchical
- b. Character

- c. Tax revenue
- d. empathy

Guidance: level 1

:: ::

_____ is a means of protection from financial loss. It is a form of risk management, primarily used to hedge against the risk of a contingent or uncertain loss

Exam Probability: **High**

55. *Answer choices:*

(see index for correct answer)

- a. similarity-attraction theory
- b. surface-level diversity
- c. co-culture
- d. Insurance

Guidance: level 1

:: Notes (finance) ::

A _____, sometimes referred to as a note payable, is a legal instrument, in which one party promises in writing to pay a determinate sum of money to the other, either at a fixed or determinable future time or on demand of the payee, under specific terms.

Exam Probability: **Medium**

56. *Answer choices:*
(see index for correct answer)

- a. Principal protected note
- b. Note issuance facility
- c. Treasury Note
- d. Large-sized note

Guidance: level 1

:: Banking ::

A _____ is a financial account maintained by a bank for a customer. A _____ can be a deposit account, a credit card account, a current account, or any other type of account offered by a financial institution, and represents the funds that a customer has entrusted to the financial institution and from which the customer can make withdrawals. Alternatively, accounts may be loan accounts in which case the customer owes money to the financial institution.

Exam Probability: **Low**

57. Answer choices:

(see index for correct answer)

- a. Standing order
- b. Savings account
- c. Commercial finance advisor
- d. Bank account

Guidance: level 1

:: Stock market ::

_____ is a form of stock which may have any combination of features not possessed by common stock including properties of both an equity and a debt instrument, and is generally considered a hybrid instrument. _____s are senior to common stock, but subordinate to bonds in terms of claim and may have priority over common stock in the payment of dividends and upon liquidation. Terms of the _____ are described in the issuing company's articles of association or articles of incorporation.

Exam Probability: **High**

58. Answer choices:

(see index for correct answer)

- a. GXG Markets
- b. Erie War
- c. Instinet

- d. Voting interest

Guidance: level 1

:: Asset ::

_____ s, also known as tangible assets or property, plant and equipment, is a term used in accounting for assets and property that cannot easily be converted into cash. This can be compared with current assets such as cash or bank accounts, described as liquid assets. In most cases, only tangible assets are referred to as fixed. IAS 16 defines _____ s as assets whose future economic benefit is probable to flow into the entity, whose cost can be measured reliably. _____ s belong to one of 2 types:"Freehold Assets" – assets which are purchased with legal right of ownership and used, and "Leasehold Assets" – assets used by owner without legal right for a particular period of time.

Exam Probability: **Low**

59. *Answer choices:*
(see index for correct answer)

- a. Current asset
- b. Asset

Guidance: level 1

INDEX: Correct Answers

Foundations of Business

1. a: Outsourcing

2. b: Bankruptcy

3. d: Insurance

4. a: Employment

5. a: Target market

6. c: Initiative

7. b: Social security

8. : Size

9. b: Focus group

10. c: Venture capital

11. d: Utility

12. : Publicity

13. b: Globalization

14. c: Economic Development

15. c: Information systems

16. d: Currency

17. b: Bribery

18. c: Patent

19. b: Need

20. : Perception

21. a: Import

22. c: Foreign direct investment

23. b: Money

24. b: Trademark

25. d: Arthur Andersen

26. a: Strategic alliance

27. b: Investment

28. b: Expense

29. a: Industry

30. d: Financial services

31. b: Frequency

32. b: Raw material

33. a: Brainstorming

34. : Policy

35. d: Error

36. a: Entrepreneur

37. c: American Express

38. b: Variable cost

39. b: Strategy

40. a: Feedback

41. c: Capitalism

42. : Six Sigma

43. c: Purchasing

44. a: Building

45. b: Direct investment

46. b: Health

47. a: Market share

48. d: Logistics

49. d: Franchising

50. a: Total quality management

51. a: Resource management

52. c: Financial crisis

53. d: Chart

54. d: Credit card

55. : Bank

56. d: Description

57. a: Explanation

58. : Tariff

59. c: Authority

Management

1. c: Entrepreneurship

2. c: Brand

3. c: Overtime

4. b: Labor force

5. d: Labor relations

6. b: Partnership

7. b: Specification

8. a: Fixed cost

9. d: Decision-making

10. a: Business process

11. a: Intellectual property

12. c: Job satisfaction

13. d: Offshoring

14. a: Law

15. : Hotel

16. c: Cost

17. : Collective bargaining

18. c: Virtual team

19. b: Mediation

20. : Human capital

21. a: Reason

22. : E-commerce

23. b: Frequency

24. d: Dilemma

25. d: Bottom line

26. a: Merger

27. c: Arbitration

28. a: Kaizen

29. c: Transactional leadership

30. d: Enron

31. : Total cost

32. : Variable cost

33. : European Union

34. c: Assembly line

35. d: Tariff

36. c: Asset

37. c: Individualism

38. c: Environmental scanning

39. b: Officer

40. : Quality circle

41. d: Logistics

42. d: Stereotype

43. d: Inventory control

44. b: Knowledge management

45. : Control chart

46. d: Management by objectives

47. a: Reinforcement

48. a: Task force

49. : Customer

50. a: Management process

51. : Sharing

52. : World Trade Organization

53. : Collaboration

54. a: Bargaining

55. d: Information

56. c: Supply chain

57. c: Analysis

58. b: Goal

59. a: Cooperation

Business law

1. d: Statutory Law

2. a: Substantive law

3. b: Commercial Paper

4. d: Corporate governance

5. b: Criminal procedure

6. a: Parol evidence

7. d: Duty

8. a: Property

9. b: Certiorari

10. : Resource

11. c: Categorical imperative

12. c: Contract law

13. c: Real property

14. c: Warranty

15. a: Fair use

16. c: Hearing

17. b: Securities Act

18. a: Social responsibility

19. c: Health insurance

20. c: Jurisdiction

21. : Labor relations

22. b: Wire fraud

23. b: Buyer

24. a: Punitive damages

25. d: Issuer

26. a: Requirements contract

27. b: Clayton Act

28. b: Firm offer

29. b: Consumer Good

30. a: First Amendment

31. b: Fee simple

32. b: Output contract

33. a: Industry

34. d: Criminal law

35. d: Brand

36. c: Breach of contract

37. d: Trial

38. : Standing

39. c: Insurable interest

40. c: Security interest

41. a: National Labor Relations Board

42. c: Consideration

43. : Creditor

44. b: Writ

45. : Board of directors

46. a: Utility

47. c: Respondeat superior

48. c: Lien

49. a: Contract

50. d: Litigation

51. a: Defamation

52. a: Opening statement

53. c: General partnership

54. c: Contributory negligence

55. a: Federal question

56. b: Appellate Court

57. c: Rescind

58. a: Directed verdict

59. d: Indictment

Finance

1. c: Liquidity

2. b: Perpetual inventory

3. : Net asset

4. : Schedule

5. : Rate risk

6. : Price

7. : Competition

8. c: Intangible asset

9. c: Arbitrage

10. : S corporation

11. c: Finished good

12. d: Capital market

13. : Taxation

14. a: Accounts payable

15. d: Risk premium

16. b: Adjusting entries

17. a: Bank statement

18. c: Accrual

19. c: Yield curve

20. c: Manufacturing overhead

21. : Free cash flow

22. d: Financial Accounting Standards Board

23. c: Underwriting

24. c: Forecasting

25. c: Brand

26. d: Net worth

27. : Relevance

28. c: Capital lease

29. a: Pricing

30. : Long-term liabilities

31. d: Commercial bank

32. c: Debt-to-equity ratio

33. b: Gross profit

34. d: Indenture

35. : Capital asset pricing model

36. b: Capital gain

37. : Net profit

38. a: Aging

39. a: Book value

40. b: Insurance

41. d: Accounting

42. a: Pension

43. : Monte Carlo

44. : Industry

45. : Conservatism

46. d: Callable bond

47. d: Deferral

48. c: Security

49. a: Bank reconciliation

50. : Loan

51. b: Amortization

52. a: Capital structure

53. b: Worksheet

54. : Buyer

55. a: Receipt

56. c: Dividend yield

57. : Future value

58. c: Mutual fund

59. b: Income tax

Human resource management

1. a: Asset

2. b: Labor union

3. d: Hazard analysis

4. b: Bottom line

5. a: Halo effect

6. d: Needs analysis

7. a: Realistic job preview

8. c: Internship

9. b: Part-time

10. d: E-learning

11. d: Global workforce

12. d: Recruitment advertising

13. a: Picketing

14. b: Overtime

15. c: Employee benefit

16. d: Best practice

17. c: Intellectual capital

18. b: Employee stock ownership plan

19. d: Proactive

20. d: Ownership

21. b: On-the-job training

22. : Total Reward

23. a: New Deal

24. b: Executive compensation

25. b: Job fair

26. : Career development

27. b: Affirmative action

28. b: Scientific management

29. d: Scanlon plan

30. d: Faragher v. City of Boca Raton

31. : Profit sharing

32. a: Distance learning

33. a: Local union

34. a: Strategy map

35. b: Exit interview

36. b: Job performance

37. b: Kaizen

38. b: Succession planning

39. b: Talent management

40. d: Background check

41. d: Skill

42. b: Piece rate

43. : Payroll

44. : Telecommuting

45. a: Arbitration

46. c: Expert power

47. c: Worker Adjustment and Retraining Notification Act

48. c: Virtual team

49. : Cost leadership

50. a: Theory Z

51. : Six Sigma

52. d: Lilly Ledbetter

53. : Data collection

54. b: Love contract

55. a: Glass ceiling

56. c: Trainee

57. b: Unemployment

58. b: Persuasion

59. : Self-assessment

Information systems

1. d: Freemium

2. c: Semantic Web

3. c: Microprocessor

4. b: System software

5. c: Business process reengineering

6. c: Automated teller machine

7. : Netscape

8. d: Dimension

9. : Business intelligence

10. : Social commerce

11. d: Change management

12. : Chief information officer

13. : Data aggregator

14. : Online advertising

15. : First mover advantage

16. c: Geocoding

17. d: Sustainable

18. a: Switch

19. d: Supply chain management

20. : Web analytics

21. a: Long tail

22. d: Code

23. c: PayPal

24. c: Personalization

25. c: Google Maps

26. c: Viral marketing

27. : Executive information system

28. b: Big data

29. c: Downtime

30. a: Disaster recovery plan

31. c: Fraud

32. b: M-Pesa

33. a: Authorization

34. b: Commercial off-the-shelf

35. : Carnivore

36. c: Common Criteria

37. c: Smart card

38. c: Star

39. c: Expert system

40. b: Keystroke dynamics

41. a: Intranet

42. c: Craigslist

43. c: Global Positioning System

44. c: Geographic information system

45. d: Facebook

46. c: Epicor

47. c: Chart

48. a: Critical success factor

49. a: Service level

50. c: Click-through

51. c: Tacit knowledge

52. : E-commerce

53. d: AdWords

54. a: Yelp

55. b: Reputation management

56. b: Decision support system

57. : Decision-making

58. d: Data integrity

59. d: Business process management

Marketing

1. c: Brand equity

2. a: Secondary data

3. b: Marketing channel

4. : Disintermediation

5. a: Market research

6. c: Evolution

7. a: Shares

8. c: Distribution channel

9. b: Productivity

10. : INDEX

11. b: Supermarket

12. d: Market segmentation

13. b: Corporation

14. a: Ford

15. d: Frequency

16. b: Creative brief

17. d: Trademark

18. : Value proposition

19. c: Loyalty program

20. c: Performance

21. a: Subsidiary

22. c: Advertising agency

23. b: Mobile marketing

24. : Social marketing

25. c: Intranet

26. c: Warranty

27. : Auction

28. d: Monopoly

29. b: Sales management

30. : Total cost

31. d: Direct selling

32. b: Partnership

33. a: Direct marketing

34. a: Marketing communications

35. : Return on investment

36. : Image

37. a: Small business

38. : Technology

39. a: Intangibility

40. c: Aid

41. a: North American Free Trade Agreement

42. a: Argument

43. a: Intellectual property

44. c: Mass customization

45. : Choice

46. a: Regulation

47. b: Adoption

48. a: Database marketing

49. b: Early adopter

50. b: Psychographic

51. b: Total Quality Management

52. : Business marketing

53. d: Commercialization

54. a: Cost

55. a: Buyer

56. b: Business-to-business

57. : Brand

58. d: Consumer Protection

59. : Sales promotion

Manufacturing

1. a: Sequence

2. : Good

3. : Information management

4. a: Prize

5. c: Raw material

6. b: Purchasing process

7. c: Rolling

8. : Cost estimate

9. a: Manufacturing

10. c: Asset

11. d: Cash register

12. b: Bullwhip effect

13. d: Vendor relationship management

14. a: Sunk costs

15. c: Consensus

16. : Opportunity cost

17. c: Purchasing manager

18. c: Supplier relationship management

19. a: Global sourcing

20. c: ROOT

21. b: Thomas Register

22. a: Inventory

23. b: Service level

24. a: Heat exchanger

25. b: Scope statement

26. b: Reverse auction

27. a: Quality assurance

28. a: Scheduling

29. c: Resource

30. a: Total cost of ownership

31. a: Quality by Design

32. c: Distillation

33. d: Design of experiments

34. a: Virtual team

35. b: Supply chain

36. d: Furnace

37. d: Zero Defects

38. : Goal

39. c: Turbine

40. c: Kaizen

41. a: Solution

42. : Reorder point

43. a: Consortium

44. : Accreditation

45. d: Material requirements planning

46. c: Vendor

47. c: DMAIC

48. a: Cost driver

49. b: Sputnik

50. : Schedule

51. c: Total quality management

52. a: Project team

53. b: Bill of materials

54. c: Workflow

55. c: American Society for Quality

56. a: Production schedule

57. : Mary Kay

58. b: Business process

59. c: Sales

Commerce

1. b: European Union

2. b: Credit

3. d: Interest

4. b: Issuing bank

5. b: Household

6. b: Permission marketing

7. b: Stock

8. b: Consortium

9. d: Public policy

10. c: Product mix

11. d: Subsidiary

12. a: Encryption

13. b: Advertisement

14. : Leadership

15. d: Organizational structure

16. a: Consumer-to-consumer

17. b: Firm

18. a: Bill of lading

19. b: Purchasing manager

20. a: Pension

21. : Affiliate marketing

22. d: Inflation

23. a: Merchant

24. b: Committee

25. d: Confirmed

26. : Bank

27. c: General manager

28. c: Resource

29. d: Variable cost

30. : Argument

31. c: Board of directors

32. : Competitive advantage

33. d: Appeal

34. d: Empowerment

35. : Consideration

36. b: Netflix

37. a: E-procurement

38. c: Subsidy

39. d: Supply chain management

40. d: Raw material

41. c: Procurement

42. c: Investment

43. : Economies of scale

44. c: Marketing strategy

45. d: Buyer

46. d: Manufacturing

47. : Mass production

48. c: Complaint

49. d: Credit card

50. a: Expense

51. c: Production line

52. d: Disintermediation

53. a: Economic regulation

54. c: Outsourcing

55. b: Collaborative filtering

56. b: Strategic plan

57. d: Brand

58. b: Supranational

59. d: Revenue management

Business ethics

1. c: Patent

2. c: Electronic waste

3. b: Workplace bullying

4. c: Kyoto Protocol

5. a: Trojan horse

6. d: Conscience

7. c: White-collar crime

8. a: Skill

9. c: Sustainable

10. d: Dress code

11. d: Invisible hand

12. b: Partnership

13. c: Siemens

14. a: Lead

15. d: Fannie Mae

16. a: Pollution

17. c: Criminal law

18. : Medicaid

19. c: Stanford Financial Group

20. b: Ethics Resource Center

21. : Community development financial institution

22. a: Coal

23. a: Stanford International Bank

24. d: Clayton Act

25. d: Solar power

26. : Trade

27. d: Human nature

28. d: Locus of control

29. d: Tobacco

30. : Micromanagement

31. a: Auditor independence

32. c: Workplace politics

33. b: Collusion

34. b: Feedback

35. b: Corporate citizenship

36. d: UN Global Compact

37. a: Global reach

38. : Guerrilla Marketing

39. : Insider trading

40. d: Enron

41. d: Internal control

42. : Foreign Corrupt Practices Act

43. a: Consumer Protection

44. b: Constitutional law

45. b: Ethical leadership

46. d: Medicare fraud

47. a: Urban sprawl

48. : Principal Financial

49. a: Dual relationship

50. a: Supply Chain

51. d: Federal Trade Commission Act

52. b: Consumerism

53. c: Utopian socialism

54. d: Corporate structure

55. d: Biofuel

56. c: Lawsuit

57. a: Lanham Act

58. d: Individualistic culture

59. : Statutory law

Accounting

1. : Accounting management

2. c: Pension

3. d: Trend analysis

4. a: Statement of retained earnings

5. c: Calendar year

6. b: Transfer pricing

7. d: Ownership

8. : Stock Market

9. d: Management by exception

10. : Paid-in capital

11. d: Liquidation

12. d: Income tax

13. b: Finished good

14. c: Debt ratio

15. : Revenue

16. a: Cost basis

17. : Incentive

18. : Single Audit

19. b: Internal Revenue Service

20. b: Benchmarking

21. d: Time value of money

22. : Capital expenditure

23. a: Accounts receivable

24. a: Inventory turnover

25. b: Adoption

26. b: Separation of duties

27. : Operating leverage

28. d: Net income

29. a: Amortization

30. : Ledger

31. b: Accelerated depreciation

32. a: Zero-based budgeting

33. a: XBRL

34. d: Overdraft

35. d: Capital loss

36. d: Error

37. b: Free cash flow

38. a: Fair value

39. d: Securities and Exchange Commission

40. a: Independent contractor

41. d: Embezzlement

42. c: Gross margin

43. a: Bookkeeping

44. : Earnings per share

45. c: Subsidiary

46. c: Adverse

47. b: Current asset

48. b: Periodic inventory

49. : Accrued liabilities

50. a: Loan

51. d: Property tax

52. a: Hedge accounting

53. d: Relevant cost

54. c: Tax revenue

55. d: Insurance

56. : Promissory note

57. d: Bank account

58. : Preferred stock

59. c: Fixed asset

CPSIA information can be obtained
at www.ICGtesting.com
Printed in the USA
LVHW041023301019
635717LV00002B/80/P